The Nonprofit Mergers Workbook

Part II: Unifying the Organization after a Merger

La Piana Associates

AMHERST H.
WILDER
FOUNDATION

SAINT PAUL,
MINNESOTA

We thank The David and Lucile Packard Foundation and the
Amherst H. Wilder Foundation for supporting the production of this publication.

The Amherst H. Wilder Foundation is one of the largest and oldest endowed human service and community development organizations in the United States. Since 1906, the Wilder Foundation has been providing health and human services that help children and families grow strong, the elderly age with dignity, and the community grow in its ability to meet its own needs.

We hope you find this book helpful! Should you need additional information about our services, please contact:

Wilder Center for Communities
Amherst H. Wilder Foundation
919 Lafond Avenue
Saint Paul, MN 55104
phone 651-642-4022

For more information about other Wilder Foundation publications, please see the back of this book or contact:

Wilder Publishing Center
Amherst H. Wilder Foundation
919 Lafond Avenue
Saint Paul, MN 55104
800-274-6024
www.wilder.org/pubs

Edited by Vincent Hyman and Judith Peacock
Text designed by Kirsten Nielsen
Cover designed by Rebecca Andrews

Manufactured in the United States of America
First printing, June 2004

Library of Congress Cataloging-in-Publication Data

The nonprofit mergers workbook. Part II, Unifying the organization after a merger / by La Piana Associates, Inc.
    p. cm.
 Includes bibliographical references and index.
 Sequel to: The nonprofit mergers workbook / David La Piana. c2000.
 ISBN 0-940069-41-5 (pbk.)
 1. Consolidation and merger of corporations. 2. Nonprofit organizations--Management.
I. Title: Nonprofit mergers workbook. II. Title: Unifying the organization after a merger.
III. La Piana, David, 1954- Nonprofit mergers workbook. IV. La Piana Associates.
 HD2746.5.N66 2004
 658.4'02--dc22
                               2004005685

This workbook was made possible by the generous support of the James Irvine Foundation, the David and Lucile Packard Foundation, and the William and Flora Hewlett Foundation. For five years these funders supported the Strategic Solutions project, which generated the research and practice expertise that inspired us to write this workbook.

This work is dedicated, with admiration and respect, to our clients who have successfully struggled to make their mergers work. The importance of their mission and the strength of their devotion are what make our work worthwhile.

—David La Piana

About the Authors

David La Piana

David La Piana is founder of La Piana Associates, Inc., a consulting firm specializing in strategic issues for foundations and nonprofit organizations nationally. He has been an adjunct professor at the University of San Francisco's Institute for Nonprofit Organization Management and a lecturer at the Haas School of Business at the University of California, Berkeley. David has worked extensively with funders and nonprofits in every subsector, and he coined the term "strategic restructuring." He has facilitated more than seventy mergers. A popular speaker, David is the author of *Strategic Restructuring: Mergers, Integrations and Alliances* (2003), *The Start-Up Assessment Tool* (2003), *In Search of Strategic Solutions* (2003), *Real Collaboration* (2001), *The Nonprofit Mergers Workbook Part I* (2000), *Beyond Collaboration: Strategic Restructuring of Nonprofit Organizations* (1997), and *Nonprofit Mergers* (1994), as well as numerous articles and opinion pieces on nonprofit boards, strategy, and executive leadership. He is currently at work on a book on competition in the nonprofit sector.

Robert Harrington

Robert Harrington, MSW/LCSW, is director of consulting at La Piana Associates. Bob came to the firm with more than thirty years of experience in social services management. He was previously executive director of Children's Garden of California, a mental health and educational services nonprofit. In 1999, Bob led Children's Garden through a successful merger and became the chief operating officer of the merged agency. Bob leads strategic planning and strategic restructuring processes for the firm's clients.

He has worked with arts and culture, health, environmental, youth development, education, faith-based, workforce development, and mental health organizations. Bob has trained hundreds of consultants and nonprofit leaders around the country on strategic restructuring and other organizational development and strategy issues.

Michaela Hayes

Michaela Hayes, MHSA, is director of marketing, research, and development at La Piana Associates. She has an extensive background in all aspects of marketing including strategic planning; marketing communications; population, market, and survey research; and program development and evaluation. Michaela has held senior-level marketing positions with several organizations, as well as having served as senior and managing consultant with national consulting firms. Her professional experience spans the for-profit, nonprofit, and government sectors. Michaela has served as a board member and volunteer for several nonprofits. She is active in professional organizations including the American Marketing Association and the International Association of Business Communicators, where she serves on the board of the San Francisco chapter.

Liza Culick

Liza Culick, Esq., MPH, is director of capacity building initiatives at La Piana Associates. She has a background in law and public health, and more than nineteen years of experience in the nonprofit sector. Her work with nonprofits and foundations has focused on organizational effectiveness and capacity building, strategic restructuring, strategic planning, board leadership, learning communities, and program planning and development. Liza led implementation research efforts for La Piana Associates' Strategic Solutions project. She studied Chinese and political science at Wellesley College and has completed language study programs in both China and Taiwan.

William J. Coy

William J. Coy, MA/MFT, senior associate at La Piana Associates, has particular skills in helping organizations to manage their human resources, develop their leadership talent, and integrate their changing cultures. He is an adjunct professor at the University of San Francisco's Institute for Nonprofit Organization Management, where he teaches the graduate-level course on human resource management. Bill has been director of human resources for the Catholic Diocese of Oakland and for Yosemite National Institutes. He was also training coordinator for George Lucas's Industrial Light and Magic (ILM), a film special-effects company, and he was responsible for organizational and management development at both ILM and Skywalker Sound. Bill is the only consultant known to have facilitated meetings at both the Vatican and Skywalker Ranch! He has acted as a coach to forty nonprofit executive directors.

Heather Gowdy

Heather Gowdy, MBA, brings experience in both the private and nonprofit sectors to La Piana Associates. She has worked with nonprofits as a volunteer, staff member, consultant, trainer, and board member. As a consultant, her work has focused on strategic restructuring, organizational analysis and structure, strategic planning, business plan development, and management information systems design and implementation. She played a lead role in designing and implementing La Piana Associates' Strategic Solutions project. Heather received her master of business administration degree from the University of California at Berkeley's Haas School of Business, where she concentrated on nonprofit management. Prior to attending Haas, she worked as a technical specialist at Wilmer, Cutler & Pickering, a large corporate law firm in Washington, DC. There she designed, developed, and implemented proprietary information management systems for large litigations, specializing in case management and business development.

Kristen Godard

Kristen Godard, MP (master of planning), associate consultant at La Piana Associates, has a background in research, organizational development, communications, and advocacy. She consults on projects involving strategic planning, assessment, strategic restructuring, and market and survey research for nonprofits from a wide range of sectors. Previously, Kristen was director of Silicon Valley Training Programs at CompassPoint Nonprofit Services; worked as an independent consultant; and was a program officer at the W. Alton Jones Foundation with responsibility for a national grassroots environmental grantmaking portfolio. Prior to that, Kristen worked on environmental policy issues at several nonprofit and governmental organizations. She currently serves on the board of the Alliance for Healthy Homes in Washington, DC, and is the founding director for the Mockingbird Foundation, a philanthropic organization that supports music education.

Contents

Preface

This workbook is a sequel to *The Nonprofit Mergers Workbook Part I—Considering, Negotiating, and Executing a Merger,* also published by the Amherst H. Wilder Foundation. The previous work thoroughly addresses the motivations, negotiations, and processes of merger. However, it left unanswered the question that most often arises *after* a merger agreement is struck: *"How do we make this merger work?"*

We refer to this post-merger phase as "implementation" of the merger. In our work with nonprofits, we have found this phase to be even more challenging than the negotiations that produced the partnership in the first place. Implementation typically takes more time and energy than negotiation, and it directly or indirectly involves everyone in the merged organization, both board and staff. Most specifically, implementation of a merger requires *integrating* the organizations to create an essentially new organization.

For several years, La Piana Associates, Inc., through its Strategic Solutions project, researched mergers and the larger field of strategic restructuring[1] among nonprofit organizations. Recently, we've focused almost exclusively on the question, When it comes to integrating organizations after a merger, what works? We reviewed the business and nonprofit literature and interviewed dozens of nonprofit leaders who have experienced strategic restructuring. All sources, and our own experience, agree: most people embark on this process unaware of the massive effort required. Most integration "survivors" say they wish they'd had more support in navigating this process—a planning guide would have helped!

---

[1] *Strategic restructuring* is the creation of an ongoing relationship among two or more organizations to increase administrative efficiency or mission impact by sharing, transferring, or combining services, resources, or programs. Administrative consolidation, joint programming, joint ventures, parent-subsidiary relationships, and mergers are all forms of strategic restructuring. See the sidebar Types of Strategic Restructuring, page 11.

We created this workbook to help nonprofit organizations develop an integration plan that supports success. Additionally, we want to prepare *everyone* involved—nonprofit organizations, as well as the foundations and consultants who serve them—with a solid understanding of what it takes to achieve successful integration.

When we were researching *The Nonprofit Mergers Workbook Part I*, we found the extensive literature on corporate mergers of little use. The motivations, processes, and desired outcomes involved in negotiating nonprofit mergers differed too much from those of the corporate world for the lessons learned in corporate America to be helpful. This changed dramatically when we turned our focus to merger implementation and, specifically, to integration.

About Strategic Solutions

Strategic Solutions is a five-year (1998–2003) foundation-funded initiative dedicated to achieving a major and lasting positive impact on the nonprofit sector's perception, understanding, and use of strategic restructuring, thereby increasing the capacity of organizations to advance their missions.

Strategic Solutions has been a collaborative effort of the David and Lucile Packard Foundation, the James Irvine Foundation, the William and Flora Hewlett Foundation, and La Piana Associates, a management consulting firm specializing in the issues faced by nonprofit organizations in today's challenging and ever-changing world. Although the project officially concluded in 2003, La Piana Associates continues much of the research and dissemination activity, as well as the consulting work on which our ongoing learning is based.

For more information on Strategic Solutions, please see www.lapiana.org.

The voluminous literature on merger integration among corporations is, for the most part, right on point for nonprofits. It deals primarily with the people issues that are central to merger integration in both the corporate and the nonprofit worlds. In both sectors, successful integration largely hinges on people, and good communication plays a central role. In sum, the strategies and methods described in this book are built on the many lessons we learned directly from nonprofit leaders, but they also integrate the insights of those who study corporate mergers—insights we translated to the nonprofit reality.

This workbook represents a true team effort. The entire La Piana Associates staff was involved in the research, writing, and editing. Each person in our firm is both a consultant and a researcher. Nonetheless, we identify ourselves primarily as consultants, and we were intent on making this book, while research-based, a wholly practical tool. Each chapter was drafted by the person or persons with the most expertise in the relevant area. The authors of the individual chapters are, alphabetically: Bill Coy, Liza Culick, Kristen Godard, Heather Gowdy, Robert Harrington, Michaela Hayes, and David La Piana. Once this initial work was completed, David La Piana, Heather Gowdy, and Liza Culick pulled the final manuscript together and edited it.

The research reflected in this book, and the writing of it, would not have been possible without the financial and moral support of the Strategic Solutions funders. Specifically, these included Terry Amsler and Renu Karir from the William and Flora Hewlett Foundation, Jim Canales and Marty Campbell from the James Irvine Foundation, and Barbara Kibbe and Richard Green from the David and Lucile Packard Foundation. These individuals formed the Strategic Solutions Advisory Group, which provided direction and invaluable advice on every aspect of the project from the outset.

Whether you are a nonprofit leader, a funder, or a consultant to nonprofits, we hope you will find this book to be a useful tool in your work to help nonprofit partnerships succeed.

Introduction

Negotiating a merger between nonprofits is tough, but implementing it successfully is tougher still. Our work on the Strategic Solutions project[2] revealed that while many nonprofit leaders understand the process of *getting* to a merger decision, they still need more and better guidance on how to implement such a decision once it has been reached.

Implementation has two components: legal execution of the merger and integration. While legal execution creates a single organization on paper, it is really through integration that the merged organization becomes a reality. Often, in the heat and anxiety of merger negotiations, nonprofit leaders—management staff and board members—either ignore or delay consideration of key integration questions. Consultants assisting the process have their hands full just keeping the talks moving forward. Once the deal is struck, organizational leaders quickly become immersed in the daily work of the nonprofit, which piled up while they were negotiating the merger. Often, the consultant's involvement ends when the deal is struck. Moreover, some of the organization's leaders may leave the nonprofit because of arrangements made in the merger agreement, and others may simply be burned out and turn away from the process.

Whatever the scenario, many nonprofits begin implementing a merger with only a vague idea of what awaits them or how to navigate the difficult waters ahead. Distracted by obvious details—designing a new logo, printing new letterhead—or even by such important decisions as who comprises the management team, they ignore the larger strategic issues related to weaving organizations together and presenting the new organization to constituents.

[2] For information on Strategic Solutions, see the sidebar on page xiv.

This book will help you, the nonprofit leader, create a comprehensive plan to achieve successful integration—a plan that addresses large, strategic issues, as well as small, but no less essential, practical issues. This plan will guide your integration and inform everyone involved where they are going and what to expect when they get there.

Making a Merger Legal

First, let's briefly review the legal aspects of implementing a merger. Merger is, before all else, a legal process. Exhibit 1: Legal Execution of a Merger—Two Methods, page 3, illustrates two typical paths from decision to legal execution. States regulate mergers, so this process will vary somewhat from state to state. It is always best to work with an attorney who understands the relevant procedures for nonprofit organizations in your state. (For more information on the process leading up to legal merger, see *The Nonprofit Mergers Workbook Part I—Considering, Negotiating, and Executing a Merger.*) We will not go into the legal aspects of implementing a merger in this book, as this is one area where there is no substitute for obtaining legal counsel experienced in the law of your state.

Making a Merger Integrated

This book focuses on the nonlegal aspects of implementing a merger—specifically, the *integration* of the merging entities. While legal execution of a merger is relatively straightforward, and once completed is, in fact, permanently done and over with, integrating the people, systems, and processes of two or more nonprofits is far more difficult, complex, and timeconsuming.

Two Components of Implementing a Merger

Implementing a merger involves two things: the *legal execution* of the merger decision—filing paperwork, transferring assets and liabilities, and so forth—and the *integration* of the merging organizations.

Merger integration is the process through which two or more organizations bring together their people, programs, processes, and systems into a single, unified organization.

A long-term process

Merger integration is the process through which two or more nonprofit organizations bring together their people, programs, processes, and systems into a unified new organization.

The literature on mergers in both the corporate and nonprofit worlds is clear: deciding to merge is only the first step in a long process. The new entity emerges through the careful interweaving of a wide set of systems and practices—everything from finance and development to phone systems, from volunteer management policies and practices to a new, unified board of directors.

Further, nonprofits have strong cultures, deeply ingrained beliefs, and closely prescribed ways of doing everything from providing services to throwing retirement parties. Inattentive or insensitive handling of any aspect of corporate culture can lead to misunderstandings, hurt feelings, and ill will among the staff, volunteers, board, and other stakeholders. Negative feelings toward the "other" organization may have existed even prior to the merger

Exhibit 1: Legal Execution of a Merger—Two Methods

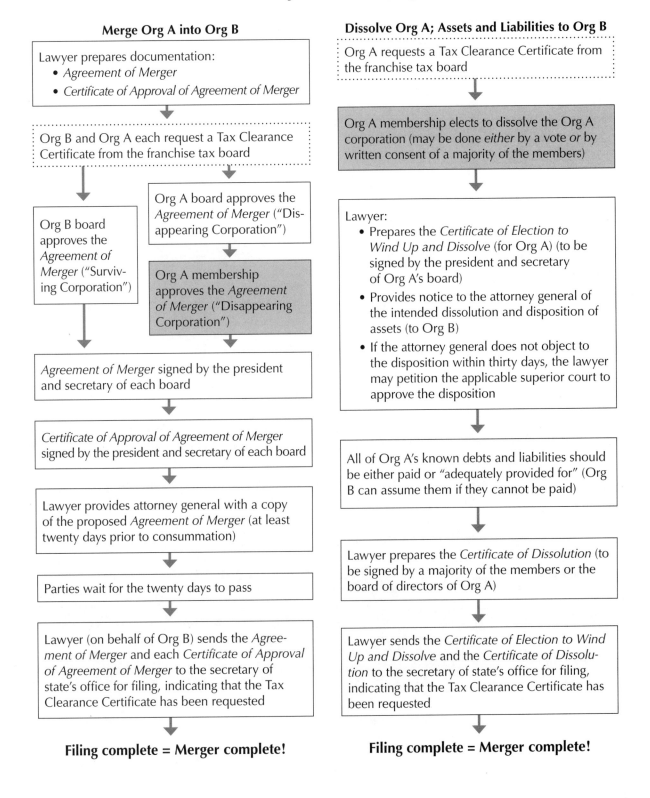

NOTE: *This is an illustration only. Laws and procedures differ by state.*
This assumes that Org A is a membership organization.

Merge Org A into Org B

Lawyer prepares documentation:
- *Agreement of Merger*
- *Certificate of Approval of Agreement of Merger*

↓

Org B and Org A each request a Tax Clearance Certificate from the franchise tax board

↓

Org A board approves the *Agreement of Merger* ("Disappearing Corporation")

↓

Org B board approves the *Agreement of Merger* ("Surviving Corporation")

Org A membership approves the *Agreement of Merger* ("Disappearing Corporation")

↓

Agreement of Merger signed by the president and secretary of each board

↓

Certificate of Approval of Agreement of Merger signed by the president and secretary of each board

↓

Lawyer provides attorney general with a copy of the proposed *Agreement of Merger* (at least twenty days prior to consummation)

↓

Parties wait for the twenty days to pass

↓

Lawyer (on behalf of Org B) sends the *Agreement of Merger* and each *Certificate of Approval of Agreement of Merger* to the secretary of state's office for filing, indicating that the Tax Clearance Certificate has been requested

↓

Filing complete = Merger complete!

Dissolve Org A; Assets and Liabilities to Org B

Org A requests a Tax Clearance Certificate from the franchise tax board

↓

Org A membership elects to dissolve the Org A corporation (may be done *either* by a vote *or* by written consent of a majority of the members)

↓

Lawyer:
- Prepares the *Certificate of Election to Wind Up and Dissolve* (for Org A) (to be signed by the president and secretary of Org A's board)
- Provides notice to the attorney general of the intended dissolution and disposition of assets (to Org B)
- If the attorney general does not object to the disposition within thirty days, the lawyer may petition the applicable superior court to approve the disposition

↓

All of Org A's known debts and liabilities should be either paid or "adequately provided for" (Org B can assume them if they cannot be paid)

↓

Lawyer prepares the *Certificate of Dissolution* (to be signed by a majority of the members or the board of directors of Org A)

↓

Lawyer sends the *Certificate of Election to Wind Up and Dissolve* and the *Certificate of Dissolution* to the secretary of state's office for filing, indicating that the Tax Clearance Certificate has been requested

↓

Filing complete = Merger complete!

negotiations, and they may have diminished or increased through that period, depending on a number of factors. Time spent addressing these *people issues* at the outset will pay off handsomely in better, faster integration of the merging entities.

Poor integration and mission failure

When merged entities fail to fulfill their new mission, it is usually because they fail to integrate successfully. The signs of a poorly integrated merger are readily apparent:

- Conflict throughout the organization at every point the predecessor organizations touch: board, management, staff, and volunteers.
- The "unconsummated merger syndrome," in which little, if anything, changes after the merger. People remain aligned with their previous affiliations, co-workers, or ways of doing things. The merger becomes an uncomfortable standoff.
- Inability to chart a unified strategic direction or, often, even to discuss the future without a high degree of conflict.
- Lack of unified data and systems—for example, failure to merge the fundraising databases or accounting systems.
- Lack of unity among staff, leading to ongoing duplication of functions.
- Inability to create a unified management structure.
- Inability of the board to select an executive director for the merged entity, or to appropriately support the person selected.
- Primary loyalties to predecessor organizations remain, often quite visibly so.

The results of a failed integration effort can be devastating. You, as the nonprofit leader, may have favored merger because you wanted to achieve synergies, reduce costs, avoid duplication, or strike out in new directions. But now you find yourself overwhelmed with work, spending more and more time in unproductive and conflict-filled meetings, continually approached by staff and board members alike with complaints about "the other." Every management decision, every board discussion, every seemingly innocent or routine move you make carries the possibility of opening old (or still-fresh) wounds and derailing the organization's progress for hours, if not days or weeks.

Not only do these problems wreak havoc on your organization internally, but also—unresolved—they spill over to the external world. The result can be damaged relationships with clients, donors, funders, vendors, and the community at large. *Merger integration is critical because without successful integration, the new organization will not achieve its mission.*

Beginning before the legal merger

While legal execution of a merger has a clearly delineated start and end, integration spans a more diffuse and longer time frame. Successful integration begins in the negotiation stage. A well-conducted and thorough negotiation that builds trust between the parties lays the groundwork for successful integration. Some decisions regarding integration are, in fact, best made by the negotiations committee, and some of the research and information gathering necessary to negotiations is likewise useful for successful integration. Whether you began working through integration issues at the first negotiations session or avoided the subject entirely until the boards approved the deal, you need to get it right, now.

Who Should Read This Workbook?

While this book addresses the leader of the organization undergoing merger integration, it is intended to benefit all affected by a merger, including board members, managers, funders, and consultants who work with nonprofits. As with *The Nonprofit Mergers Workbook Part I*, most of these intended audiences will have had little exposure to the integration of nonprofits after a merger. Board members who have participated in corporate mergers can use this book to compare and contrast the process as it unfolds in the nonprofit sector, while consultants who have not previously worked on merger integration will find the book a helpful orientation and guide.

Both our research and our consulting work encompass every subsector of the nonprofit world. We have found that the substantial programmatic differences among arts and culture organizations, environmental advocacy groups, human services agencies, management support organizations, and other specialized types of nonprofits do not significantly change the basic strategies and processes required either to negotiate or to implement a merger. We are confident this book will apply to the situations encountered by any nonprofit experiencing a merger.

This book will help you, the nonprofit leader, create a comprehensive plan to achieve successful integration—a plan that addresses large, strategic issues, as well as small, but no less essential, practical issues.

Overview of This Workbook

Through our direct experience and research, we've found the two things nonprofit organizations need most in order to successfully implement a merger are a well-conceived and detailed integration plan, and the leadership to carry it out. This book will help you quickly create your own integration plan and show how you, as a leader, can best guide the organization through a successful integration process.

The book has two sections, which we suggest you read in order. Section I (Chapters 1 through 5) provides a broad view of integration, its challenges, and how to meet them. This section highlights the leader's role, skills, and mindset and describes the need for an integration team to support the process.

Chapter 1 reviews the basic tenets of organizational change. Integration has a better chance of succeeding when there is effective change leadership. This chapter provides tips for leaders on how to implement a successful merger.

Chapter 2 defines what success looks like in a well-implemented merger. This chapter describes where you are heading—the promised land of a well-functioning, "new" organization—and stresses the importance of focusing on that goal.

Chapter 3 discusses the purpose and content of an integration plan, and the requisite leadership skills, qualities, and structure. This chapter introduces the concept of an *integration team* responsible for certain components of the integration plan.

Chapters 4 and 5 discuss two aspects of integration that are involved in all components of the process: people and communication. Successful integration depends on how well these are handled. Chapter 4 discusses how people issues can be addressed through effective leadership and planning, while Chapter 5 reviews the relationship between effective leadership and effective communication, and their combined contribution to integration success.

Section II (Chapters 6 through 13) focuses on the creation of an integration plan, built on the strategies discussed in Section I.

Chapter 6 explains the process for creating the integration plan and describes how best to utilize it over time. It also introduces a software tool, packaged with this workbook, which can help you create a plan tailored to your organization.

Chapters 7–13 introduce the content of the integration plan section by section: board integration, cultural integration, management integration, staff and volunteer integration, program integration, communications, and marketing integration, and systems integration. One by one, we focus on each aspect of the plan, providing details on the necessary steps for creating that section; the most common challenges and crises that will arise; and the processes, procedures, and interventions likely to be most helpful and necessary. Worksheets, checklists, tips, and quotes from leaders of merged organizations help you in your own merger. Write in this section, take notes, make copies of the worksheets—whatever helps you and your organization.

To make the book more useful, the worksheets and other helpful tools are available online at the Wilder Publishing Center's web site. Enter the following URL into your web browser to download these materials:

http://www.wilder.org/pubs/workshts/pubs_worksheets1.html?069415

Integration is not linear. While we have broken out the different focus areas in integration for the purposes of discussion—board integration, cultural integration, management integration, and so forth—you can't pursue these strategies sequentially. Nonprofits are far too dynamic and complex for that to be possible. Successfully implementing a merger is like juggling; you will need to keep many balls in the air at once. We hope that this book will help you not only to avoid dropping an important ball, but also to enjoy the process of organizational change. Change is inevitable, so why not try to enjoy it!

SECTION I
Going the Distance

CHAPTER 1

Effective Change Leadership

Even the simplest merger usually involves enormous changes to the participating organizations. Some changes are specific, predictable, and visible (such as a new name or a larger budget); others are general and often less easily discerned (such as a changed culture and the need to work with additional people). Both kinds of change require people to give something up, something they have known. This is difficult. Do not expect their reaction to the loss—which is how people often experience change—to be proportional to the seeming importance of the thing lost. We know of a merged organization in which staff from one of the previous entities mourned the change in location of the annual retreat. They had been accustomed to going to a much loved seaside hotel, but the hotel was now too small to accommodate the new organization.

Making things worse, there is often no immediate replacement for the thing lost, only the uncertainty of the future. And for many people that uncertainty can be the most troubling aspect of the change. Additionally, merger involves change on many levels at once, so that coping mechanisms are stressed, and they continue to be so as each new change unfolds over the succeeding months.

The Importance of Leadership

The degree of success organizations achieve in implementing a merger depends on how well equipped they are to deal with, and capitalize on, intense and widespread change. As the merged organization's leader, the skills you need to understand and manage merger-related change are the

---

From the Field . . .

"In a merger you're asking people to become something new. And without knowing what that new is, it's very hard for them to not do what they already know. In Chinese medicine they say that if you don't give something up, you can't accept something new. And that's very applicable. But in the merger, you're asking staff and board to give something up for something they don't yet know. So it's a very difficult process."

— *Executive director of an arts organization that merged with a similar nonprofit*

same skills required to grow an organization from a local nonprofit to a regional presence, to take a board from small-time to big-time fundraising, to restructure staff after the loss of a major government contract, or to cope with the retirement of a beloved founder. *The essential required skill is the ability to navigate the unknown with both the competence and confidence that will inspire others to follow.*

Take a moment to scan Section II in the table of contents. It lists the specific areas where change is to be expected: you will need to tend to the board, corporate culture, management, staff and volunteers, programs, marketing, and systems. This chapter, however, focuses more generally on the concept of change, and on what you, the nonprofit leader, can do to better understand, manage, and *cause* changes that bring success.

While the topic of change management has spawned an enormous body of literature, we present what's most helpful when integrating organizations—*change leadership*. This chapter includes some basic tools for you—the change leader—to use as you lead your organization through this period of intense change. These include tips on the mindset and attitudes that will help you maintain focus and momentum, and that will provide support and strength to those who look to you for guidance. We then describe how to use these tips to produce the changes necessary for integration to succeed.

The Leader's Job

Key to successful organizational integration is a desire to move beyond where either organization is at the time of the merger, and to go forward together to create a truly *new* organization. Unfortunately, the fear and uncertainty that can arise around a merger often compel nonprofit board and staff members to cling to their known world, and to hold on with uncommon vigor to comfortable (if ineffective) practices.

Fear of change is natural and broad, and not always rational on the surface; it also sometimes seems to be seeking problems where none exist. Thus, what looks like an irrational fight over which copier contract is the most favorable is really a battlefield for some deeper struggle: Who has the power in this organization? Who is favored? Whose choices and traditions will be honored? Such questions lurk beneath the overt conflict. And these questions arise again and again as each change is discussed.

Merging nonprofits often strive to replicate within the new organization the processes and functions that existed in the previous entities. This can be especially dangerous if the pre-merger organizations did not function very effectively. In addition, many nonprofits have adapted and often maladapted themselves to the needs and views of particular individuals within the organization, instead of to the exigencies of the organization's mission. It can be difficult to step out of this mindset and let go of old patterns and ways of doing things.

Ideally, however, merging organizations will not strive to get back to what they had, but instead will attempt to transcend the status quo and create something greater. A merger is not the time to drag forward old, familiar, and less than optimal ways of doing things. Rather, it presents an opportunity for leaders to invent new practices from the

Types of Strategic Restructuring*

Strategic restructuring occurs when two or more independent organizations establish an ongoing relationship to increase the administrative efficiency or further the programmatic mission of one or more of the participating organizations through shared, transferred, or combined services, resources, or programs. Strategic restructuring ranges from jointly managed programs and consolidated administrative functions to full-scale mergers. Whatever type of strategic restructuring you choose, it will involve change.

- An *administrative consolidation* is an alliance that includes the sharing, exchanging, or contracting of administrative functions to increase the administrative efficiency of one or more of the organizations.

- *Joint programming* is the joint launching and managing of one or more programs to further the programmatic mission of the participating organizations.

- A *management service organization (MSO)* involves the creation of a new organization in order to integrate some or all of the administrative functions of the partnering organizations, thus increasing their administrative efficiency.

- A *joint venture corporation* is a new organization created by two or more partnering organizations to further a specific administrative or programmatic end.

Partner organizations share governance of the new organization.

- A *parent-subsidiary* structure integrates some administrative functions and programmatic services. The goal is to increase the administrative efficiency and program quality of one or more organizations through the creation of a new organization or designation of an existing organization (parent) to oversee administrative functions and programmatic services of another organization (subsidiary). Although the visibility and identity of the original organizations often remain intact in a parent-subsidiary relationship, some organizations involved in such restructurings consolidate to the point where they look and function much like a merged organization.

- A *merger* involves the integration of all programmatic and administrative functions to increase the administrative efficiency and program quality of one or more organizations. Mergers occur when one or more organizations dissolve and become part of another organization's structure. The surviving organization may keep or change its name. A merger also occurs when two or more organizations dissolve and establish a new structure that includes some or all of the resources and programs of the original organizations.

* Adapted from Kohm, Amelia, David La Piana, and Heather Gowdy. "Strategic Restructuring: Findings from a Study of Integrations and Alliances Among Nonprofit Social Service and Cultural Organizations in the United States." June 2000: The Chapin Hall Center for Children and the University of Chicago.

best of the merging organizations. A senior staff member at a national health nonprofit who has been integrally involved in many mergers among affiliates of her organization highlighted this point in an interview: "I don't know if I can overemphasize the necessity of getting people on board in terms of new things. And I think 'the new thing' is a really important concept. There were these two things over here; now there's this new thing. It's not just a continuation of this big thing. It's a *new* thing."

In times of threat and transition, self-interest and self-preservation hamper rational decision making. As a leader, you need to believe—and demonstrate—that change is not only inevitable, but also full of promise and opportunity. That means you've got to accept reality, have a change-friendly mindset, and accept your role in motivating change.

Dispelling myths, accepting reality

As the change leader, you must have a clear understanding and expectation of what lies ahead, and must accept it, rather than ignore or fight it. Here are three myths about change, and the realities you should prepare for.

Myth #1: Things will calm down. You expect that a merger will cause some turmoil for the organizations involved. Viewed from the merger negotiations table, the period of envisioned turmoil might be the time until the merger is legally completed. You may say, "If we can just get through negotiations, things will settle down."

The Reality: It will become clear after making your way through this workbook that the legal moment of merger is more of a starting line for organizational change than a finish line.

Myth #2: Planning can adequately prepare us for change. People desperately want to predict the future. Nonprofit leaders may believe that creating a plan will remove the uncertainties inherent in implementing a merger.

The Reality: This workbook will help you to create an integration plan, but realize that no plan can fully prepare you for the human responses of your board, staff, volunteers, funders, clients, and other constituents. You plan because it is good discipline, because it reduces the impact of the unknown, and because it allows you to act assertively with regard to those things you can know. But you will still be surprised.

Myth #3: We can control change. People often think that reading and learning about change will somehow help to control it. The number of books and articles on the topic attest to this belief.

The Reality: You cannot ever fully control change. When the economy periodically takes a prolonged dive, for example, and both individuals and foundations find themselves with less money to give, could you have impacted that development? You can try to anticipate change, try to take advantage of it, and hedge your bets, but in the end you cannot control the future. As you go about the process of organizational integration, it can be a dangerous self-delusion to imagine otherwise. September 11, 2001, and its aftermath demonstrate the impact of unforeseeable events on well-made plans.

Be prepared to "ride" the change through which you are trying to guide your organization; you can't control it, but you can help direct others through it.

Having a change-friendly mindset

There is a lesson to be learned from the myths. It is not: "Give up; you can neither predict nor control the future." The lesson is to understand what you can control and what you cannot in a dynamic world in which you don't know what is going to happen tomorrow, let alone in a year.

This approach might be expressed as having a change-friendly mindset. Mindset is the all-important element. Mindsets are mental positions or outlooks from which people approach problems. Mindsets can be either self-limiting or expansive. As the change leader, your mindset will be emulated by those around you. It can either help you or work against you. What mindset do you need in order to successfully implement a merger?

Mindset #1: This is an opportunity. To effectively anticipate and respond to the challenges of post-merger integration, assume an aggressive stance toward the future: "This is an opportunity" should be your motto. Do not be daunted by impending change, and certainly do not fear it. Learn to use change to improve the management of your organization and to advance its mission.

Take a simple example. Let's say you need to integrate the two merging organizations' fundraising databases. Don't limit yourself to choosing between the two current systems. Assess your needs and it may become clear that you require a more robust system to serve the current and projected needs of the merged entity. Absent the merger, this upgrade might not have risen to your attention, or garnered the organizational will to make it a reality. However, since you must integrate the current databases anyway, why not use the opportunity to obtain a better overall system?

Change equals opportunity; this mindset is contagious. If the leaders exhibit it, the staff, volunteers, and even the board will likely follow, at least to a degree. Post-merger integration will not go smoothly. Be prepared for the bumps in the road and respond to them with a can-do attitude. Seek opportunities in the chaos and uncertainty. It will work wonders.

Change Is Constant

The nonprofit world is never calm, and the political, economic, and social outlooks all point to continued chaos in the coming years. In fact, it has become generally accepted that change is a constant in our world. Drivers of ongoing change in the nonprofit sector include:

- Demographic changes, including emerging minority majorities in many communities.

- Lack of sufficient capital and reliance on a narrow base of support, resulting in regular fiscal crises.

- Massive demands of the aging baby boom demographic group on society.

- The political, economic, and psychological aftermath of September 11, 2001.

- The trillions of dollars being passed from the World War II generation to the baby boomers.

- Ever-shifting funder priorities, often driven by the interests of a few leading foundations.

- The full weight of welfare reform and devolution, particularly in down economic periods.

- The competitive force of the approximately 35,000 new nonprofits that are created each year and the entrance of for-profits into many fields once considered to be the exclusive domain of nonprofits.

Mindset #2: Everything is negotiable, except the mission. To keep on course in a changing world, your best rudder is clarity about the difference between mission and "what we do today." Many nonprofit leaders do not see a difference between mission and practice. For example, ask the director of a food pantry what her mission is and she might answer, "To provide packaged, nonperishable food to the folks who drop in here." This is a fine statement of the work she does each day, but it is an overly narrow statement of the mission, which is about feeding the hungry, bestowing dignity, keeping families together, and many other things beyond packaged food.

This nonetheless typical answer leads to a tendency to resist even small operational changes because they are perceived as threatening the mission. In fact they threaten only the accustomed way of doing things. In the food pantry example, will expanding from one distribution site to three imperil the mission? What about adding a hot-meals component? Or initiating an arrangement for meal delivery to a nearby shelter? Of course not. Yet any of these opportunities might be presented to the food pantry through a merger and resisted as being inconsistent with the mission, narrowly defined as "what we do today."

Where does mindset come in? Nonprofit leaders need to focus everyone's energy on how to best advance the mission in a turbulent world.

Mindset #3: We exist to serve our clients and communities. During times of change, and never more so than during a merger, internal constituencies accept great pressure to keep things as close as possible to how they were—to maintain the status quo. To remain clear about what is most important during times of change, nonprofit leaders must remember that they are not in business to make their board members or staff comfortable and happy. Rather, they are in business to serve their clients and communities.

While good leaders care deeply about the morale of their people, and never forget that an unhappy board can make life difficult, they do not let fears of the unknown, or resistance to change, be the determining factor in organizational decisions. Statements such as "We can't work in that neighborhood; it is too dangerous" and "Changing the board meeting day will cause us to lose board members" really reflect the needs, desires, fears, and interests of these internal constituencies. The leader is challenged to respond by focusing on the needs of the clients or community served. For example, "Now that we have merged with XYZ, their clients are our clients. We will serve them, and we will find a way to do it safely." And "We are going to find a time that works for the new board, and it may not be our old time. We'll work it out together so no one gets left out."

Mindset #4: What you see is what you get. To motivate staff, volunteers, and board members to embrace impending change, you must help them to understand the reason for the change. Chapter 5 addresses in detail communication, but a primary point is this: the leader's mindset must be that "we are hiding nothing." If, prior to the merger, the organization had a history of clear and honest communication with its stakeholders, particularly its staff and board, those stakeholders will be more likely to trust what you tell them about the impending changes brought about by the merger. Thus, a long-standing and absolute commitment to "transparency" in all dealings will enable the organizational leader's communication about the changes to be heard and believed. If the organization's communication has been less than open in the past (or at least is perceived by some to have been so), then continuously clear and honest communication must begin at once. Credibility is essential to change leadership.

Motivating change

You have put yourself into a situation where change is inevitable—a merger. Now you are trying to figure out how to bring about the changes you need in the quickest, least expensive, and least painful way possible. That's a tall order. Nonetheless, let's look at some effective ways to motivate change.

The leader's role in motivating change is to define what is needed, and then to persuade others of its urgency. This is our definition of *change leadership*. One of the first tasks you face is to give shape to the multitude of feelings, fears, and misapprehensions your people may have developed about the merger. That is, before you can expect your board or staff members to accept change, you must first help them to identify what they are experiencing as change—the difficult, necessary, natural consequences of the merger decision.

> Until people see themselves as involved in a change process, resistance will be highly charged, irrational, and difficult to address.

For example: "Those guys want to put in a whole new accounting system! They're nuts. You're not going to let them, are you?" is an expression of horror on the part of a staff person who sees the change as a mad intrusion by barbarians into what had been a stable world. You would prefer to hear "Changing the accounting system is going to be a real pain, and expensive. This is nuts! Do we have to?"

The difference is subtle but essential. In the second case the person is just as upset and "unsold" on the new system as the person was in the first case. The difference is that the second person sees the problem as change, and he owns it as his problem. "They" is replaced by "we," and the new accounting system has been labeled as change.

A small step forward? Yes, but an essential one. Until people see themselves as involved in a change process, and until they are able to link their particular change-related problem to other problems throughout the organization, resistance will be highly charged, irrational, and difficult to address. Once they see their difficulties as part of the post-merger change process, you can educate them about the change itself, the reasons for the merger, and the potential benefits. You can then ask them to pull together behind you. Keep leadership guru Max De Pree's famous pronouncement in mind: "The first duty of the leader is to define reality."[3]

Think your way through the following steps to achieving positive change:

Motivator #1: Make a strong case. Much as you would for a fundraising effort, list in writing all the reasons why things must change in the way you are envisioning. This is for your own use. If you cannot convince yourself of the need, you will have real trouble

---

[3] Max De Pree, "What the Leader Owes," interview by Peter F. Drucker, in *Managing the Non-Profit Organization: Principles and Practices* (New York: HarperBusiness, 1990), 40.

attempting to convince others. Keep the list brief, no more than one or two pages. Resist the temptation to simply e-mail your masterpiece to the entire organization; they won't be sold. Making a case for change will take a far more intensive and personal communication effort. (See Chapter 5 for details.) In thinking about your case,

- Consider the situation—how did the organization get to this point, and what needs to happen next?
- Examine the urgency—are both the need for change and the time frame envisioned evident and compelling?
- Assess the feasibility—is the change even possible? Don't ask people to do the impossible.
- Describe the problem (not the symptoms), then the consequences.
- Describe what can be done.
- Describe ways you could make things better.
- Describe the consequences of the change.

Motivator #2: Send a clear and consistent message. Use your written analysis of the situation to craft the change message you will send to your people. Remember, you must both model and champion the change you wish to produce. That means you must align your speech, behavior, and reward systems with the change. Modeling change entails a great deal more than giving a pep talk or printing T-shirts. People believe the message they see you embody. Your behavior is at least as important as your words.

- Communicate the message consistently and at every opportunity.
- Start with likely allies who will be amenable to the message.
- Get others who share your commitment to spread the message.

Motivator #3: Secure the buy-in of the people who will carry out the change. A change imposed without at least some support from those having to implement it is doomed. Examples of people "living the change" will be essential to convincing the majority of people that this is real. Do not issue sweeping fiats for major change initiatives. Find those in the organization who already think the change is a good idea and give them a chance to shine. Then celebrate their accomplishments in front of others. Let these "early adopters" be first in line for the best assignments and promotions. All this sends the message that the change is real and mission-critical.

- Do not expect massive change to occur all at once; work incrementally.
- Find the 20 percent of the people who are ready to change and work with them first.
- Showcase their work to the 60 percent who will accept the change if it is seen as safe enough.
- Deal with the 20 percent who will not willingly change, no matter what. Some may need to go.

The Speed of Change

As you plan your integration, realize that you cannot, and need not, do everything at once. In some situations incremental change is appropriate, while others require rapid action. Even among the urgent issues, you can focus effectively on only a few key changes at a time. As the change leader, it is important that you distinguish among these types of change, and that you are prepared to speed up the pace of change when necessary.

Incremental change is appropriate in many circumstances:

- Implementing ongoing quality improvement efforts
- Moving to larger fundraising goals
- Lowering staff turnover
- Learning to work across the old organizational lines
- Communicating externally as one entity rather than as two
- Implementing new software
- Building a unified staff and board

Radical change is sometimes necessary:

- When health or safety is in question
- When ethical or legal issues are in question
- When financial collapse is imminent
- When moving more slowly only prolongs the pain

This last point is essential. Sometimes an incremental approach is tantamount to no change at all. Consider the true story of a counseling clinic that merged with a larger mental health center. The clinic had a long waiting list, but its staff therapists did not seem especially busy. The executive director of the mental health center found that the clinic's caseload standard was far below that adhered to in her other clinics. The executive director first tried an incremental approach: she asked the staff to each add two new clients from the waiting list in the next month; then, in the next month, two more clients. Through this approach the clinic would eventually attain the caseload standard. "We wanted to give them time, since this was such a huge change," recalled the executive director. At the end of the first month, the waiting list was longer than ever; no therapist had taken on a new case, and two therapists had actually lost cases. "They all felt so busy taking care of four or five clients that it just seemed an impossible demand to them," the executive director stated. Finally, with the clinic hemorrhaging money, she realized that this problem was not amenable to further negotiation or delay. "I told the staff that they each had to take on twenty new clients from the waiting list that week, or we would have to close." A week later the clinic did indeed close. Clients were referred to other resources in the community. This is not a programmatic success story, but closing the clinic did prevent the organization from losing even more money and got clients on their waiting list help.

Where do you begin instituting change? Pick those areas that are most urgent and, if you have a choice, those that are most visible to the staff and board. Quick, highly visible wins should be mixed into the early work. For example, a national federation of advocacy groups was formed several years ago. One of its first changes was to unify its public relations campaign, addressing a generally held concern that each member had not been able to individually access the media very successfully. The new campaign garnered millions of dollars in pro bono advertising support and airtime, and it cemented everyone's loyalty to the new name.

Remember, no matter how well you plan the integration, chances are the changes you seek are not going to just happen "over time." Remember also to let the mission of your nonprofit organization drive changes or large improvements. Otherwise, you may feel like you have your shoulder against the rear of a big old Buick stuck in the mud, and all you can see is your own feet.

Tips for the Effective Change Leader

The qualities that you demonstrate are even more important than what you, as the change leader, do. The change leader must lead by example.

La Piana Associates conducted a series of in-depth interviews with twenty-five leaders of organizations that have lived through strategic restructuring. While most of the individuals with whom we spoke described certain practical implementation tasks for which the leader was responsible, all of them focused on the less tangible things that the leader did to facilitate change. These included modeling a positive, forward-looking, mission-oriented attitude; acknowledging, absorbing, and attending to the emotions of the staff; naming and dealing with the resistance that emerges among staff; and concentrating on communication.

Based on this and our other research, we concluded that no matter how effectively a leader implements the technical aspects of a merger, that merger will not succeed without sufficient attention to all of the nontechnical aspects.

Leaders are made, not born. Leadership skills can be acquired. Further, leadership takes experience; the most effective change leaders are individuals who have been through large-scale organizational change themselves. As your organization's change leader, you must

- Be a cheerleader and champion for the change, showing confidence and conviction
- Have a vision of the new entity—the promised land
- Communicate that vision throughout the organization
- Be patient—except when impatience is needed (and know when that is)

The Role of the Executive Director

When we use the term *leader* in this chapter, our focus is primarily on staff leadership, and in particular the executive director (sometimes known as the chief executive officer or CEO) of the merged organization. This does not negate the importance of the board, which played a key role in the merger negotiation process and must continue to lead as the integration process moves forward. However, once the issue of who will lead the merged entity is settled, the executive director is the individual who will be at the forefront of the transition process.

- Understand what needs to be done, and focus on those priorities
- Keep everyone in the organization focused on the ultimate goal
- Build trust
- Be an excellent communicator—a master at both listening (asking others for their opinion) and persuading
- Maintain the balance between process, relationships, and results
- Focus on continual learning and improvement

Let's combine a few of these nontechnical aspects and look at them in more depth.

Have a vision and the focus and conviction to realize it. A strong leader has a clear vision for the merged organization and communicates it broadly and with enthusiasm. Staff at all levels will look to the leader to set the tone for the merged organization; that tone must be positive, energetic, and focused on a compelling vision that is clearly understood by all.

Explain the change and the rationale for it. The leader must be able to describe the change and why it must happen. In other words, how will the organization's mission be advanced by the change? Making this connection can help staff more easily accept uncertainty, as well as the less appealing (to them) but necessary aspects of the change.

Focus on the mission. The mission is the reason for the existence of a nonprofit organization, and the ultimate goal of any merger should be to create an organization that is better able to fulfill its mission. The leader should be able to articulate, clearly and convincingly, how the merger advances the mission. When the integration process encounters a roadblock—and it will encounter many—the leader must remind everyone where the organization is going, and why. A focus on mission can often help reduce the influence of individual personalities and positions in a discussion, bringing the group back to a larger and longer-term focus.

Have a plan for integration, and communicate it broadly. The leader, along with any designated integration team, must carefully plan the details of the integration, assign responsibilities, track progress, and make adjustments where necessary. The plan must reflect the leader's anticipation of people issues and plan for addressing these if and when they arise. Essentially, the plan is a road map for the integration process. It must be shared with everyone in the organization, so that everyone understands the requisite roles and responsibilities. The plan helps ease people's uncertainty and fear. It communicates strength and confidence. It keeps people focused on the reason for the merger. But even the most comprehensive and sensitive plan will not accomplish any of this if people do not know of its existence.

From the Field . . .

"I think if I had one piece of advice for somebody else approaching the same challenge, it would be to make sure you invest the time in building a common picture, a common strategic vision, and that you actually force the organization to give that time. You can't rush this."

— *President of the board of a merged youth service organization*

"Our number one concern throughout all the drama was making it [the merger] as fluid for clients as possible. That was the prize we could keep our eyes on. People saw that the mission was important, and valuable, and relevant."

— *Post-merger executive director of an HIV/AIDS service organization*

Respect the old organizations, but create a new organizational culture. Successful leaders of merged organizations both understand and convey that the integration process is really about transforming several organizations into something new. They work actively to create new cultural norms, activities, and traditions, and to leave behind older, dysfunctional organizational patterns. Culture is embodied in both attitude and behavior. The leader must model the attitude and behavior that is expected in the new organization, and foster an environment where the "new" is emphasized and celebrated.

Summary

A merger involves tremendous change, and successful mergers require strong, effective change leadership. An organization's leaders must be able to navigate the unknown with both competence and confidence, clearly articulating both a vision of the future and a path to success. When tensions or roadblocks arise—as they inevitably will—an effective leader will recognize and address them in a way that both respects the old and encourages and champions the new.

Good leaders are visionary, but they are also clear and concrete. They both understand and communicate the rationale for the change, as well as what success will look like. The next chapter looks more closely at when and how an organization can define success.

CHAPTER 2

Defining a Successful Post-Merger Integration

The last chapter looked at the leader's role in managing the change process to effect a successful merger. The leader's mindset, attitudes, approach to change, and decisions about change all impact how successfully the organization meets the challenges of merger. But, to have a truly successful change process, it is essential to know where the change you have engineered is leading. What are your performance targets? What areas do you need to work on? What will success look like in each area?

This chapter discusses how successful post-merger integration is defined and how to achieve it. The most successful mergers are those in which organizational leaders consider these questions from the beginning of the merger process, not just once the agreement to merge has been signed. This is especially true when it comes to people issues. The impact of a merger on the staff and organizational culture, for example, should be considered when assessing whether a merger might be right for an organization, when negotiating the merger with potential partners, while waiting for the merger to become a legal reality, and throughout the integration process. A *lack* of attention to these issues at any point can make the process much more challenging, and can even contribute to its ultimate failure.

How a Merger Unfolds

Before we discuss how to define success, it is helpful to review the phases of the merger process. It's important to see how the phases unfold, because successful integration depends on the outcomes of each phase.

Exhibit 2: Key Issue Areas by Stage of the Merger Process, page 23, illustrates the various issues that arise in each phase of a merger. Across the top of the chart (the column headings) are the six discrete stages of the merger process. These are, in general, time sequenced; that is, one follows the other, and any successful merger will probably move through all six. In fact, in appraising the success of a merger, it is useful to review whether and how well the organizations addressed and passed through these stages. The leftmost column in the chart identifies the areas that those leading the merger process will need to attend to. The checks within the chart indicate which areas need to be most closely considered at each stage.

Assessment and Readiness—This phase, addressed in detail in *The Nonprofit Mergers Workbook Part I—Considering, Negotiating, and Executing a Merger*, is where each party first assesses its own suitability for merger and its assets and liabilities as a partner, and then examines itself in light of a potential partner or partners. While many factors must be considered, even at this early stage attention must be paid to the concerns of (at a minimum) the board and management, and how the culture and program mix of the organization would affect and be affected by the negotiation process. The need for effective communication—primarily internal at this point—begins here.

Negotiation—This phase, also treated in depth in *The Nonprofit Mergers Workbook Part I*, is where the entities come together to determine if, and under what circumstances, a merger will occur. At this point some questions are likely to be raised in each issue area. There will be a need to communicate with both internal and external constituents about the process.

Immediate Pre-Merger—This is the often uncomfortable period between the point at which the merger decision is ratified by the boards, and the day on which the merger legally takes effect. It can often last several months, and is unique in that the organizations' futures are joined but their present identities are still separate. It is crucial to pay attention to the concerns and anxieties of the staff, management, and board during this stage, as well as the impact of these concerns on the overall culture. Many organizations get a head start on integration at this point, and begin planning for, and to a small degree implementing, the necessary changes. Announcements to the public about the merger are typically made at this stage as well. A proactive stance can often help alleviate the natural anxiety felt by many in this stage.

Legal Merger—This is a moment in time—the date the merger becomes legally effective. It is significant as a legal event, but it is not an actual span of time.

Immediate Post-Merger—Immediately after the merger legally takes effect there are many changes, often great confusion, and usually high emotion. New ways of doing things have yet to be established, and true integration is just beginning. Many a merger begins to go off track in this stage, and, once again, the first priority needs to be attending to the "people" issues.

Integration—This is the process, often lasting years, through which the entities truly become one. Full integration involves the people, programs, and systems of the entire

Exhibit 2: Key Issue Areas by Stage of the Merger Process

		Pre-Merger			Legal Merger	Post-Merger	
		Assessment and Readiness *the suitability of a merger for us*	**Negotiations** *making decisions, coming to agreement*	**Immediate Pre-merger** *waiting...a sort of limbo*	**Legal Merger** *a moment in time*	**Immediate Post-merger** *the immediate emotional aftermath*	**Integration** *engagement, experimentation, learning, competence*
Structure	**Legal Execution**		✓		✓		
People	**Board**	✓	✓	✓		✓	✓
	Senior Management	✓	✓	✓		✓	✓
	Staff and Volunteers	✓	✓	✓		✓	✓
	Organizational Culture	✓	✓	✓		✓	✓
Program	**Program**	✓	✓				✓
Systems	**Finance and Fundraising**		✓				✓
	Human Resources		✓				✓
	Technology		✓				✓
	Facilities		✓				✓
	Other Systems		✓				✓
Communication	**Communication and Marketing**	✓	✓	✓	✓	✓	✓

(merged) organization. The process also involves considerable attention to communication, both internal and external.

The goal of this workbook is to prepare and support you as you lead your organization through the unstable post-merger phase and into and through the later stages of formal integration as quickly and successfully as possible.

It is important not to consider these stages as completely discrete. Be aware that it is *not* necessary to complete one stage before you can begin working on the next. Successful leaders often look far ahead when moving through the merger process. For example, during the immediate pre-merger stage, some organizations are hard at work on staff and systems integration, developing a cohesive board, and reviewing how programs can work together. In other mergers, nearly all progress stops when the negotiations are complete and does not resume until the immediate post-merger stage begins. While both paths are common, successful merger-makers tend to move seamlessly from negotiations to approval by the boards to integration activities, without a hiatus between immediate pre-merger and immediate post-merger.

Determining and Articulating Desired Outcomes

Ideally, early in the merger negotiation process the negotiating committee, with input from the various stakeholders of each of the organizations involved, puts together a list of desired outcomes for the merger. (Worksheet 2 in *The Nonprofit Mergers Workbook Part I* describes how to do this.) Now that you have concluded negotiations and agreed to the merger, this list becomes even more important.

Before disbanding (with its negotiations work complete), the negotiating committee should revisit the list of desired outcomes and make any adjustments deemed necessary in light of the current situation. Give this list to the integration team—that group of individuals charged with leading the integration effort—for "safekeeping." (Chapter 3 describes the integration team concept more fully.) As part of its work, the integration team makes sure the leadership of the merged organization—both board and staff—reviews and adds to or adjusts the desired outcomes list early in the integration process. The integration team then takes responsibility for maintaining the list and using it as a "scorecard" for monitoring progress. At this point, you might think of the items on the list as the "outcome targets" toward which integration is proceeding.

It's possible your negotiating committee did not use *The Nonprofit Mergers Workbook Part I*, and whoever negotiated the merger may not have explicitly stated the desired outcomes. However, this information is usually expressed in some form during the merger negotiations. If not, now is the time to clarify the desired outcomes for the merger.

An important consideration as you enter into the integration process is how you define "success"—both internally and externally. This definition will vary from merger to merger. One way to define success is to look at the organizations' greatest challenges pre-merger, specifically those challenges you thought the partnership would aid, and ask if the merger agreement itself addresses them. If not, how can the merged entity best address the challenges?

At a minimum, a successful merger will result in the following ten outcomes. Use this list as a starting point for creating your own scorecard:

1. A cohesive governing body capable of leading the merged entity forward in a unified manner.

2. A single executive director who is supported by the board and staff.

3. A merged vision statement and mission statement expressed in a sound strategic plan that is supported by the entire organization.

4. A clear management structure representing the best skills of the pre-merger management teams.

5. An evolving, integrated organizational culture that staff feel connected to.

6. A sound, realistic budget and budget-monitoring system.

7. A unified human resources management system, including a single set of personnel policies and a unified and equitable compensation system.

8. A method for measuring the success and outcomes of the organization's efforts.

9. A coordinated set of high-quality, effective programs aligned with the new organization's mission.

10. A combined information system that meets management's needs.

> **Look at the Big Picture**
>
> During integration planning, always keep the big picture in mind. Why are we doing this? What do we want the end product to look like? It is easy for these questions to get lost in the hectic post-merger period.

Obviously, many nonprofits that have *not* just undergone a merger would yearn for the presence of these ten attributes. They are, in fact, the bedrock of success for any nonprofit, newly merged or not. We include them here because no post-merger integration effort will succeed without these fundamentals. If your primary goal in merging was to capture a larger market share, undertake a new capital campaign, raise your nonprofit's public profile, or attract highly skilled board members or staff, you will not truly succeed unless you achieve these fundamentals.

Using Worksheet 1: Outcome Targets, page 209, as a guide, add your own specific desired outcomes to this basic list. These become your outcome targets for the overall integration effort. These outcome targets will shape the content of the integration plan, and will inform the strategies and activities undertaken in the merger integration process.

Ultimately, a merger will succeed more fully in some areas than in others. Perhaps your programs are better integrated and better meet client needs, but the financial success you hoped for remains out of reach. Or your organization is better known and respected, but internal cultural tensions persist. Gauging success is not about giving yourself a report card. Rather, it is an effort to understand what has happened as a result of the merger, so you can hone your strategies. Because nonprofit organizational life is hectic, it is easy to move on and forget about the impact of the merger after a few months. Do so, and you will find that the problems you face a year after the merger either grew out of or are heavily influenced by the merger itself. Keeping this in mind will help you to understand the genesis of your post-merger problems, and to find workable solutions.

Consider this example of not dealing with the fallout from a merger. After the merger of two museums, it became clear that layoffs would be necessary at one merging party's site, because of long-standing financial difficulties that were only brought to light during the merger process. When the layoffs were proposed, both the staff and board members of this predecessor organization blamed the decision on the "cold-blooded" management style of the executive director, who came from the other predecessor museum. Thus, responsibility for an old problem was conveniently placed on the shoulders of the new leader. Weeks of painful discussions finally resulted in most people seeing the necessity for the cutbacks, but many still blamed the merger decision for the need to cut back.

Going deeper: Identifying desired outcomes for each integration area

Once you begin creating an integration plan (see Chapter 3 for an introduction to the integration plan concept, and Chapter 6 for a description of how to create and use a plan), you will revisit your list of outcome targets and add detail in each of the primary integration areas: board, culture, management, staff and volunteers, program, marketing and communication, finance, fundraising, human resources, information technology, and facilities. For each area, the merged organization's integration team should work with relevant staff to articulate a more detailed set of desired outcomes specific to that area. For example, a list of board-specific desired outcomes might include the following:

- An integrated, unified board with members who are engaged, enthusiastic, and mission-driven.
- A board with between ten and fifteen members, with at least two specifically representing our client population.
- A clear understanding of both our skills and our needs, and a recruitment plan that takes both into account.
- A formal orientation process for new members.
- A commitment from all members to participate in fundraising.

Such desired outcomes should be considered *part* of your integration plan. They describe what you are striving for, and they should be the natural end result of the action steps articulated in that section of the plan. Such detail will come later, however. For now, simply identify your "big-picture" outcome targets and set them aside until you have read Chapters 3 and 6.

Looking ahead to evaluation

Outcome targets, like the more detailed, area-specific desired outcomes you will articulate later, serve both a motivational and an evaluative purpose. At any stage of the process they can be held up as concrete statements of what the (exciting, inspirational) future holds. They can also be used to "check in" on your progress during the integration process. It is often wise to commit to certain milestone dates—say, every three months—where you review your outcome targets and discuss how close—or not—you are to reaching them. As mentioned above, such a process is not meant to "grade" you (or your staff), but to encourage reflection and discussion on what is working well and not so well, why, and what changes to strategy or action plans might make reaching those targets easier or more likely. Each time you check in, celebrate your successes and reenergize people around those outcomes that have yet to be realized.

Summary

A successful merger entails the creation of a well-run, highly integrated organization. This will of course be easier to achieve if the predecessor organizations were also well run and effective. Similarly, any faulty aspects of the former organizations that are carried forward into the merged entity will detract from the success of the merger.

As noted in Chapter 1, having an open mind about how to integrate the previous practices of the merging organizations will allow you to see the opportunities that change offers—opportunities to "train-up" staff, and also to develop and refine systems that have long-needed attention. Having an open, positive attitude will help you to take advantage of these opportunities to create a new organization that is better than the sum of the predecessors' parts. Articulating outcome targets, and reviewing them regularly, are a vital part of this process.

CHAPTER 3

Managing the Integration Process

To succeed, a merger must be actively *managed*. There are three keys to managing a successful merger: planning, leadership, and ongoing evaluation and adaptation. Each depends on the others—this chapter explains how.

We begin our discussion of these three keys to success with a discussion of the integration plan. We then look at leadership in the context of an integration team, a group of individuals who, along with the executive director, takes responsibility both for creating the integration plan and for managing the integration process, evaluating results, and adapting actions as the plan proceeds.

The Integration Plan

The *integration plan* is your map to the highly complex process of creating a new organization out of those that have merged. It includes a clear set of desired outcomes and objectives for each major area of organizational integration, along with an action plan and timeline for achieving those objectives.

The plan addresses each of the following areas of integration:

- The management of the integration process itself
- Board
- Management
- Staff (paid and volunteer)
- Programs
- External communication and marketing
- Systems (finance, fundraising, human resources management, information technology, and facilities)
- Evaluation

It also addresses organizational culture and internal communication; we find it best to integrate the *activities* related to both of these areas within each of the other integration areas, however.

The plan should be concrete and easy to use. Everyone in the organization—board and staff alike—contributes to the development of the plan and uses it when setting priorities and developing more detailed work plans over the course of the integration process.

Appendix A includes two sample integration plans. The content (the desired outcomes, activities, and information about the activities) is the same in both plans; the difference between the two is in presentation only. The first presents the action plan—a series of activities, with a lead person, team, and start date and goal date for each—by integration area. For example, it groups all board integration activities together, all management integration activities, all finance function activities, and so forth. The second presents integration activities in the order in which they must be done—those with the earliest start dates are listed first, regardless of the kind of activity.

Chapters 6–13 explain in detail how to create your own plan. If you choose to use the software tool included in this book (and available on the Wilder Publishing Center's web site) to create your plan, you will be able to generate a hard copy organized like either of the samples in Appendix A—or in still other ways. Regardless of how you choose to present the information, the overarching theme is the same: a well-conceived plan will show anyone interested where you are going with your integration, and how you propose to get there.

Elements of an Integration Plan

Desired Outcomes: What are you hoping to achieve within each integration area? What does successful integration look like?

Activities: What activities need to be accomplished to get you from where you are to where you want to be?

Lead Person: Who has primary responsibility for making sure each activity is accomplished?

Team: Who else will be working on that activity?

Start Date and Goal Date: When does work on that activity need to start, and—if it's not an ongoing requirement—by what date does it need to be completed?

Integration plan versus strategic plan

Often, nonprofit managers considering how best to pull their merging organizations together decide to embark on a strategic planning process. A strategic planning effort—whether the traditional model or a slimmed-down, more flexible approach—provides a context for viewing the newly merged entity as a new organization with a newly enlarged mission and programs. Strategic planning can be an invaluable tool after a merger.

At the same time, any *actions* resulting from a strategic planning effort are at least several months off. Recently merged organizations need to take immediate action across a broad front to ensure the new organization's success. For this reason, this book provides a model for integration planning that does not include strategic planning. However, if you wish to engage in a strategic planning process at the same time as you plan and pursue integration, the two processes should fit together. Integration planning, as you will see, deals with many of the same topics considered during strategic planning: programs, organizational culture, communication, and finances, to name a few. However, while the strategic planning process aims to chart a future course building on the unique strengths of the organization, integration is intended to *develop* those very strengths through the merging of two different organizations.

Do not forgo integration planning because you intend to develop a strategic plan. The two processes can work together, but you cannot replace one with another. If you have time for only one plan at this point, make it an integration plan.

When to create an integration plan

In an ideal world an integration plan would be ready immediately after the decision to merge has been announced. In reality, most organizations emerge from merger negotiations with a map for *legal* implementation, but no clear plan for *organizational* integration.

In some situations, the joint merger negotiations committee has a good feeling for when integration planning makes sense. For example, negotiations sometimes reach a tipping point at which it's obvious the merger will happen. That's an excellent time to assemble an integration team to begin addressing the big-picture goals and overall timeline of an integration plan. If you are using this book along with *The Nonprofit Mergers Workbook Part I* in preparation for a merger, then by all means begin integration planning early.

But that's not the norm; in fact, you may have come to this book with a merger in place and no plan. Usually actual integration is begun informally, without thought of creating an overall plan. If you are in this situation, quickly assemble an integration team to develop a plan to see you through the integration process.

Establishing an Integration Team

In many small organizations the executive director of the merged organization creates and implements the integration plan. This, however, is often not the best model. The executive director has many other responsibilities—not least of which is setting the tone, both internally and externally, for the entire integration process—and often cannot single-handedly give the time and attention to detail required to manage the process. We recommend that the executive serve as the *overall leader* of the integration process, but delegate primary responsibility to an *integration team*, which he or she assembles with consultation from both predecessor groups. The integration team, reporting to the executive director, is then responsible for

- Leading the development of an integration plan for all aspects of the new organization, and setting overall objectives, policies, and a budget for integration.
- Establishing planning, coordination, tracking, and reporting mechanisms for the process of organization-wide integration.
- Acting as focal point for all decision making and dispute resolution related to the integration process.
- Functioning as the communication hub for the successes, challenges, and status of the integration process to staff, board, volunteers, and other key internal and external stakeholders.

Do not forgo integration planning because you intend to develop a strategic plan. The two processes can work together, but you cannot replace one with another. If you have time for only one plan, make it an integration plan.

- Maintaining oversight of the integration process, and keeping others focused on the big picture—mission, vision, and desired outcomes.
- Setting up working groups to accomplish specific integration tasks.

Integration team members

Ideally, people on the integration team possess the following attributes:

- The ability to lead the organization in balancing integration activities with everyday business needs in order to keep productivity up.
- The ability to focus on, and get others focused on, the big picture—and those big-picture objectives that are most critical in the first year.
- Skill at achieving real progress while forging good relationships. You cannot afford to sacrifice good relationships for progress.

Include one or two board members (if more than one, include one from each of the pre-merger organizations) and several senior managers on the integration team. Since this group oversees the entire integration process, it needs to be in touch with all the organization's departments and key constituencies. Team members must not only communicate *to* these groups, but also hear *from* them, and be alert for signs of unease or discord throughout the organization.

Working groups

Truly successful integration teams do not create or implement an integration plan alone; they work with staff and volunteers throughout the organization, soliciting, encouraging, and rewarding involvement at all levels. In many functional areas the "on-the-ground" staff will actually have the best idea of what is working and what isn't; of what might work well and what might prove difficult. More importantly, getting staff involved increases their sense of ownership of both the process and the plan—an essential ingredient to success.

Thus for each integration area, appropriate staff should form working groups to flesh out the integration plan for their area and focus on the details of the integration process. This work should feed back to the integration team. The team then ensures that all integration activities fit together and advance the overall integration process.

Let's look at an example: the integration of technology. You don't need multiple information-technology people from each of the merging organizations to be on the integration team. But you might want them in a working group for a nuts-and-bolts discussion of what needs to happen to effectively integrate the merging organizations' hardware, software, and technical support systems. The same is true for integration of programs. You want at least one program director on the integration team, but you do not necessarily need more than that. Instead, gather key staff from across the various programs, with at least one member of the integration team present, to pool their expertise and brainstorm what needs to happen at the program level. Perhaps one meeting to talk through the issues and "flesh out" the integration plan is enough; perhaps more will be necessary. Working groups should be fluid—use them as you need them to gather input, plan, do the "work" of integration, and build commitment to the process.

Exactly *when* you create such working groups should also be fluid; but, in general, the sooner you do so, the better. In all but the smallest organizations they are likely to be a key resource for the planning process, and you will need the type of input they can provide before you will truly understand the full scope of work ahead of you.

Exhibit 3: The Integration Team, below, shows the relationship between the integration team and the rest of the organization and its leaders.

Exhibit 3: The Integration Team

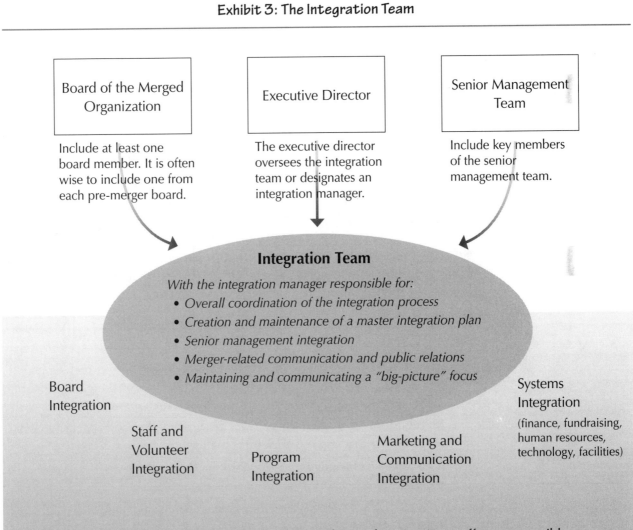

Board of the Merged Organization

Include at least one board member. It is often wise to include one from each pre-merger board.

Executive Director

The executive director oversees the integration team or designates an integration manager.

Senior Management Team

Include key members of the senior management team.

Integration Team

With the integration manager responsible for:
- Overall coordination of the integration process
- Creation and maintenance of a master integration plan
- Senior management integration
- Merger-related communication and public relations
- Maintaining and communicating a "big-picture" focus

Board Integration

Staff and Volunteer Integration

Program Integration

Marketing and Communication Integration

Systems Integration (finance, fundraising, human resources, technology, facilities)

In each integration area, "working groups" made up of appropriate staff are responsible for developing and implementing a more detailed, area-specific integration plan.

Day-to-Day Management of Integration

Whether or not you choose to form an integration team, someone must ultimately oversee the integration and ensure that its processes are coordinated and completed on time.

The executive director often plays the role of integration manager—a role reflected in Exhibit 3. As mentioned, given the executive's significant challenges of business as usual (programs, fundraising, staff issues, keeping the board engaged), the hands-on management of the integration process may be too much.

Some organizations create a new, temporary role of *integration manager* to see the organization through this stage. Especially in a larger, more complex organization, designating a specific manager can keep the integration on track. This role can be played by a senior staff person with clout, credibility, and the appropriate skills. Some organizations hire a consultant to be the integration manager. With either option—staff or consultant—the executive director retains oversight and *must* continue to be the overall visionary and champion for the merger, but remains free from the day-to-day challenge of managing the integration process.

Characteristics of a good integration manager

The integration manager must be a person who can see the big picture while at the same time managing a multitude of specific tasks with different deadlines and resource demands. Requisite attributes include skill at managing relationships and motivating people in difficult times, credibility as a leader within the organization, and authority (in position and among staff) to make decisions that keep the process moving forward. The integration manager must also have the complete trust of the executive director.

As leader of the integration team, the integration manager has day-to-day responsibility for

- Taking the lead in creating the structure for the integration process: an integration team, an integration plan, a process for decision making, and a process for communication of progress to all internal and external stakeholders.
- Managing the integration team and the integration process, keeping it moving in such a way that goals and deadlines are met.
- Overseeing the integration of people within the organization (board, staff, and program volunteers).
- Overseeing the development of the new organizational culture.
- Working with each department to set goals that define success for the merger, and action plans that lead to the attainment of those goals.

Using outside consultants

Many of the nonprofit leaders we interviewed recommended hiring a consultant for one or more of the following purposes:

- Helping to develop a plan
- Taking on some of the actual implementation work
- Providing ongoing guidance to the integration team
- Facilitating the integration of organizational cultures
- Attending to the important people and communication issues

Beware of the trap of hiring a consultant, at a consultant's hourly rate, to simply follow the executive director or integration manager around, accomplishing what amount to support tasks. If you prefer this model, you will probably do better, and save money, by hiring an executive assistant. For example, one executive said: "I don't need a consultant who is going to advise me, and essentially give *me* more tasks to do. I need someone to sit next to me, whom I can hand tasks *to*."

Remember, it takes time to use a consultant, too. A consultant needs direction and feedback to be successful. You cannot simply hire a consultant and forget about integration. But, if you have the needs described above and lack the time or additional staff to handle them, by all means, find a consultant and budget time to manage the person.

Evaluation: An Ongoing Responsibility

Even nonprofits that are *not* going through a merger struggle with evaluation. Funders increasingly require evaluation efforts as a condition of their grant or contract. Aside from all the external pressure to "measure outcomes," there are internally focused reasons to do it. For one thing, the prospect of evaluation forces you to state clear goals, so that you can later ask yourself how well you did against those goals at the outset. Many nonprofit leaders avoid evaluation, feeling that they know in their hearts they are doing the right thing, and perhaps fearing any analysis that might prove otherwise.

For a merger, evaluation helps you measure the degree to which you have achieved the changes you sought through the merger in the first place. The desired outcomes articulated in the negotiations process, and refined with the outcome targets worksheet, were and are central to your merger decision. Thus, it makes sense to measure how well you do against them. If you achieve 50 percent or 80 percent of the intended aims of the merger, is that a success or a failure? Neither; it is really just a reality check on where you are at any given time.

Common Errors of Integration Project Management[*]

- Lack of a clearly defined project leader. Be sure to have only one person in charge, and be clear on this person's role and responsibilities.
- Failure to follow the plan. The role of the integration team is to make sure the integration plan is manageable and that progress is not sidetracked.
- Declaring victory on the twenty-yard line.
- Skimping on investing in the integration effort.
- Presuming that all people are at the same point.
- Failure to design an active and comprehensive communication plan.

[*] Adapted from Robert J. Kramer, *Post-Merger Organization Handbook* (New York: The Conference Board, 1999).

At the beginning of the integration process, decide how often you will measure your progress against the goals you have set. At a minimum, aim for such a review at six months and one year post-merger, and annually after that for as long as seems necessary. Better still, check in every quarter in the first year. Be as explicit as possible when you articulate desired outcomes and goals for each integration area, and again when you are conducting your evaluation. The more quantitative your goal statements (for example, "we will increase the number of clients served by 50 percent") the easier it will be to measure their accomplishment.

Here are questions to ask at each evaluation point:

- How many of our desired outcomes have we fully achieved at this point? How many have we partially achieved?
- What three factors contributed most to our success in these areas? Can we bring these factors to bear on those areas where we *haven't* yet reached our goals?
- What has kept us from reaching those goals? Do we need to change our strategy in any way, or do we simply need more time?
- Is our timeline still realistic? Do we need to make any other changes to the integration plan?

The sample integration plans in Appendix A include references to evaluation "check-in" points. We recommend you do the same. Including evaluation in your task list can help to remind people of its importance to the overall integration effort.

Appendix B includes La Piana Associates' Pre- and Post-Merger Organizational Profile, a measurement tool that looks at some of the most common indicators of merger success. Feel free to use this tool to establish a baseline analysis of your organization at the point of merger, and then to use it again annually post-merger to assess changes.

Summary

Successful management of the integration process requires clear leadership, an organized approach to planning, and a commitment to ongoing evaluation and adaptation. Leadership of the process must ultimately reside with the executive director, but he or she can—and often does—delegate the day-to-day responsibility for *managing* the process to an integration team and/or integration manager. This team, or person, must work with staff throughout the merged organization to create, modify, and implement a comprehensive plan for integration. Ideally, such a plan includes not just a task list, but also a summary of the desired outcomes, or goals, for each integration area (board, staff, culture, finance, fundraising, and so forth), and a schedule for evaluation of the organization's progress toward those goals. Such evaluation is critical to the long-term success of the merger, as it is impossible to plan for every eventuality in a merger integration process.

CHAPTER 4

The People Issues

The greatest threat to merger success is the impact that change has on the people in the organization. Studies have reported that 70 percent of mergers in the business sector fail,[4] and that a good part of these failures are due to the ways management handles the people, emotions, and communications that surround merger.[5]

In nonprofit organizations, people are the greatest asset. As management guru Peter Drucker states in *Managing the Non-Profit Organization*, "No organization can do better than the people it has ... In the end, what decides whether a nonprofit institution succeeds or fails is its ability to attract and to hold committed people. Once it loses that capacity, it's downhill for the institution, and this is terribly hard to reverse."[6]

This chapter focuses on the people issues that arise in merger integration, drawing on both our experience and the research literature. Leadership's role in helping people handle change and move forward is the key to successful merger integration. Leadership's failure is equally key, as reported in a recent Booz-Allen study of corporate mergers: "Whether tactical or strategic, problems in merger performance land on the same doorstep: they are attributed to poor leadership."[7]

As head of the organization, the executive director is crucial. But the board, the integration team, and human resources staff also lead the organization and make an enormous difference. Chief among the merger issues that these leaders will need to confront is the fear of change.

---

[4] Kristina Lucenko, *Implementing a Post-Merger Integration, Research Report* 1257-99-CH (New York: The Conference Board, 1999), 8.

[5] Nathan D. Ainspan and David Bell, *Employee Communications During Mergers, Research Report* 1270-00-RR (New York: The Conference Board, 2000), 13.

[6] Peter F. Drucker, *Managing the Non-Profit Organization: Principles and Practices* (New York: HarperBusiness, a division of HarperCollins, 1990), 145, 155.

[7] Gerry Adolph, et al, *Merger Integration: Delivering On a Promise* (McLean, VA: Booz-Allen & Hamilton, 2001), 5.

Fear of Change

While some people find change exhilarating, most fear it. Faced with the uncertain outcome of a merger, these people experience fear, uncertainty, and doubt—the "FUD" factor, to use a term coined by the Conference Board. It's a frustrating irony for change leaders: people are essential to the successful merger, but they are also the source of significant challenges in post-merger integration. In the worst case, the FUD factor is realized in staff becoming roadblocks to change and attempting to sabotage processes and integration in general.

Despite the business sector's greater experience with and research on mergers, it still struggles with the people issues. In some ways, the nonprofit sector, with its inherently greater focus on people and its ability to attract employees with nonmonetary incentives, may have greater people strengths. Brookings Institution researcher, Paul Light recently made this point in his article "The Content of Their Character: The State of the Nonprofit Workforce." Light reports that 60 percent of nonprofit employees joined their organizations in order to help the public, rather than for job security, as opposed to 32 percent of federal government workers and only 20 percent of private sector workers.[8]

People and change

Who are "the people"? In a nonprofit organization, many different stakeholders may be affected by a merger, and their concerns, if not addressed, can create major barriers to success. These stakeholders include

- Staff
- Volunteers (essentially unpaid staff)
- The board
- Donors
- Members (if the organization is a membership organization)
- Clients
- The community that "owns" the nonprofit
- The public at large

This chapter focuses on paid staff. However, many of the concerns of the other stakeholder groups and, hence, the approaches to addressing their concerns, are similar.

At the "end" of a merger, you want all these stakeholders to embrace the new organization's vision and mission. You'll know this has happened when the separate constituents of the merged organizations

- See themselves as "us" rather than "us and them"
- View the merger as a good thing
- Have a sense of shared culture and values
- Share stories of the new organization, and celebrate its past, present, and future

---

[8] Paul Light, "The Content of Their Character: The State of the Nonprofit Workforce," *Nonprofit Quarterly* 9, no. 3 (Fall 2003): 6–16.

Achieving staff integration is a tall order. It may take a long time to reach this point, and the path may be convoluted. The objective in addressing the people issues is to make the path as direct as possible, and to undertake all integration activities with this end point in mind.

The organization's leaders, supported by the human resource function and ongoing communication efforts, must focus on this goal.

Helping People Change

How can you get people over the rocky road of integration? Three emotional issues typically arise during post-merger integration: a sense of loss, uncertainty about the future, and fear of the unknown.

According to researcher and writer William Bridges, people must move through three distinct phases in order to embrace change: they must first say good-bye to the old; then they must shift into a neutral zone of uncertainty and confusion; and finally they must move forward.[9] Leadership's responsibility is to help people move through this process. Organizations must invest time and resources in this effort. Leaders must be carefully selected and prepared for their responsibility to lead the organization through change.

Leaders can do a host of things to overcome people's fear. The thread that runs through all these activities is great communication. That means leaders must be optimistic and consistent in delivering a message of moving forward. They must listen willingly to the concerns and fears of staff and take them seriously. And they must communicate regularly and consistently. (Communication is so important that we've devoted Chapter 5 to it.) Listed below, and described on pages 40–43, are actions commonly taken by successful change leaders.

Leading People Through Change

Here are actions that help guide staff, board, volunteers, and other stakeholders through the uncertain times after a merger.

- Act quickly and decisively, especially with regard to leadership.
- Be sensitive to people's needs and concerns.
- To the extent possible, take care of those individuals who are leaving the organization.
- Have high expectations and help people meet them.
- Focus on those individuals who are most supportive of, and enthusiastic about, the merger.
- Give people a sense of involvement and control.
- Create cross-organizational and cross-functional teams to work on challenges and problems.
- Talk with people face-to-face.
- Continually check the "pulse" of the organization.
- Make adjustments where needed.
- Acknowledge that there will be bumps along the road, and address them when they are encountered.
- Acknowledge people who have put in extra effort.
- Celebrate!

[9] William Bridges, *Managing Transitions: Making the Most of Change* (Cambridge, MA: Perseus Books, 1991).

Act quickly and decisively, especially with regard to leadership. The worst aspect of change for most people is the accompanying uncertainty. Most people worry about how the change will impact them personally and are unsettled by their lack of control. Information eases the discomfort. Therefore, people need both *clarity* and *stable direction* from you.

Clarity starts with the appointment of the executive director for the merged organization. The executive director should be named quickly, followed as soon as possible by the appointment of the rest of the leadership structure.

Decisions about top leadership positions should be made with an understanding of the skills and experience that contribute to effective change leadership. These attributes will be a critical component of all such positions throughout the integration process. In fact, managers who are good at change leadership will be an asset to the organization long beyond the merger integration process.

Just as the decision about the executive director should be made quickly, so, too, should the decision about the role (if any) of the former executive directors of the merging organizations. This is one area where the nonprofit sector often diverges from business. In the nonprofit sector, former executive directors often remain involved, even if they are not selected to lead the merged organization. In general, however, we have found (both through research and our own experience) that having a former executive director remain to work "under" the new leader is unproductive. The arrangement can confuse staff, divide loyalties, and perpetuate the "us-and-them" syndrome. The former executive directors must be treated well, however—because it is right, and because their treatment will be watched by the staffs they once led.

Following the decisions about the organization's leadership, make all other staffing changes as soon as possible. For example, if there is to be a reduction in staff, make the announcement and the reduction in quick succession. The results of a survey of post-merger leaders underscore this point: 90 percent of those surveyed said they would make staffing changes more quickly.[10]

The flip side of quick action is patience. People need time to adapt to change; true and lasting integration takes time. It will likely be several years before the merged organization truly feels like one seamless entity, both internally and externally. Patience demonstrates that you do not expect the impossible. However, some people interpret patience as indecision or as an excuse to foot-drag. Therefore be patient—except when impatience is needed.

Be sensitive to people's needs and concerns. When leading an integration, you need to listen to and address the concerns of people throughout the organization—both paid

---

[10] Mark L. Feldman and Michael F. Spratt, *Five Frogs on a Log* (New York: HarperBusiness, 1999), 8.

staff and volunteers. Communicate with respect and care. Be sure to welcome *everyone* into the "new" organization; avoid communications that perpetuate feelings of "us" versus "them" in discussion, action, or demeanor.

To the extent possible, take care of those individuals who are leaving the organization. Although large-scale layoffs are almost unheard of in nonprofit mergers (we have never encountered one), often a small number of employees will leave through choice or through elimination of a duplicated position. Treat them fairly and humanely and provide severance, out-placement services, and/or time and support for a job search (for example, the use of office space or telephone). Remaining staff will be watching to see how well the new organization takes care of those who are leaving, and they will form opinions about the new organization's management philosophy and attitude toward staff based on what they see. This is particularly true when the departing individuals are former leaders. Staff will have natural allegiances at this point and will watch to see how their leaders are treated.

You may lose some staff because they are not comfortable with change and uncertainty. This is something to expect, and it should be accepted as a normal part of restructuring.

Have high expectations and help people meet them. While it is important to be sensitive to the difficulties of transition, the leader must also be clear about what behavior is and is not acceptable. Never let individual acting-out take over and derail progress toward integration.

An important component of change leadership is to emphasize performance. Board, paid staff, and volunteers need clear assignments and responsibilities. To most effectively engage them in the transition, assign specific responsibilities for creating the new organization, allow them to do their job (paid or volunteer), and emphasize and evaluate performance. If an individual's performance is not up to the agreed-on standards, state what needs to change and the consequences if improvements aren't made.

Emphasizing performance means making an effort to match people with positions in a way that both empowers them and paves the way for positive outcomes. The integration process must consider individual employees and volunteers by quickly matching skills to organizational needs, opening growth opportunities, and addressing each employee's pay and position issues. It also needs to attend to the *collective* needs of the organization—to have a talented, merged staff that contribute individually and as a team to mission success.

Focus on those individuals who are most supportive of, and enthusiastic about, the merger. In most cases at least, 10 percent to 20 percent of staff enthusiastically support the merger. Convert these people into ambassadors for change. The more ambassadors you have, the more quickly and easily the positive message will filter through the organization and take hold.

From the Field . . .

"You have to have clearly focused executive leadership on the ground the day the merger occurs. Once you announce it you should have a plan in place, instantly have a management structure in place, and instantly give executive leadership to the new organization."

> — *Post-merger chief executive officer of a nonprofit educational and cultural center*

"I didn't want to announce the new management structure right away, but I would have started that process sooner. Too much was in limbo for too long."

> — *Post-merger executive director of a nonprofit human services organization*

Peter Senge, a management expert, expressed this change action as follows: "One of the most simple and basic lessons for leaders is to find where the energy wants to go and work with it. Sometimes there's a part of us that wants to correct the people that are wrong, rather than finding the people who are passionate to build something and supporting them . . . Change starts with the passionate few." [11]

Give people a sense of involvement and control. Delegate any decisions that can be delegated, and give staff appropriate levels of control. This involves staff directly in the change. Through this process, the leader transfers ownership of the change to the staff. An important indicator of successful integration is the degree to which the staff own the change, rather than seeing it as something imposed on them. Their sense of ownership and control will go far to alleviate the uncertainty of merger.

Create cross-organizational and cross-functional teams to work on challenges and problems. In interviews with nonprofit leaders, we consistently found that organizations that brought staff members together to work on a time-limited, shared project (such as creating a strategic plan for the new organization) early on in the integration process tended to move through that process more quickly and successfully than those that did not. Such a step allows people to focus on the new organization and its mission, and gets them involved in creating and then owning that new organization. Once invested in the new organization, they will be less likely to undermine it or to leave it.

Talk with people face-to-face. Leadership and communication go hand in hand—and the most effective form of communication is face-to-face. Memos, a web site, and the employee bulletin board are all helpful, but they should support, not replace, personal contact. This communication needs to be frequent and the message consistent. It also needs to be two way—where the leader listens to the opinions and feelings of the employees and volunteers as well as communicates where the organization is going with the change.

Continually check the "pulse" of the organization. Effective leaders are in touch with the people they lead. The best way to do this is in person, through conversation and active listening. Walk around, talk to people, listen, and generally tune in to the environment. Ask the change ambassadors to be sounding boards for their colleagues and channels for information within the organization.

Make adjustments where needed. No process can be perfectly predicted, nor perfectly planned. A successful leader continually monitors the change process and the integration plan, and adjusts as necessary. Accept that the plan will change; involve people in fine-tuning it. This shows staff that you do not have all the answers, that the plan can respond to changes in organizational reality, and that they can impact where the organization is going—all good messages after the merger (or at any time, for that matter).

Acknowledge that there will be bumps along the road, and address them as they are encountered. There will be rough spots in the integration process. For example, some people may leave the organization, either initially or at a later point in the process. This creates upheaval for those remaining, and can cause a new wave of fear and loss

> An important indicator of successful integration is the degree to which the staff own the change, rather than seeing it as something imposed on them.

[11] Frances Hesselbein and Rob Johnston, eds., *On Leading Change* (San Francisco: Jossey-Bass, 2002), 13.

and uncertainty. The leader needs to help people get through rough spots. The most successful strategy for handling the unexpected is to accept the fact that something unexpected will most likely happen, and then to communicate openly about it when it does occur.

Acknowledge people who have put in extra effort. It is extremely important to publicly recognize those who support the integration effort. This tells everyone what behavior and attitudes the new organization values. It demonstrates that those who support the new organization will be rewarded, at the very least by being publicly recognized. Encourage people who have accomplished something during the merger to tell others about it—at staff meetings or other gatherings—and visibly show your appreciation for their success. Such recognition helps the organization hold on to its people assets—employees and volunteers who feel valued are much less likely to leave. Recognition is a very effective, and often under used, reward in any organization.

Celebrate! Celebration in various ways and at multiple levels helps integration succeed. Celebration shows people that change is occurring. It brings them together, and acknowledges that the change effort is making a positive difference within the organization and the community. Celebrations can be large and public, or small and internal for a few staff; both types are important.

Board, Volunteers, and Donors

While paid staff will present the most challenges in leading people through change, board members, volunteers, and donors will present some unique people issues of their own.

Issues related to board members

For board members, the most pressing people issue is the risk of burnout—especially for those who were most involved in the merger negotiations. Watch for this and prepare to help those members shift out of the most intense roles. On the other hand, those tired board members who have been through the negotiation process are just the ones most likely to carry a strong commitment to making the deal work. A board that excludes all or most of these experienced warriors will have a more difficult time integrating. After all, they crossed the organizational divide and formed the partnership in the first place.

Some board members who were active in the negotiation process may have a difficult time when they shift into a less prominent role as others take on the oversight of the integration. These board members should be recognized for their contributions to the merger process.

Sometimes board members become quite active in operational matters during a merger negotiation; for example, negotiating staffing structures or reviewing the other party's

---

From the Field . . .

"The staff really needs you as a leader. They need you to reassure them. They need you to trust them with decisions. They need you to trust them with participation. They need you to be there to hear what's going on from their point of view, from their perspective."

— *Post-merger executive director of a nonprofit serving victims of domestic violence and sexual assault*

financial health. They will need support in understanding their new roles and responsibilities, letting go of former roles, and returning their focus to ongoing governance.

A newly merged organization presents an opportunity to engage board members who may have been on the sidelines in the past, but whose skills are needed by the new organization. Do your best to motivate to increase their involvement going forward.

Chapter 7 deals at length with the challenges and opportunities related to the board of directors in post-merger integration.

Issues related to volunteers

Volunteers are often emotionally tied to their organizations. After all, they work for free and have a choice about contributing those hours elsewhere. Because of this, they may be more closely tied to "the way things were" than paid staff, who at least have a monetary or career-related incentive to change with the organization. Make sure to attend to the needs and feelings of volunteers, and communicate closely with them. They are also a part of your staff.

Early in the integration process, meet with the volunteers of the former organizations, and assure them that you value their contributions. Bring them together at least once, and keep them informed at every step of the process.

From the Field . . .

"If there's going to be real cultural issues, it's probably among the volunteers. Staff will adjust if they want a job. With the volunteers it's an ownership issue."

— *Coordinator of strategic alliances for a national youth-serving organization*

Just as you must integrate other human resources systems and functions, you will need to integrate volunteer systems. As with paid staff, you must determine what volunteers need to do their jobs effectively. Often volunteers are the closest link to the organization's customers; they frequently serve as the face of the organization to the community.

Similarly, volunteers can provide a communication channel back to the organization, letting it know how the merger and the integration process is perceived in the community and among the organization's external stakeholders. Take advantage of your volunteers' knowledge and connections to learn about the community's perception of the merger, and adjust your community and public relations efforts as needed.

Issues related to key donors

As with volunteers, key donors may be emotionally attached to a pre-merger organization, and you will need a plan for addressing their concerns. Donors are similar to volunteers in that they receive intrinsic rewards (satisfaction) as well as rewards in the form of appreciation and recognition for their involvement with the organization. The merger and integration may threaten their perceived status within the nonprofit. Listen to donors and attend to their interests; otherwise, they may take their support elsewhere.

Smaller donors may simply write a check each year because they receive a solicitation. Because of changes in the organization's name, logo, or fundraising style, these donors may fail to connect your most recent mailing with their long-loved organization. Or they may make the connection, but not like the changes. In either case your appeal may end up in the wastebasket. To avoid this problem, give careful thought to communication strategies that will bring these donors along as the organization changes. Chapter 12 discusses such communications in more detail.

Summary

Because people are central to any organization, a successful merger depends on the skill with which you tend to the people issues brought about by the change. Expect fear, uncertainty, and reactions that seem illogical to you (but are perfectly logical to constituents). Help people overcome these normal responses by reducing the uncertainties: act quickly and decisively; be honest and transparent; delegate as much as possible; give people, especially staff, a role (and sense of control) in shaping their future with the new organization; recognize and reward accomplishments; and, most of all, celebrate your successes. Remember to keep everyone focused on the mission—something better than the merging organizations could have accomplished separately. By demonstrating effective and proactive leadership; communicating frequently, honestly, and clearly; and drawing on the support of the integration team and the human resources function, you can successfully address the challenges raised by people's natural, adverse reaction to change.

CHAPTER 5

Communication

Successful mergers require significant changes in attitudes and behavior. Communication is at the heart of change management. As communication expert Michael Blakstad states: "The best strategy in the world is ineffective unless properly communicated to the people whose support is needed to effect new policies."[12]

The overriding objective of merger communications is to win the understanding and commitment of stakeholders to the merger and the new organization. Effective internal and external communications can significantly improve the integration process and outcomes.

A well-planned communication campaign, ideally initiated in the negotiation period and continuing through the merger announcement and the integration process, can make the change process smoother. It can shorten the integration time frame; reduce stress surrounding the change process; and mobilize board, staff, and volunteers to make constructive contributions to the new organization. Effective communications can stimulate board enthusiasm and support, improve employee and volunteer morale, increase client satisfaction, enhance public and media perceptions of the organization, and increase the appeal of the new organization to donors and funders.[13] (Of course, no amount of communication can make an ill-conceived merger successful.)

---

[12] Nancy Welch and Mark Goldstein, *Communicating for Change: Ideas from Contemporary Research*, Report 01-FN010 (San Francisco: International Association of Business Communicators [IABC] Research Foundation), ii.

[13] The research bears this out. For example, a recent Conference Board survey found a correlation between effective communication and positive merger results. (Ainspan and Bell, *Employee Communications*, 5.) Other studies show that business mergers fail to meet their objectives 50 percent to 85 percent of the time, and that communication activities were found to be one of the most crucial determinants of successful business mergers. (Welch and Goldstein, *Communicating for Change*, 11–12.)

Organizations that use communications most effectively consider communication to be a fundamental management system, encompassing a plan, strategy, accountability for outcomes, and education and training.[14] The communication system facilitates the exchange of ideas, messages, and information using a variety of vehicles and media, tailored to the needs of the organization and its stakeholders. It is a two-way channel, supporting both the sending and receiving messages.

While organizational leaders usually agree that communication is essential to change management success,[15] all too often communication is shortchanged. As you embark on your integration process, we urge you to avoid this mistake. Invest in communication from the start.

In this chapter we describe the role of, and rationale for, internal and external communication in the merger integration process. In doing so, we discuss the following:

- Characteristics of effective change communication
- Assembling a communication working group
- Internal and external audiences for communications
- Messages and the timing of their delivery
- The importance of promoting the new organization
- Communication vehicles and media
- Monitoring, evaluation, and revision of the communication plan

Much of our discussion focuses on internal communication, as this is where organizations must expend significant energy throughout the merger process, and where most of the communication efforts are focused in the early stages of the process.

This is not to give short shrift to external communication; much of external communication mirrors internal communication. Having a sound internal communication plan in place early in the process will lay a foundation for the creation and execution of an external communication plan.

This chapter lays the groundwork for the creation of your own communication plan; Chapter 12 walks you through steps designed to help you build an actual plan—one tailored to the needs of your newly merged organization.

Communication: A Two-Way Street

Communication involves not only disseminating information, but also receiving and interpreting information. Organizations often communicate "top down," and ignore the impact of such communication on their constituents. Lack of attention to stakeholders' questions and concerns can thwart efforts to integrate.

---

[14] Roger D'Aprix, *Communicating for Change: Connecting the Workplace with the Marketplace* (San Francisco: Jossey-Bass, 1996), 49.

[15] Welch and Goldstein, *Communicating for Change*, ii, 5–7.

To avoid this, develop a communication plan that includes a means of obtaining feedback from stakeholders and of continuously evaluating the communication campaign. Feedback obtained early in the process will help shape the plan and the messages, as well as the vehicles, media, and time frames for their delivery. This feedback—solicited through formal and informal surveys, focus groups, one-on-one and group meetings, telephone calls, telephone hotlines, e-mail, suggestion boxes, and other channels—can pinpoint stakeholders' concerns, questions, and needs for additional information.

Besides being two way, effective communications about organizational change share other characteristics. Assess your ongoing communications and your communication plan against the list that follows. (For a quick reminder, use the sidebar Effective Communications on page 50.)

Proactive. At all times, and most of all during periods of organizational change, communication must be *proactive.* If not addressed up front, the fear, uncertainty, and doubt that abound during periods of change will run rampant and threaten to destroy the change process. This is especially true in a merger situation. The communication team must be prepared for the questions and concerns that will arise during the change process and address them before they become serious roadblocks.

Interactive. As noted, communication is a two-way street. Listen and interact—and be sure communications are bottom up and top down. Add mechanisms (staff surveys, focus groups, telephone hotlines, and informal one-on-one and group meetings) to learn what questions, concerns, and issues stakeholders have and to address these proactively.

Candid. While you can't know all the answers, be honest about what *is* known. When you can't answer a question, tell people when you will know the answer. Then follow up to either provide the answers sought or indicate that you need more time.

Clear. Clarity is always important in the uncertain environment of organizational change, and it is essential during merger integration. Ambiguous communications can lead to misinterpretation and rumors, exacerbating the fears and doubts that hinder integration.

Continuous. Communications must also be *continuous* during the integration process. Experts in merger integration consistently admonish: "Communicate, communicate, communicate." When in doubt, err on the side of over-communication.

Content-rich. While it is better to over-communicate than under-communicate, communication must also have *content.* Strike a balance: don't overwhelm people with too much raw (unprocessed) information, and don't lose them with empty fluff about the ideal world to come once the merged organization is up and running.

From the Field...

"You've got to keep communicating with everybody because there's a tendency to rely on old patterns. To establish new patterns, you need new forms of communication. You have to keep communicating the message that it's a new organization."

— *Executive director of an arts organization that merged with a similar nonprofit*

Consistent. Choose your messages and consistently reinforce them among all stakeholders. While messages will be framed somewhat differently depending on the audience, the content of the messages should be consistent.

Customized. The interests and concerns of stakeholders vary, so customize your messages to different stakeholder audiences. For example, donors may need to know that the good work they've supported will continue but under a new name; staff may need to know that they will still have the same jobs, but some of the processes will change. The message of good service is consistent, but the form is customized. When possible, customize to the extreme: each person you deal with experiences the merger differently, so be personal. One-on-one meetings are great for this.

Courteous. Under the stress of merger, volunteers may feel depressed as they mourn the loss of the old. Employees may express anger and resentment to others, especially as fears and uncertainty over their personal futures arise. Donors may seem irrationally upset over the changed name of a program. Defensive reactions to these emotions only fuel the fire. Douse the fire with courtesy and true respect, even when you feel you are under personal attack. Even as you calm fears, you'll be modeling the behavior you want from all constituents.

Credible. It doesn't matter what you say if people don't believe you. Some stakeholders may experience merger as a fracturing of trust—and most stakeholders will be less trusting when they are stressed by change that's out of their control. Rebuild trust through honest communication. Make the communication credible by following it up with consistent action.

Effective Communications

Excellent communication is the best tool for alleviating the stress of merger. Regardless of the means of communication, it should have the following characteristics.

- *Proactive.* Anticipate and address questions before they harden into roadblocks.

- *Interactive.* Find out what people think and respond.

- *Candid.* Say what you know; if you don't know, say so and say you *will* know.

- *Clear.* Ambiguous statements only heighten fear and distrust.

- *Continuous.* Better to hear "you told us that before" than to miss someone.

- *Content-rich.* Don't communicate fluff; don't be too general.

- *Consistent.* It's fine to reframe for different groups, but the core message should stay the same.

- *Customized.* Alter the framework for the message to fit the audience.

- *Courteous.* Respect your stakeholders—even when they seem hostile or needy.

- *Credible.* You can only build trust through honest, believable messages that are followed up by action.

Assembling a Communication Working Group

As discussed in Chapter 3, the integration team will be a key communicator throughout the integration process. Ideally, at least one person responsible for communication at each of the merging organizations should be appointed to the integration team as soon as possible after the decision to merge. Together these individuals should invite other staff to form a communication working group and develop a communication plan for the merger announcement and subsequent integration.

Choose these people carefully; not only will they shape and guide the communication plan, but also they must model effective communication for the rest of the organization. Some nonprofits have specific communication staff on board. If the merging organizations have such staff, your choice should be obvious and easy. But many nonprofits spread communication-related functions throughout the organization. If this is the case, select those people with the most experience communicating to both internal and external audiences. Likely candidates with internal communication skills can be found among those staff who focus on internal communications. Human resources or operations and information systems (IS) staff are often responsible for electronic or print communications to staff and volunteers.

For external communication skills, look to the development director, particularly with respect to donor and funder communications. This person, who often wears numerous hats—media relations, public relations, customer service, and marketing—knows how to create promotional materials, such as brochures, newsletters, and annual reports.

Additionally, board members might be tapped as resources for external communication. They will know people and organizations in the community that should be kept informed of the integration process. Board members may also have experience preparing communications to constituent groups.

Thus, as you assemble both your integration team and communication working group, be sure to include people who already have the skills and connections needed to shape key messages and collect information from constituents. Try not to let your group grow too large, however. While you ultimately want *everyone* in the organization to serve as communicators, more than five to six people in the working group could get unwieldy.

At this point—and you should reach this point *very* early in the integration process—the working group needs to get busy identifying the different audiences for your communications; your messages; your marketing goals and process; your communication vehicles and media; your methods of gathering feedback on the integration process; and your plans for monitoring, evaluating, and revising your communication plan. We will cover some of these topics in this chapter; the rest will be made clear in Chapter 12.

The Role of Information Technology and Human Resources in a Communication Plan

Information Technology. Because of the large and increasing role technology plays in communication today, the information technology function should be represented not only on the integration team, but also on any communication working group. One important responsibility of the information technology professional will be to inventory the merging organizations' information systems (telephones, hardware, Internet, intranet). Until these systems are merged (which may take months and even years), information technology staff must ensure that the systems can talk to each other.

This may seem more of a systems issue than a communication strategy. But information technology systems—such as e-mail, listservs, web sites, intranets, online bulletin boards, and so forth—can help deliver key messages. If, for example, the merging organizations have different e-mail systems, this channel may not be fully available to support integration.

Human Resources (HR). Throughout the integration process, staff with internal communication responsibilities should work closely with those responsible for human resources functions. Human resources staff have a major role in translating words into actions. The new organization's philosophy about treatment of staff will be reflected in the way staff are treated during the integration process. Equitable integration of fringe benefits is one way these words are reflected in actions. As the new organization takes shape, it will be important to work closely with human resources staff to provide clear descriptions of roles, responsibilities, and expectations.

As with information technology, the human resources function may seem more of a systems issue than a communication issue. But at a minimum, human resources is responsible for formal communications about jobs. More important, the way in which human resources shapes and fulfills promises made by the leaders of the merger will influence the credibility of all communications.

Identifying Audiences

Your organization's stakeholders can be categorized into internal and external audiences. Each audience needs to be addressed during the integration process.

Internal audiences include staff, board members, and volunteers. These stakeholders should always be the first to be informed of the decision to merge and subsequent plans for integration.

External audiences include funders and donors (current, past, and prospective), other community leaders, consumers and clients, the media, collaborating or partner organizations (such as referral agencies, organizations with complementary programs), and the community and public at large. Depending on the nature of the merging organizations, external audiences may include government agencies (when the nonprofits are funded or regulated by public agencies) and lobbying groups. Other external audiences include any professional associations or affinity groups to which the organizations belong.

Delivering the Message

Chapter 12 discusses the types and timing of communications to your stakeholder groups in detail. Following is a list of the basic messages that need to be communicated to the internal and external audiences.

From the beginning: Explain the merger

Too often, communication focuses on the who, what, and when questions. These are important, but the response to why has the most powerful influence on behavior and acceptance of the merger. This is particularly true during negotiations and in the days immediately after the decision to merge is made. Research and experience attest to the fact that people are much more accepting of change, even if they stand to lose their jobs, if there is a clear, understandable reason for the change.

Answering why involves presenting the opportunities or challenges that predicated the decision to merge. In essence, a merger will be justified in the minds of stakeholders if they understand why it is occurring and the negative consequences likely if it did *not* occur. One of the first charges of the integration team is thus to craft a merger message that includes who, what, and when, but emphasizes why—especially, the benefits of merging and the downsides if merger does not occur. Remember to check your message against the characteristics of effective communication listed earlier in this chapter on pages 48–50.

> **From the Field . . .**
>
> "Focus on the mission and big picture—stress that the best interests of the clients was a primary motivator for the merger."
>
> — *Executive director of a legal services organization after the merger of his organization with two others that did similar work*

From announcement to integration: Announce name, staff, and service changes

Once the decision to merge has been made, it must be announced both internally and externally. From this point onward significant information will need to be communicated. The main message continues to be the rationale for the merger, but communication should expand to address all the major changes occurring as a result of the integration. These include

- The identities of the new leadership (staff and board)
- The merged organization's name, and the process for selecting and adopting it
- Staff reductions and additions
- Changes in roles and responsibilities (for management, staff, and volunteers)
- Changes to location of staff
- Changes to programs and services

Decisions regarding these and other issues may not be made at the time of the initial merger announcement. Ideally, these decisions will now be made quickly. The longer it takes to make decisions regarding staff roles and responsibilities, the more stressful the situation for staff, and the greater the likelihood of rumors and other negative communications circulating that will threaten the stability and success of the new organization.

Both internal and external stakeholders will want to know how you handle critical changes, such as new leadership appointments, staff reductions, or closing of offices (if applicable). Be sure to accurately and honestly describe the decisions and actions in both internal and external communications. Be direct and as transparent as possible, knowing that while some constituents will dislike (and challenge) your decisions, most will respect your candor.

Throughout the process: Update stakeholders using every media

During the merger integration stage, send out regular updates to all stakeholders. For example, use newsletters (print and e-mail) and the organization's web site and intranet to keep stakeholders up-to-date on the integration process.

It is important to have interactive communication with stakeholders to ensure that the integration proceeds smoothly. This includes face-to-face meetings (one-on-one, in groups, in town hall forums) and phone and e-mail communications, where the organization's leadership can listen to concerns and address them. Remember, too, unanticipated situations always arise and require a quick response.

Promoting the New Organization

Once the merger has taken place, turn energy and resources to a specific form of external communication: promotional activities. The sooner such materials for the new organization can be created and disseminated, the better.

Often, nonprofits do not give sufficient attention to promoting themselves. To fully advance their mission, however, nonprofits must market their vision. This involves selling donors and other constituents on the value of the nonprofit's work and its effectiveness in advancing its mission. This marketing motivates funders and donors to invest in the nonprofit's work. They are, essentially, "buying" the nonprofit's services and, in the bigger scheme of things, its vision.

To attract and keep the best-qualified board, staff, and volunteers, nonprofits must market themselves to these stakeholders. These individuals invest their time and energy in the organization, "buying" the status and personal fulfillment they receive from supporting its vision and mission. The press and community leaders are also valuable resources to nonprofits. If they buy the organization's vision and mission, they can be powerful supporters. Press coverage (when it's positive!) can help nonprofits gain needed visibility with external audiences.

The nitty-gritty of promotions

The introduction of the "new" nonprofit is essentially a branding process—one that requires expertise to execute. Staff and board experience will help you determine whether or not you need outside assistance. Regardless, many details must be considered when developing a plan to integrate the marketing activity of merging organizations. These include the following:

- *The new organization's name.* There are several options: one of the former organization's names, a blended name, or a new name altogether.

- *Program names.* These may also be changed, especially if similar programs are being merged. However, program names are often valued as dearly as corporate names; sometimes more so. All naming activity should begin and end with consideration of the Hippocratic oath: "First, do no harm." An organization's greatest asset is constituent and public recognition of its name.

- *Image: logo, color schemes, "look and feel."* The branding process will also incorporate a "look" for the organization, which may include a new logo, a new color scheme, and new design work.

- *Promotional messages.* New tag lines, key messages, and value statements may be developed.

- *Promotional materials.* The changes listed above affect all marketing materials. Conduct a complete inventory of all marketing materials to identify those that need revision. For example, the text of a program brochure may not change, but the old logo will need to be replaced. Or the entire text may need to be revised. Marketing materials include a broad spectrum of communications: brochures, flyers, letterhead, second-page stationery, envelopes, labels, report covers, business cards, web sites, intranet, signage, posters, promotional items (mugs, bookmarks, and other giveaways), advertising, and trade show materials. Boilerplate language for grant and federal proposals must also be reviewed and updated.

- *Communication systems.* If any organization locations close or new ones open, addresses and telephone numbers will change. Similarly, web site and intranets will need to be integrated. Integration of these communication systems—telephone, regular mail, interoffice mail, Internet and intranet sites—requires the active involvement of staff responsible for information technologies and facilities.

Two Types of Communication

Communication can be divided into two types: *broadcast* and *interactive*.

Broadcast communications are one-way communications that are intended to reach many audiences. They typically do not allow for interaction between the communicator and those receiving the message. These media include newsletters, announcements delivered on a web site, letters and memos, video presentations, press releases, advertisements—any one-way communication delivered en masse.

Interactive communications are two-way communications that, as their name implies, allow for interaction. They include telephone discussions, in-person presentations with time set aside for questions, answers, and discussion, town hall forums, one-on-one and group meetings, e-mail exchanges, online bulletin boards, and chat rooms on Internet or intranet sites.

Communication Vehicles and Media

Communications can be delivered via a variety of vehicles, including print, audio, visual, and electronic. Each of these can use a variety of media:

- Print: newsletters, brochures, flyers, press releases
- Audio: radio, live or recorded presentations, telephone, mass voice mail
- Visual: TV, video, images, pictures
- Electronic: e-mail, web sites, online bulletin boards, chat rooms
- Combination: for example, voice and visual—one-on-one meetings or interviews, group meetings, focus groups

All of these options can be useful in a comprehensive communication campaign. However, make sure that all stakeholders whom you wish to reach have access to the communications. If they do not, some important constituents may be excluded—an invitation for trouble.

Face-to-face: Still the most effective vehicle

Despite all of the options available through electronic media, the optimal method for communicating is still face-to-face. In-person communication should be used throughout the integration process and, in fact, is the primary method of communicating in the pre-merger (negotiation) stage. Because they are time and resource intensive, face-to-face communications should be supplemented by broadcast communications.

Depending on the location of the merging entities and their staffs, there may be constraints on the use of face-to-face communication. In some instances, telephone calls and e-mail messages can substitute. But neither is a completely adequate substitute for

---

More Tips for Effective Communication

Here are more things to remember for effective communicating during a merger.

Listening: an often overlooked communication skill. In any organizational change, interactive communications are essential; this is especially true in the initial stages of post-merger integration. The only consistent "known" in such a time is that there will be many questions regarding the change. Those in charge of communication must *listen* to those who are impacted by the change—to hear their concerns, questions, and issues. These *must* be addressed in order for the integration to proceed smoothly. Interactive communication provides a means of measuring the success of the integration process on

an ongoing basis, as well as gauging the audience's response to communications.

Everyone is a communicator. Effective communication should be part of everyone's job description, particularly those in management and leadership positions. Staff and volunteers should be responsible and accountable for their communications. Use surveys, focus groups, and performance evaluation processes that draw on input from other staff members and clients or customers to ensure accountability. Provide educational and training resources for those who need to improve their communication skills.

in-person communication. Many nonverbal messages (facial expressions, body language) will not be captured in other forms of communication.

Actions speak louder than words

Remember that actions communicate far more than words. Actions that are inconsistent with verbal and written messages can undermine trust and be detrimental to your goals. For example, the verbal communication may be that the merging organizations will be treated as equals. However, if all pre-merger meetings are held at Organization A, and none at Organization B, this may communicate to the staff of both organizations that one group is less important, or less valued.

Feedback

We have already touched on the importance of establishing a feedback loop to gather input from stakeholders throughout the integration process, beginning with the negotiation stage. This loop helps you shape and guide the integration, as well as evaluate the effectiveness of the communication plan and communication materials. Design the feedback loop so that all board and staff members have a role in it. Encourage everyone to provide input and to capture input from others, while preserving confidentiality.

Both formal (surveys, focus groups) and informal (telephone calls, one-on-one meetings) methods should be in place to obtain feedback and channel it to communication staff. This will mean training staff to interact with external stakeholders to capture questions, issues, and concerns, and to report on these at the regular meetings of the communication working group. This group should summarize the feedback and report on it at the integration team meetings.

To complete the feedback loop, the integration team should communicate back to the stakeholders themselves (or to those who have contact with stakeholders) via updates to a talking-points document, a questions-and-answers document, web site information, intranet information, or other communication vehicles. Chapter 12 provides more detail on all of these options.

Evaluation

The communication working group, under the guidance of the integration team, should evaluate the degree to which it meets the goals and deadlines of both the communication plan and the overall integration plan. For example, consider a plan in which a key objective is to rally stakeholders behind the "problem" facing the merging organizations, to understand and buy into the rationale for the merger, and to support the vision of the new organization. The communication working group could measure achievement of

Grieving and Griping

Communication embodies the "people" aspect of the integration. By openly acknowledging that integration involves losses, communication helps people move through this period. Pretending that losses don't exist upsets people. However, it is equally important to draw a line between acceptable grieving and unacceptable acting out. Communications should encourage people to take charge of the situation, and to become involved in both the formation of the new organization and in career self-management. Some leaders, wanting to acknowledge their staff's need for grieving and carping while still moving forward, allow a ten-minute gripe session at the beginning of staff meetings. During this period, while all complaints, laments, and other feelings of loss are expressed, management listens quietly. When the period is over, the staff leader moves on to the agenda.

this objective using surveys and focus groups with the different stakeholder groups: staff, clients, customers, community leaders, funders, and donors, to name a few. Other measures might include the degree and nature of media coverage of the merger.

Such evaluation mechanisms really serve two purposes: they help the team know if it is accomplishing its goals, and they help it adjust the messages and media used to accomplish the goals. Ideally, the evaluation cycle (and surveys and focus groups, if called for) begins during negotiation, and continues through merger implementation—say, at three, six, and twelve months after the announcement. The communication working group itself can undertake actual evaluation activities. Outside evaluators are rarely required.

Summary

Effective communication—both internal and external—is critical in a merger situation. Careful planning and attention to both "outgoing" and "incoming" communications are required. This chapter described the characteristics of effective communication; make sure that everyone in the organization understands these—especially the leaders—and that all of your messages embody them.

Change is difficult, but it is much less threatening when understood. Announce your decision to merge and make the benefits clear as soon as possible after the decision. Update stakeholders throughout the merger process, using a variety of methods and media. Remember that face-to-face communication is always most effective; arrange for meetings, focus groups, and social gatherings to share information whenever possible. Lastly, remember that even the best-laid plans can go awry. Establish feedback loops and evaluate the effectiveness of your communication strategy at regular intervals throughout the integration process.

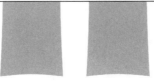

SECTION II
Creating an Integration Plan

CHAPTER 6

Creating and Using an Integration Plan

As discussed in Chapter 3, the purpose of an integration plan is simply to help you organize the work required in the many important integration areas into a comprehensive plan, with responsibilities, expectations, and time lines clearly spelled out. The plan you create will be a living, changing document, but it will also serve as a touchstone for all future integration activity. This chapter suggests two possible processes for getting started on the plan, and then offers a tool to assist you.

Jump-Starting an Integration Plan

There are two basic approaches to creating the *initial* version of your integration plan. You can use a small group—usually the integration team—or you can use the entire staff (or, minimally, a large group of staff leaders). We'll examine both approaches here.

The integration team as driver for the plan

Some organizations choose to have the integration team develop the integration plan. The team involves lead staff from all departments in setting key outcomes and creating an action plan.

This approach typically takes several weeks, assuming two to four meetings of three or four hours each over the course of that time. We recommend that you commit to an intensive work schedule to get the plan done within a few weeks, so you don't dilute momentum.

It is easier to coordinate the schedules of the limited number of people on the integration team. If the team includes good planners and big-picture thinkers who can clearly see (and articulate) where the merged organization is heading and what needs to be done to get there, it can rapidly set out an action plan. After creating a draft of the plan, the team gains department-head approval of the time frame and action steps, since department heads know best what their staffs can accomplish.

Speed and ease are clear benefits of this approach, but there are several potential drawbacks. It depends largely on the makeup of the integration team; the wrong mix can hinder good planning. The approach also reduces staff involvement and buy-in. Instead, a team creates the plan, the department heads modify and approve it, and then staff must commit to their respective roles in the process.

The staff-wide planning approach (one version of which is described next) can overcome these drawbacks.

Staff as driver for the integration plan

Some organizations hold a one- or two-day staff retreat to jump-start integration planning. This is a great way to get the entire staff (or staff leadership, depending on the size of the organization) to work together toward a new future for the merged organization. It can be very effective in building a sense of teamwork throughout the newly merged organization, while at the same time accomplishing a key planning activity with everyone's buy-in more assured. Because the staff drafted the plan and the timeline, they can feel confident that the tasks and deadlines are achievable. They will have built a sense of commitment to and ownership of the plan. The staff-retreat approach has drawbacks as well: retreats are difficult to coordinate, they can be costly (in budget and lost work time), and they can be cumbersome.

The product that comes out of such a retreat won't be a "final" plan, but it should be as comprehensive as possible. Like a plan jump-started by an integration team, it will need to be reviewed and approved by the various department heads, and it should always be viewed as a "work in progress." Integration never goes exactly as planned, and you always need to be ready and able to modify tasks, dates, and even team assignments as circumstances change. In this approach, once the plan has been approved, an integration team could assume responsibility for managing it.

Developing the Content

Regardless of who creates the initial plan, it must contain certain types of information:

- Desired Outcomes: What are you hoping to achieve within each integration area? What does successful integration look like?
- Activities: What activities need to be accomplished to get you from where you are to where you want to be?
- Lead Person: Who has primary responsibility for making sure each activity is accomplished?

- Team: Who else will work on that activity?
- Start Date and Target Date: When does work on that activity need to start, and—if it is not an ongoing requirement—by what date does it need to be completed?

Exactly *how* the planning group answers these questions can vary. We recommend doing the initial work in a room with a lot of wall space. Post large sheets of paper on those walls to represent a twelve- to eighteen-month timeline. List the months horizontally along the top of your charts, and the activities vertically. As you add activities, ask yourself: is everything in the right order? That is, if A has to happen before B, is A *scheduled* to happen before B? Your goal is to organize activities so that they all happen at the right time relative to each other.

One key to developing a useful integration plan is not getting bogged down in details. Those responsible for each activity will lay out the specific tasks to be accomplished. In this level of planning, you want to get the big-picture "must do's" out on the table and organized into the same plan.

Recording the Plan

Once the initial planning group—however you have defined it—has laid out the full set of activities necessary to accomplish integration, you need to record this information in a form that can be modified and adapted over time and serve as a guide through the integration process. You can do this on your own, using a word-processing program, database, or spreadsheet, or you can use the integration planning tool that accompanies this book. The software tool, which is based on a database, is also available on Wilder Publishing Center's web site. This workbook assumes that you will be using this tool, but it in no way requires you to do so—the material presented will help you create a plan in whatever format works best for your organization.

Once you have, and are able to print, a first draft of your plan, get input from organizational leaders, affected line staff, board members, volunteers, and anyone else with a stake in the integration effort. Remember, you want these people on board. Make changes to the plan until you have a document that everyone on the integration team and everyone in management buys into.

If you are using our tool to create your plan, note that at any time you can either print and use the plan "as-is," or you can export it to a word-processing file for further editing. The latter can be helpful in that you can invite each department and staff working group to add detail to the sections for which they are responsible, creating their own "living documents" in the process.

Monitoring Your Progress

Assign someone to be responsible for regularly updating the plan (using the software tool or your own document), and make sure that you incorporate changes to both activities and timeline as you move forward.

The integration team should meet regularly to review progress in each integration area. Use these meetings to learn what is working well and where you are encountering problems. Always keep the articulated desired outcomes at the forefront of your mind.

Questions to guide these discussions can include the following:

- What actions have been accomplished— what have we learned?
- What problems or challenges are we encountering?
- Does anything need to be changed—any midcourse adjustments?

The integration team should set a clear milestone—such as a full year of joint operations or completion of a budget cycle—that tells the organization that integration is complete, and it's time for "business as normal."[16] This clear goal keeps the process accountable to key deadlines, and helps employees set and work toward a goal, and then move on. Reaching that milestone is a great time to gather the staff together for a celebration of their accomplishment.

We now move into the "nitty-gritty" of integration planning.

How to Use Section II

Chapter 3 provides an overview of how to manage the integration process. Be sure to read it before proceeding into this section, where you will actually create the plan itself.

Section II includes Chapters 6 through 13. Starting with Chapter 7, each chapter discusses the integration of one particular area of the organization. You'll note that each chapter follows a similar format:

- First, a portion of the text entitled Envisioning the Future describes what the *future* of that area should look like. It helps you picture how a fully integrated board or a fully integrated human resources department (for example) should look and act. It will also help you think through your organization's desired outcomes for this area.
- Next, the chapter describes the steps necessary to achieve successful integration of that area according to the timeline that naturally occurs in a merger. It starts with steps that begin (ideally) *before* the merger, often when the organizations are just beginning to size each other up. It ends with steps that result in full unification. (Of course, this pattern varies based on the particular organizational element being integrated.)
- Finally, the chapter highlights the key challenges and roadblocks that organizations usually encounter *during* the integration of that area.

---

[16] Kristina Lucenko, *Implementing a Post-Merger Integration* (New York: The Conference Board, 1999), 19.

Once you are ready to begin, read each chapter in this section and complete any applicable worksheets. Throughout Chapters 7–13, you will find exhibits summarizing common desired outcomes and activities related to the various aspects of integration—board, management, staff, and so forth.[17] Exhibit 4: Managing the Integration Process, page 66, provides a list of tasks for the integration team. Make notes on these exhibits if you wish, and bring them to your planning meeting(s). Use them to "seed" your discussions when creating your own lists. Remember to include those activities that are most important for *your* integration process. Also remember to keep your activities general enough so that you don't get bogged down in details. Use the software tool or whatever tool works best for you to record your desired outcomes and activities. From this point on, follow the process described on page 64 (Monitoring Your Progress) and in Chapter 3 to refine and use your plan over time.

No treatment of integration planning can address all the variations likely in each integration process. The size, scope, mission, culture, location, and history of each merging organization all impact the specifics of the integration plan and dictate what is most appropriate for a given merger. Our discussion in the following chapters represents a middle-of-the road merger situation—one that applies to most situations and that addresses the most commonly encountered issues and challenges. We presume a merger between two organizations that are sufficiently complex to involve challenges within each area of integration, but not so complex that the necessary steps to integration will be beyond the scope of what is relevant to most mergers. Further, we assume that the two nonprofits are located in the same geographic region and that staff from each can move somewhat freely between various offices and service provision locations.

Creating the integration plan is a critical step in bringing your organizations together. The value of the plan is about equally divided between the substantive work it lays out and the process of coming together that it requires. Keep that balance in mind if you are tempted to sit in your office and create an integration plan by yourself.

---

[17] Note that Chapter 8 does not include an exhibit for cultural integration; instead, cultural integration activities appear in the other lists, specifically those covering the integration of staff, volunteers, and management.

Exhibit 4: Managing the Integration Process

Key Activities

The following list, while not exhaustive, includes activities that need to be accomplished during the early stages of integration planning. You may want to include some or all of these activities in your integration plan.

The Integration Team

❑ Define the "ideal" integration team for this situation.

❑ Draft integration team "job descriptions" including roles, responsibilities, and time frame.

❑ Select and invite individuals to join the integration team.

❑ Select an integration manager.

❑ Clarify the team's role, goals, and channels of communication.

❑ Designate working groups for key integration areas.

The Integration Plan

❑ Decide *how* to create the first draft of an integration plan.

❑ Articulate the desired outcomes for integration, the necessary action steps, and a timeline.

❑ Enter planning data into the software tool and generate reports for staff and board members in "lead" roles.

❑ Review reports and make any changes necessary; finalize the plan.

❑ Design a process for monitoring progress toward integration.

❑ Establish methods for gathering and incorporating feedback on the plan, ensuring that it remains a "living document."

CHAPTER 7

Board Integration

B oard integration is the process of creating a new, effective board of directors from the boards of previously separate organizations. It involves the creation of a new cultural identity, as well as new roles and responsibilities. Most importantly, it involves developing a sense of shared ownership for the enterprise.

Envisioning the Future

As a first step in developing a plan to integrate your boards into a new governing body, take time to visualize the board you will need for your newly merged organization. If you could describe the board of your new organization one year after its merger, what would you say are its most important characteristics? Every organization's board will have its own particular character, but there are important goals to work toward as you create the board of your new entity.

Here are things to think about as you plan your new board:

- A successfully integrated board provides the leadership necessary to serve the mission of the new organization and works as a unified team.
- The new board includes individuals from each of the merging organizations, as well as new members brought on after the merger is complete.
- The new board takes the best practices from each of the former boards, creates new ones as necessary, and develops a governance style that works for the merged organization.
- The new board assesses its capacity to oversee an organization that is considerably larger or more complex than the organizations that formed it. New skills, and thus new board members, may be needed.

Though the new board is not being created entirely from scratch, the integration process serves as a valuable opportunity to carefully consider its roles and responsibilities. The key is to understand the nature of the board's governing role, and to develop practices that suit that role.

As you think through this chapter, make notes on what some of your organization's desired outcomes and activities would be with respect to board integration. Develop a plan with the integration team and staff, and use the software tool to record it. Exhibit 6: Board Integration, page 76, provides a list of possible desired outcomes and activities.

Following are integration lessons learned from other organizations that have been through merger integration. These can help ground your vision of the immediate future as the boards merge into one.

The board's role is to model a commitment to the vision of the new organization. Many of the leaders with whom we spoke emphasized the board's crucial role in setting and keeping people focused on the organization's vision after the merger. Everyone on the new board should agree on the vision and be completely committed to it. Similarly, the board needs to model strong support for the executive director's efforts to achieve that vision.

Recognize that the board is governing a new organization. The boards must integrate knowing that they are governing a *new* organization. It isn't possible to simply transfer the practices of the old boards to the new organization and expect a perfect match between leadership practices and organizational needs. The new organization is usually larger than the former organizations, and the new board must consider its role in light of this and other changes brought by the merger.

A new organization will develop its own culture, drawing on practices from the former organizations and also creating new practices that suit new circumstances. Honor the practices of the former organizations, but don't cling to them. Board members can serve the organization most effectively by seeking the best practices applicable for the new organization. Moreover, change is challenging, and focusing on the new helps boards move forward with greater ease.

New members can energize the board and bring important fresh perspectives. The board often benefits from the addition of new members who weren't formally associated with the pre-merger organizations. Board members and executive directors interviewed for our study of integration leadership noted the benefit of bringing in people new to the organization as a way of solidifying the new board. These new members brought fresh perspectives, they weren't wedded to the way things used to be, and, in some cases, they provided an important bridge between members of the former organizations.

Further, as noted in Chapter 4, board members who have been involved in the merger process are often fatigued. New board members, spared

---

From the Field . . .

"The board was used to running two smaller organizations. I never heard people say, 'We're running a much larger organization now. What does that mean?' It would have been helpful to get the board ready, so that they got off on good footing."

— *Interim executive director of a merged HIV/AIDS organization*

the often-grueling process of merger negotiations and decision making, can bring new energy to the post-merger board.

The board leads the way in setting the tone for the new organization. Symbolic acts are important. The board must create something new in the name of the new organization. Hold an event or function that can serve to focus your board, staff, and the community on the merger. Consciously create new ways of conducting business, new patterns of doing things to distinguish the new organization from the old. The killer sentiment is "We've always done it this way." Try to prevent anyone—staff or board—from falling into the trap of wanting to stick with a previous approach just because it's tradition.

Board members should serve on the integration team. Several board members should be part of the integration team, and they should be involved in creating and implementing the integration plan.

A "quick win" builds team spirit among board and staff. Our research indicates that having the board plan an event or a special activity that gives the organization a tangible accomplishment can jump-start the integration process. This could be a successful press conference, a well-attended fundraising event, or a new program that garners high visibility in the community. The key is to get board members working together on an effort that is new and can feel like theirs.

A consultant can be very helpful in facilitating the challenges of integration. We encourage boards to seek the assistance of an outside consultant. A consultant can help to plan and facilitate a board retreat for team building or strategic planning, for example. Consultants are also useful as neutral sounding boards in resolving conflict or as guides in leading board members through the inevitable rough spots. Expertise in areas such as communication and human resources management can be invaluable to a board moving through an integration process.

There should be strong board leadership from BOTH (or all) organizations. Both (or all) organizations in a merger integration should put forward strong leaders to plan and manage the board integration. In our research, organizations that merged most successfully drew on leaders from both of the merging organizations. The board and staff feel equitably involved and valued in such situations, which dissuades rumors that the deal was an acquisition.

Pre-Merger Steps to Successful Integration

As soon as possible after the decision to merge, establish a board integration committee comprised of board members representing each of the merging organizations. If the executive committee is representative of the merging organizations, it could function as the board integration committee. Note that you do not need to wait for the merger

---

From the Field . . .

"The board decided not to recruit new board members for a year after the merger. This created a kind of 'us-and-them' dynamic for longer than it had to be. Once we had new board members that dynamic quickly evaporated."

— *Executive director of a nonprofit training, consulting, and research organization*

"The directors we acquired actually came in without having allegiance one way or the other. It helped on the board level to lower the feeling of territoriality."

— *Chief executive officer of a nonprofit educational and cultural center*

to *legally* take effect before beginning board integration. As we've stressed several times now, the earlier you begin planning, the better.

The board integration committee will serve as a watchdog and champion of the integration process for the board of directors, and it will anticipate the needs of the board. It will create a process to support and train board members during integration. The board integration committee should remain in place for six to nine months after the actual merger.

Certain types of people will be especially beneficial as members of this committee:

- Board members committed to the same vision for the successful new organization
- Board members from each of the former boards who are generally held in high regard
- Individuals who consistently look at the big picture
- Individuals with good people skills, who can help integrate the board into a new team

The board integration committee should immediately begin developing a plan to guide the board integration process. As a first step, start planning a joint board retreat. At the retreat, if not before:

- Clarify and agree on the new organization's mission, vision, programs, character, and so forth. Arm every board member with the information needed to be an ambassador to the community for the new organization and a supportive leader for the staff.
- Assess the board composition and determine what new skills and characteristics are needed. Develop a recruitment plan that serves the new organization's needs.
- Review each board's prior practices, and then create a new job description for board members.
- Plan a board and committee structure that meets the needs of the new organization.
- Ask board members which committees they wish to serve on.
- Establish new meeting times and the meeting site (if this isn't obvious).

See Exhibit 5: Suggested Agenda for a First Post-Merger Board Retreat, page 71, for help in planning the retreat. Worksheet 2: Evaluating Board Policies and Practices, page 211, can be used to accomplish the goals outlined in the agenda.

Exhibit 5: Suggested Agenda for a First Post-Merger Board Retreat

NOTE: Questions for group discussion are in italic

8:30   Coffee and settling in

9:00   Welcome, purpose of the retreat, review of the agenda.............................. Board Chair

Review retreat objectives
1. To enable board members to get to know each other better and build cohesion as a team
2. To enhance board members' understanding of the challenges of integrating a newly merged organization and begin to identify integration tasks
3. To begin to establish the new board's culture, identity, and practices

Scope of work for the retreat
- Lay the groundwork for developing a new board
- Create an understanding of the new organization and the new role of board members
- See yourself in the new organization; make a commitment to it

Review agenda and ground rules

9:30   Introductions exercise: *Why did you join your former organization?*

10:00   Affirmation/discussion of mission/overview of new organization .... CEO
- Presentation of mission
- Overview of new organization: structure, programs, staff
  How will the board add value to this new organization?
  What will be the biggest challenges for the board?

11:00   Break

11:15   Roles and responsibilities

Brainstorm: *What are the key responsibilities of this board?*
Generate a list, gain agreement. For example, setting mission and purpose; selecting the CEO; supporting and assessing performance of the CEO; ensuring effective organizational planning; ensuring adequate resources (fundraising)

12:00   Lunch with no specific activities. Time to get to know each other.

1:00   Building a shared vision of the new board... Board Chair

1. What are the traits and qualities you want to exemplify as a board member?
   Large group brainstorm (20 minutes)—create the following two lists:
   - *What are our expectations of ourselves as board members? What do we expect from one another?*
   - *What does the community expect from us?*

Continued on next page . . .

Exhibit 5: Suggested Agenda for a First Post-Merger Board Retreat (continued)

2. Create a picture of the new board
   Small group work (20 minutes)—fill out and discuss Worksheet 2: Evaluating Board Policies and Practices, with respect to selection and composition; orientation and training; structure and organization; and the board at work. The goal:
   - To identify issues, questions, and priorities related to the practices of the new board
   - To identify areas of focus for board integration

   RAISE ISSUES. DON'T WORRY ABOUT FINDING SOLUTIONS.

   Discussion—each small group should report its results to the large group. Then discuss the following:
   - *What surprised you—what did you learn about boards in general, and our board specifically?*
   - *What are the priority issues we need to address?*

2:20 Break

2:30 Board/staff relationship, roles, and responsibilities

   Brainstorm key principles. (For example, there will be job descriptions for board and staff; clearly defined roles and responsibilities; annual expectation-setting sessions; commitment to settling issues while they're small; mutual respect)
   What would you add?

   Role of CEO/executive staff, role of board
   What are our shared expectations for the board-staff partnership?
   What does the board need or expect from staff?
   What does the staff need or expect from the board?

3:00 Celebrate accomplishments of the day
   Final questions for each board member to consider before next meeting:
   Can you see yourself in the new organization?
   Can you make a renewed commitment?

3:30 Evaluation and closing
   What would you change about our retreat today?
   What did you like—what would you keep the same?

Post-Merger Steps to Successful Integration

The board integration committee must provide leadership in two critical areas: it must first foster a culture where board members think in "us" terms—as opposed to "us and them." It must also take the lead in attending to the practical tasks related to getting the new board up and functioning smoothly. Early in the integration process specific tasks for the board, as led by the board integration committee and in concert with the larger, organization-wide integration effort, include the following:

- Orient all board members to the roles and responsibilities of the new board.
- Draft a statement of board commitment for each board member to sign.
- Ensure that the entire integration process is an agenda item for all board meetings, and develop discussions or presentations that enhance the board's ability to work effectively.
- Provide board training specific to the board's ambassador function so that each member can effectively smooth the transition to a merged organization with donors, clients, and the general public.

The entire board should take responsibility for two additional tasks as well:

- Approve a budget for the merged organization, to be revised over time.
- Create a fund development plan to meet the short-term resource needs of the merged organization. After strategic planning, this plan will need to be revisited.

Other board integration tasks can be considered in terms of an eighteen-month timeline.

By the end of three months:

- Complete development of a new board handbook. The handbook should include job descriptions for board members and officers.
- Complete development of an orientation to the new board, and make sure that all members of the board have participated. Orientation should include mission, program, staff, and board roles and responsibilities.
- Make sure that each board member is clear about—and committed to—a fundraising role and has received orientation to that role.

By the end of six months:

- Hold a board retreat for team building, decision-making processes, and planning.
- Establish communication practices that are understood and followed by all.
- Create a fundraising plan for the merged organization.

From the Field . . .

"We should have made it clearer with the new board who was responsible for what and who was accountable for what. Everybody is still a little fuzzy on exactly what's the responsibility of the board and what's the responsibility of the officers group."

— *Board member of the California division of a national health organization during a period of reorganization among its unit and regional offices*

By the end of one year:

- Create and implement a board self-assessment process. Periodically going through such a process serves as a good check-in regarding the effectiveness of the new board.
- Evaluate the board's composition in light of the needs of the newly merged organization. Now is the time to develop a new recruitment plan. Board members who have been involved in the merger process may be burnt out and ready to move on—it is important to anticipate the need to bring on new board members.
- Develop and begin a strategic planning process.

By the end of eighteen months:

- Develop an evaluation process to assess programs for quality.
- Put the new strategic plan in full operation.

Afterward:

At the end of two years, a well-functioning, merged board will have reviewed and updated (or created) a strategic plan for the new organization. All the members will understand and be able to fulfill their responsibilities with regard to fiscal oversight, legal obligations, evaluating and planning for organizational and program growth, and selection and evaluation of the executive director.

Challenges and Roadblocks

Issues around power and personality often surface at the board level during a merger process. Rarely do all members of each pre-merger board "live through" the merger process and become part of the new organization's board. The process by which members and officers of the merged entity's board are chosen is an important one. If there is a perception that power within the new board is held largely with representatives of one of the former boards, resentment and discontent may result. The best way to deal with this problem is to ensure that board leadership positions (officers, committee chairs) are equitably distributed among individuals from each of the former boards.

Note that "equitable" does not necessarily mean a fifty-fifty split. If one organization was much larger than the other, the split may be different. The important point is for board members to feel that they had a voice in the selection process for key positions, and that one group does not dominate the new organization.

The board–executive director relationship can be challenging in several ways. If the board chair and executive director come from different organizations, they may bring different expectations to their new roles. In addition, if the process leading to selection of a new executive director has been difficult, unresolved feelings may spill over into the boardroom. It is critical that once a candidate is chosen, all board members throw their support behind this person. Of course, this will be easier if the process

> **BoardSource: An Excellent Resource for Board Assessment**
>
> BoardSource has several excellent resources for measuring board effectiveness (www.boardsource.org, formerly the National Center for Nonprofit Boards).

was open and fair, and the selected candidate had support from the entire board (rather than being forced on a minority).

Another common challenge facing merging boards is culture clash. Individuals from each of the merging organizations will likely find that they previously had different ways of doing things, from managing meetings to norms of dress, from meeting time (daytime versus evening) to language. Expectations about what "work" board members will do often differ as well, as when one board was in the practice of actively soliciting funds, the other was not; one board had strict rules regarding meeting attendance, the other was much more lax. The key to resolving these problems is first to recognize that conflicts may be due to cultural differences, not personalities, and then to consciously work together to establish new norms.

Summary

A successfully integrated board provides the leadership necessary to serve the mission of the new organization. Board members must be role models throughout the integration process and beyond. In order to do this well, they must clearly understand what integration involves, what challenges are most likely to arise, and what they, specifically, can do to participate in addressing such challenges. They must also be clear on what their roles and responsibilities are as a governing body, and share a common understanding of the organization's mission and message. Orientation and training are thus crucial activities early in the integration process.

As we have said repeatedly now, it is the *people* in an organization that most impact the outcome of a merger. Board members lead the way in setting the tone for the new organization, but the overall culture plays an equally, if not more, important role. The next chapter looks at cultural integration in more detail.

Exhibit 6: Board Integration

Desired Outcomes

The following list includes commonly identified desired outcomes for board integration. You may want to use this as a starting point for your list.

- An integrated, unified board with members who are engaged, enthusiastic, and mission-driven
- A board that is fully "staffed" and with a diverse group that represents our community
- A plan for an ongoing nomination and recruitment process that will meet the governance needs of our organization
- A cohesive board capable of leading us in a unified and inspirational manner
- A board that understands and is committed to its roles and responsibilities

Key Activities

The following list, while not exhaustive, includes activities that need to be accomplished in order to achieve successful board integration. You may want to include some or all of these activities in your integration plan.

Getting Started
- ❏ Establish a board integration committee.
- ❏ Identify desired outcomes for board integration.
- ❏ Assess board composition; determine needed skills and characteristics.
- ❏ Develop a board member recruitment plan.

Orientation and Training
- ❏ Plan a retreat for members of the new board.
- ❏ Plan a social event for members of the new board.
- ❏ Provide training to all members re: their role as ambassador for the organization.
- ❏ Draft a statement of board commitment for all members to sign.
- ❏ Develop a board handbook.
- ❏ Develop an orientation program for incoming members.
- ❏ Ensure that all current members have been through orientation.
- ❏ Provide training to all members re: fundraising skills and responsibilities.

Practices and Culture
- ❏ Identify elements of previous cultures to bring forward, leave behind.
- ❏ Articulate a desired board culture and new "best practices."
- ❏ Establish a committee structure and job descriptions for the new board.
- ❏ Survey board members re: interests and strengths.
- ❏ Finalize board committee assignments.
- ❏ Establish a schedule for future board meetings.
- ❏ Establish a schedule for committee meetings.
- ❏ Agree on communication practices for the board and with the executive director.
- ❏ Create and implement a board self-assessment process.

Finance, Planning, and Evaluation
- ❏ Approve a budget for the merged organization.
- ❏ Create a fundraising plan to meet short-term needs.
- ❏ Create a fundraising plan for the merged organization.
- ❏ Develop and pursue a strategic planning process.
- ❏ Work with management to establish an evaluation process for the organization.

CHAPTER 8

Cultural Integration

There are two distinctly different definitions of culture: one is anthropological and one is biological. The anthropological definition is simply "a shared life." The biological definition, at first easily dismissed, is "a medium for growing something."

Each of these definitions is essential for understanding merger integration. Culture is about patterns of human interaction—often deeply ingrained patterns. Similarly, a nonprofit organization is nothing if not a shared life. Nonprofit staffs spend more hours within their organizations than anywhere else—often more time than they spend with their families. Years of work and struggle further cement the bonds within a nonprofit. But a nonprofit organization is also a place (a medium) for growing something—a vision of a better world.

Cultural integration in a merger situation means melding different "shared lives" and growing a new shared life in the process.

Note. As mentioned in Chapter 6, this chapter does not contain a separate list of desired outcomes and activities for cultural integration. Instead, cultural integration is woven into other areas.

Envisioning the Future

To integrate and create a new culture, you must spend time examining the cultures that currently exist in the merging organizations. Only then can you work together to articulate a vision of integrated culture.

From the Field . . .

"I think the biggest thing is culture. A lot of people haven't been reflective about some of that stuff. So they don't know how to say, 'Here's how we really do things around here.' They weren't able to really talk about culture that much."

— *A senior staff member at a leading national health organization who has been integrally involved in many mergers between affiliates*

The culture we have: A cultural audit

A cultural audit is an organized review of the major beliefs, traditions, history, leaders, and patterns of behavior of the merging organizations. Conducting a cultural audit is useful for anticipating and defusing potential post-merger conflicts. It is to conduct the audit early in the integration process—even before the merger legally takes effect, if possible; at this time the audit can most easily report on the merging organizations, highlighting commonalities and differences.

A full cultural audit can be a complex, time-consuming, and expensive proposition. Given that you are in the midst of a merger, you probably cannot afford either the time or the expense of such an undertaking. However, you can still benefit from a simplified cultural audit. The integration team could take responsibility for conducting the audit, or it could establish a working group to conduct the audit and do the follow-up work. If you choose the latter option, be sure that the majority of the working group members are senior managers and organizational leaders. Cultural integration is crucial and cannot be delegated to the same extent as more technical integration tasks. The issues involved must be given weight, attention, resources, and, most of all, respect. This means that the executive director, the integration team, the board, and other leaders must consider both the cultural audit and the follow-up work a priority.

To conduct a simplified cultural audit, ask individuals from each pre-merger organization (staff, volunteers, board members, other constituents) to reflect on that organization. Worksheet 3: Cultural Audit Survey, page 215, can facilitate this process. The most economical way to gather such information is through an e-mail survey, followed by a few focus groups and augmented by individual interviews with long-term members of the organizational community. After collecting the completed surveys and compiling the results of the focus groups and interviews, review the data with an eye toward the following questions:

- What heroes, values, words of wisdom, traditions, conflicts, stories, victories, and losses were mentioned most often for each organization? What do people care most strongly about?
- Do staff and board members from the same organization share similar impressions about their organization or was a wide range of opinions given?
- What values and traditions do the merging organizations have in common?
- What values and traditions might be in conflict?

Compile the results of this analysis and report back to everyone who participated.

The culture we want to create

At this point, bring groups of staff, board members, and volunteers together for additional discussions around culture. Addressing culture explicitly expedites the integration of different organizational cultures so that they can most effectively become one. Emphasize to discussion participants that cultural integration will enhance the new nonprofit's ability to serve its mission, help it meet organizational needs, *and* satisfy constituents.

Using the results of the cultural audit as a jumping off point, discuss the following questions:

- What are the most compatible elements of our former organizations' cultures?
- What elements suggest the greatest potential for conflict or tension?
- Where are our values aligned, and which should become part of the merged organization?
- What would we like the new organization's culture to look like?
- What do we want to be certain to bring forward into the new culture?
- What *new* cultural elements will we need to adopt to accommodate what is different about the merged organization?
- How can we build on the common challenges that we have all faced?
- What pre-merger experiences do we want to remember and appreciate as we move into the merger?
- What are some indicators of successful cultural integration?

Once again, summarize the results of the discussions and distribute them throughout the organization. This time, however, the summaries should include any conclusions reached by the integration team and board about what values, traditions, and so forth, will be incorporated into the merged organization's culture.

The information you glean for the cultural audit will be useful throughout the integration period. You will likely return to it again and again to answer new questions as they arise, and to help you understand some of the resistance and sense of loss that are likely to surface. Keep in mind, however, that while the cultural audit provides a wealth of data, an even greater benefit is the process of getting people to think about what they value most about their organizations and cultures.

Pre-Merger Steps to Successful Integration

Cultural integration begins with cultural awareness and sensitivity—and fostering these should be an important element of the entire merger process, from assessment and negotiations through integration. Once a decision to merge has been made, such efforts must become both more explicit and more central to the planning process. No matter how successful other integration efforts may be, if issues around organizational culture are not considered and attended to, the merger will not achieve its potential.

From the moment an agreement to merge is reached, make cultural integration an explicit part of the process. Tell all constituents that the purpose is to create a new future that is better than the past being left behind. The simplified cultural audit is the key to sending this message, and can certainly be done before the merger legally takes effect. By asking the kinds of questions contained in the audit, you create an atmosphere where two positive things can occur.

From the Field . . .

"There were some challenges that we still haven't overcome completely. We were both small organization cultures. Both very flat, very horizontal—both organizations had a very strong bottom-up component in decision making. Now that we're almost forty staff in the new organization, we find we need a little more hierarchy, a little more discipline in decision making, and that's a tremendous cultural change. You know, with a larger organization it's just much harder to spread information and decision making."

— *Post-merger executive director of a multistate environmental organization*

First, people begin to think consciously about what they value and love from their former organization. This frame of mind elevates the integration process from a power struggle to a consideration of what is important. Nonprofit people are heavily value-driven. The audit reminds them of this in a healthy way.

Second, the audit helps people to connect the conflicts, anxieties, and difficulties they are experiencing to the cultural changes brought by the merger. Rather than feeling devalued because their job title has changed from "Vice President" to "Senior Manager," they can begin to see this as a cultural shift, rather than as something aimed personally at them. The new organization simply uses a different language. Such reframing is a continual need during the integration process.

Post-Merger Steps to Successful Integration

Aside from the audit, the integration team can do other specific things to help with cultural integration. While having these in mind before the actual merger is helpful, they are most relevant after true integration has begun, and thus they are described here as "post-merger" considerations.

- Be aware that cultural issues will play out in every aspect of the integration, from scheduling staff meetings to buying software. You cannot think of culture as an isolated issue, since, above all else, culture is pervasive. It is the context within which the organization lives. Whenever you suspect that a conflict or problem is due, at least in part, to cultural differences, say so. This will help train people to identify the true cause of their difficulties before things get blown out of proportion.

- Establish a working group of line and management staff to create a few rituals for the new organization. Have the group use the results of the audit for ideas. Provide a modest budget to work with and total freedom (within the bounds of the law and propriety) to be creative. Perhaps a new ritual will be a Friday afternoon cookie break or an annual staff appreciation day. The important thing is that staff from former organizations create the rituals together.

- Be especially aware of one "hot button": workspace, both type and location. Do not underestimate the power of workspace to define and communicate culture. Are you locating formerly separate staff functions in the same area? Did one former organization operate out of a corporate office park, while the other worked from an old house? Are you integrating a cubicle culture with a culture that prized private offices? Be aware also that in many organizations the arrangement of offices (known technically as "the pecking order") is the result of a painstaking analysis of needs, both perceived and real. Change the arrangement if you must, but be prepared for a reaction.

- Be diligent in encouraging and maintaining two-way communication throughout the organization. Use as many of the "listening tools" (described in Chapters 5 and 12) as you can to keep your fingers on the pulse of the organization. The earlier you recognize and address cultural conflict, the better able you will be to prevent it from spreading.

- Create quick wins within the first one hundred days. As in the other areas of integration, it is essential to score a quick win in the cultural area. The best place to start is to conduct the cultural audit and share the results, leading to a staff-planned joint event—perhaps a picnic, a retreat, or the institution of a jointly developed ritual. In this way, staff will begin to see positive aspects of culture change.

The Role of Human Resources

The human resources (HR) function, whether a discrete function or—as is often the case with nonprofits—a role incorporated within other functions (finance, information systems), can aid the change leader in achieving cultural integration. The human resources function develops and institutes new policies. To a large extent, the culture of the new organization is implemented through these policies. Thus, human resources must work closely with the change leader to ensure that policies reflect and reinforce the direction in which the leader is heading.

Human resources issues greatly concern people. How human resources handles concerns such as job titles, roles, responsibilities, workspace, benefits, salary, volunteers, and so forth is critical to success. Here are some guidelines to follow:

- Create a common and fair approach—across all employees—to compensation and incentives.

- Revise performance and compensation reviews to reflect the need for cultural integration. For example, it's important for employees to share information across the old organizations' boundaries. Performance plans can emphasize the value of sharing, and performance reviews can measure employees' progress in this area. Compensation systems can reward the desired behavior.

- Follow through on assertions that people are the organization's most important asset. Use recognition, celebrations, communication, and compromise between previous fringe benefits packages, and rewards to show that people come first.

- In the early stages of integration, human resources can support the leadership in redefining the scope of principal positions so employees can both contribute more and find their work more rewarding. Human resources must work with leadership to define skills needed by the new organization. This can be achieved by conducting a skills inventory, and then matching people with needed organizational functions. This gives people a chance to see how they can benefit the new organization and how the new organization can benefit them (through new roles, expanded responsibilities, new learning opportunities). It helps make the change a "win-win."

- Through focus groups, surveys, and other information-gathering techniques, human resources can help monitor the pulse of the organization and provide feedback to the integration process. This helps clarify whether the goals and objectives of the integration are being achieved.

- Ensure that human resources is working with whatever volunteer management structure exists to include volunteers in communications, celebrations, and so forth. Plan one or more gatherings for volunteers to share both information and enthusiasm with volunteers, and give them an opportunity to mix with staff and experience the positive aspects of the merger and any attending cultural shift.

Challenges and Roadblocks

Many, if not most, of the challenges that arise in merger implementation can be at least partially traced back to a cultural issue or conflict. Unfortunately that cultural element is not always obvious. Thus the primary challenge in cultural integration is recognizing when, and to what extent, culture is playing a role in whatever else is going on.

Along those lines, as discussed in Chapter 1, do not underestimate the experience of loss by employees and volunteers. The precondition for grief is attachment. Good, bad, or indifferent, people become very attached to any reality they experience for a length of time. This is especially the case with organizational culture. There is a need to let go of the previous reality before a new one can be embraced. You'll do better at creating something new if you acknowledge the process of transition and deal with what is happening within the workforce. Help your employees let go by helping them to remember the old organization.

Be aware of the effect that departing employees will have on the culture—both the fact that they are leaving (no matter what the reason), and that what they say about their departure influences the new culture.

Summary

Culture is like DNA—you can't see it directly, but the limits, capacity, and health of an organization are defined by it.

Every article and book concerning mergers seems to repeat the same mantra: "It's the culture, stupid." Most merger failures are caused not by bad financial projections, but by a mismatch between organizational or managerial cultures. Early evaluation of the culture of each organization can help you identify and address problems before they derail implementation. Ignoring cultural differences, on the other hand, can be deadly.

Tips for Successful Cultural Integration

- *Respect what was.* Even if some aspect of the other organization makes no sense to you and serves no apparent purpose, do not disrespect it.

- *Keep the best.* Ensure that the most functional and the most healthy elements of the previous cultures are not lost.

- *Create what you want.* Know what you want to create. Know what the new culture should look like, what its hallmarks are, and what actions and perceptions will get you to those hallmarks.

- *Address fears.* Disregard emotions at your peril, but do not lose yourself in the emotions of others.

- *Deal with neutral-zone issues.* William Bridges, a researcher and writer on transitions, uses the phrase "neutral zone" to describe the time between leaving a previous state and entering a new one. Anxieties often surface in neutral zone and must be dealt with.

Nature abhors a vacuum, and if you do not proactively attempt to create a new culture, inevitably the vacuum will be filled with anxiety and grief at the loss of what was. An organization will always have a culture—just not necessarily the one you want.

We turn next to the integration of management teams. Managers are the "day-to-day leaders" in an organization, and they must lead cultural integration as well as program and systems integration. To do this, they themselves must make the transition to a unified and cohesive work group.

CHAPTER 9

Management Integration

Merging the management staff of two (or more) organizations involves more than just deciding who will fill key leadership roles in the new organization. It also involves creating a new managerial culture, articulating a management philosophy for the new organization, and putting structures in place to ensure that both the post-merger integration process *and* the mission-related work of the organization are done in the most effective and efficient manner possible. *Management integration* is the process of creating an effective management team and setting up the structures to support that team in its work.

Merged organizations require *more* management during the integration period, not less. After merger, the management team has multiple tasks and roles. It will have a role both in managing the integration process and in creating a new organization that realizes the goals of the merger. It must also model the new organization's culture and behavior for the staff, and shepherd the process of moving the organization from an "us-and-them" to a "we" worldview. And—no small feat—the individuals on the management team must also do the work that they were originally hired to do. (The development director must continue to cultivate donors and write grants while helping establish the new culture; the marketing director must assemble a new team, develop a new positioning statement, and create new materials, all while making the first new organizational rituals seem perfect.) It is likely management team members will also have a role either on, or in support of, the integration team.

As you think through this chapter, make notes on what some of your organization's desired outcomes and activities would be with respect to management integration. Develop a plan with the integration team and staff, and use the software tool to record it. Exhibit 7: Management Integration, page 92, provides a suggested list of desired outcomes and activities.

Qualities of Good Leaders

Researcher Daniel Goleman studied high-performing leaders in an effort to determine which personal capabilities contributed most to their competence. His conclusion: *emotional intelligence.* According to Goleman, emotional intelligence consists of five qualities:

Self-awareness: The ability to recognize and understand your moods, emotions, and drives, as well as their effect on others.

Self-regulation: The ability to control or redirect disruptive impulses and moods; the propensity to suspend judgment—to think before acting.

Motivation: A passion to work for reasons that go beyond money or status; a propensity to pursue goals with energy and persistence.

Empathy: The ability to understand the emotional makeup of other people; skill in treating people according to their emotional reactions.

Social skill: Proficiency in managing relationships and building networks; an ability to find common ground and build rapport.

Good managers call on all these skills to motivate their teams to perform well.

* Daniel Goleman, *Emotional Intelligence* (New York: Bantam Books, 1997).

Envisioning the Future

What does an effective management team look like after merger? At the most basic level, it includes those individuals filling the management positions throughout the organization, from the executive director to the finance director to the program heads. It is cohesive, while still welcoming productive dissent and debate as part of effective planning processes. It places high value on communication, both within the management team and beyond, and it is consistent in its focus on and support of the organization's mission, vision, and goals.

A successful management team gains respect through good leadership. (The sidebar Qualities of Good Leaders, on the left, describes the characteristics team members should have.) A good management team has integrity in both words and actions. It acknowledges problems, has (or develops) the capacity to solve them, provides tools and resources to staff, and shares both accountability and responsibility.

Pre-Merger Steps to Successful Integration

Successfully integrating the management teams and structures of merging organizations depends heavily on understanding how each of the merging entities approached management before the merger. Building this kind of understanding begins early in the merger process and, in fact, often begins even *before* the merger, when the organizations are sizing up each other—at the assessment and readiness stage.

The best time to begin considering how management will merge is when the organizations are assessing each other for potential merger. At that time, each organization should consider its *own* strengths, weaknesses, critical issues, and desired outcomes in the area of management. Specific questions to address during the assessment include the following:

- How is our senior management team functioning now?
- Do we have any gaps, or open positions, that need to be filled?
- How could a merger (or other form of strategic restructuring) help us build a stronger, more effective senior management team?

Answering these questions can help point you toward the particular outcomes you seek for the management function of the new organization. It also can help place these issues in the hierarchy of desired outcomes for the merger. (If you've come to this book after a merger has been decided, you can still use this process with management staff from the originating organizations to help identify ways for the new team to gel.)

During merger negotiations, the negotiating committee considers many questions that will impact the future integration of the management team. These questions include the following:

- *Who will lead the merged organization?* In our interviews of leaders of merged organizations we found that this question created perhaps the greatest uncertainty and tension. Answering it early on will help everyone to move ahead behind one leader—crucial to the creation of a team. Whenever possible, make this person the permanent (for now, of course) leader. Some organizations choose instead to designate an interim executive director for some period after the merger legally takes effect, but we have found this solution to be less effective in most cases. One of our interviewees, the executive director of an arts organization that merged with a similar nonprofit, put it well: "The process here was complicated by the fact that I was the interim executive director for fourteen months. Don't ever do that! Staff had no reason to be totally supportive of me as the executive director, or to believe that what I said was going to have any long-term impact on their lives or what they were doing. So it was very easy and very natural for them to keep doing what they knew how to do."

- *How will the senior management team be selected?* Sometimes the negotiations committee names the executive director, who then selects the senior management team. Other times, specific management positions must be filled as part of the negotiation process and before the merger decision. While the negotiations committee occasionally addresses specific issues around the post-merger senior management team, usually the committee recommends a process to select an executive director and then further recommends that the board give the new executive director the authority to build a senior management team within a defined budget. Sometimes negotiations committees specify that at least some number of management positions in the new organization be filled by individuals from each of the pre-merger organizations. Such guidelines, which are usually fairly general, aim at ensuring that one merger partner is not perceived as completely taking over the other.

- *What requirements, if any, will the negotiations committee establish regarding how management positions will be filled?* Some staffing decisions may be necessary for the negotiations committee to reach agreement, but most are best left to the appointed executive director, who is rightly responsible for staffing.

- *How will transitions be handled, both for individuals leaving the organization and those changing roles?* This is a key question in a merger situation, the resolution of which can support the success of the remaining managers as they integrate into a single team. Issues to be addressed include what, if any, severance policy will be put in place for staff, and what other forms of support will be given to those transitioning out of the organization.

The "limbo" period between the decision to merge and the actual merger is often an ideal time for the future executive director to put together a senior management team.

Here is where the true integration work begins. Some important questions to consider at this point include the following:

- *What management positions are needed in the merged organization, and what positions must be filled at the next level down?* Don't assume the answer to this question is the same as it would have been in the pre-merger organizations. There may be a need for additional positions, a need to eliminate certain positions, or a need to restructure a department. While you are unlikely to need two chief financial officers, for example, you may need an extra staff accountant or bookkeeper—or more. While both pre-merger organizations may have been able to handle the human resources responsibilities of their smaller organizations through other positions, the merger might be the ideal time to bring in a director of human resources. The executive director, with input from whatever management staff selected to date, should think carefully about what management structure will best serve the merged organization.

- Who is on the senior management team? It is wise to include at least some individuals from each of the pre-merger organizations on the merged organization's management team, but it is not necessary—or wise—to strictly divide the positions and "give" half to each. Think about the skills needed for each position, as well as the skills needed to help lead the integration process, and choose people who can both do the job and serve as leaders and role models for others during the reorganization.

Post-Merger Steps to Successful Integration

Whatever senior management positions have not been filled at this point need to be filled as soon as possible. The senior management team should hit the ground running as soon as the merger becomes official. Staff anxiety, requests for information, and the sheer volume of *work* required will not wait for a leisurely ramp-up period for the management team.

What are the duties and responsibilities of the senior management team as a group?

The makeup of the senior management team varies by organization, but typically this group includes heads of departments and programs: the executive director, director of operations, director of finance, development director, director of human resources, and any applicable program directors. Senior management is often defined as those positions reporting directly to the executive director. Each such person will have important responsibilities in an area of specialty. In addition, however, this group will need to take responsibility for leading the organization through the integration period, guiding the creation of a new organizational culture (and handling the attendant cultural challenges), and ensuring that communication—in all directions—remains a top priority throughout the organization. The management team should work together to articulate its shared duties and responsibilities as soon as possible, and begin establishing its own culture and practices.

This last point is an important one. It will take time for a new management team to develop its norms and culture, and it won't necessarily be easy. The selection process that brought the group together, preexisting unresolved conflicts, career development issues, and residue from the negotiation process will all set the stage for a management team's practice and structure. Attend to these concerns and conflicts early, as the management team has the primary responsibility for setting the tone and modeling key behaviors in the new environment. The dynamics of this group will be observed and mirrored throughout the entire organization.

Management must equal leadership

While the ultimate leader in a merged organization needs to be the executive director, the management team plays a crucial role in leading the organization through the transition as well. Some of the ways team members can do this follow.

Keep people focused. What is the new vision? What will the future look like when we arrive? Why is all this turmoil worthwhile? Will the future not only be different, but also better? Everyone on the management team needs to share a common understanding of the answers to these questions, and be consistent, realistic, and enthusiastic in conveying that understanding to staff. Management must practice the language of vision, mission, and mandate.

Keep yourself focused. Managers need to understand that the transition will put them out of their comfort zone. The integration of organizations is labor intensive and potentially overwhelming. Managers are building a new organization while ensuring that established services continue without interruption. At the same time, staff will look to managers for cues as to how the integration is going, and whether or not the process is worth the trouble. Thus managers must pay keen attention to established work plans and priorities, all while keeping in mind how their actions and reactions might impact others within the organization.

Resolve conflicts as they arise. While any well-functioning organization needs the ability to recognize and resolve conflicts, organizations in transition must have (or develop) this capacity. The process of resolution, as much as the outcome, will create credibility for the organization's leaders and promote stability within the organization. The management team must take primary responsibility for developing clear and consistent approaches to conflict and integrating those approaches into the new organizational culture.

From the Field . . .

"I did underestimate the challenge and the disruption in my life and the disruption in the lives of many of the people that took leadership roles . . . [Merger experts] talk about the effects on the organization and to the degree that they talk about the people, they usually focus on the fears and the anxieties . . . but the amount of work that it's going to take your management team, that is tremendous. I think it would do a world of good for people to know that up front."

— *Executive director of a legal services organization after merger with two similar groups*

"My job is about reassuring—reassuring staff, reassuring clients, reassuring funders, reassuring the community that we're stronger, we're better, we're more efficient. We had to keep up positive language. And that was a constant."

— *Executive director of a merged HIV/AIDS service organization*

Key integration tasks for the first year

Once key management positions have been filled, and the executive director and the management team itself have together articulated management's roles and responsibilities within the new organization, "management integration" has more to do with creating a cohesive working group and leadership team than listing and performing any particular set of tasks. Still, the executive director and the newly formed management team might want to consider certain specific tasks. Among them are the following:

- Discuss as a group the pre-merger managerial culture of each organization and contrast this with what you would like the culture to be in the merged organization. Use Worksheet 4: Managerial Culture Index, page 217, to help with this.

- Discuss as a group what successful integration of the management team will look like. Articulate what the "desired outcomes" are in this area, what goals you wish to set for yourselves over the next thirty, sixty, and one hundred days, and what milestones would indicate success to you as a group.

- Establish a regular meeting time for the senior management team, and use it to review the progress on integration; the mood and morale both among the managers and throughout the entire organization; any rumors that might be circulating about the integration process or its impact on staff and clients; and general management team functioning and effectiveness.

- Build in time early in the integration process for the executive director to meet individually with each member of the management team and "check in" on how things are going. The executive director will want to know how that person's role and responsibilities might need to be adapted to better fit the emerging organization. Continue these meetings on a regular basis.

- Create a plan for the professional development of each member of the management team. Moving the new organization forward means that you must work to get to something beyond what was—a better organization. A development and training plan for all managers in the new organization can help build not only individual skill levels and confidence, but also overall organizational effectiveness.

Challenges and Roadblocks

Managers are very visible drivers for change throughout an integration process, and thus their feelings, fears, and attitudes will be readily noticed by, and will influence, others. This means that recognizing and addressing resistance within management *as soon as it surfaces* is critical. Any lag time is an opportunity for uncertainty and discontent to begin trickling down through the organization. Being completely on top of this can be difficult, but if everyone on the management team commits to open and honest communication and to helping one another work through challenges as they arise, it is far from impossible.

Challenges can also arise when management teams are not clear on what constitutes success. They must have some idea of what an integrated, well-functioning team would look like in order to strive for that reality. If not, it will be difficult to foster such teams among the rest of the staff. While it may be tempting to launch right into the mechanics of integration, take the time up front to discuss desired outcomes and describe the future you are working toward.

Lack of clarity around the roles that individual members of the management team are to play after merger can also cause problems. Often merging organizations will put off or not fully address questions about key positions or roles within the organization. A prime example is when the former executive director of one of the pre-merger organizations "hangs around" in another capacity post-merger. This former executive director may be transitioned into a chief administrative officer or development officer role, but, for all practical purposes, retain an ambiguous role in the staff's eyes. This can make it very difficult for the new executive director to fully assume a leadership role within the organization, as staff or board that feel an affinity with the former executive continue to relate to that individual as before, often unconsciously. If *everyone* isn't 100 percent supportive of the new executive director, ambiguity can lead to serious divisions within the organization and can erode the new leader's effectiveness. Be clear on what everyone's role is within the new organization, and use every resource and communication possible to reinforce this message.

Summary

Effective management teams are critical in all organizations, but especially so in newly merged ones. They must manage the organization itself—programs, development, finances, and so forth—as well as play leading roles in the integration process. To do this, they must be successfully integrated themselves.

Successful management integration involves clarifying roles, responsibilities, and reporting structures, as well as the type of managerial culture that is desired. A well-integrated, high-functioning management team will be in the best position to guide and assist the rest of the staff through the integration process.

It is to the staff—and volunteers—that we turn next.

Management's Job

The charter of a management team is to coordinate, plan, prioritize, collaborate, clarify, celebrate, communicate, decide, and integrate both people and systems.

Management team members do this by

- Monitoring the function of the whole system
- Modeling the behavior they wish to see
- Holding each other and staff accountable
- Providing the resources necessary
- Acting as a connector of individuals, roles, and systems in service to the mission
- Noticing, articulating, and resolving conflict
- Maintaining a big-picture view

Exhibit 7: Management Integration

Desired Outcomes

The following list includes commonly identified desired outcomes for management integration. You may want to use this as a starting point for your list.

- A senior management team (SMT) with clear roles and responsibilities

- A senior management team that models our desired communication and decision-making process

- A unified senior management team with a common understanding of our organization's vision, goals, and priorities

Key Activities

The following list, while not exhaustive, includes activities that need to be accomplished in order to achieve successful management integration. You may want to include some or all of these activities in your integration plan.

The Senior Management Team (SMT)

❑ Identify management positions needed in the merged organization.

❑ Identify necessary skills and competencies for each management position.

❑ Match current (pre-merger) employees to positions where appropriate.

❑ Articulate a recruitment plan for any remaining senior management positions.

❑ Create a process to fill open positions.

❑ Articulate the integration-related duties and responsibilities of the senior management team.

❑ Articulate the general duties and responsibilities of the senior management team.

Culture and Practices

❑ Establish shared understanding of the "managerial culture" in each pre-merger organization.

❑ Define a desired managerial culture for the new organization.

❑ Identify the specific work required to achieve the desired managerial culture.

❑ Define an overall management philosophy.

❑ Articulate a shared understanding of the organization's vision, mission, and future.

❑ Establish a regular senior management team meeting time and list of "must-have" agenda items.

❑ Articulate processes, policies, and procedures around conflict resolution.

Training and Development

❑ Have the executive director work with each manager to create a personal development and training plan.

❑ Have the executive director create his or her own development plan, in partnership with the board.

CHAPTER 10

Staff and Volunteer Integration

The people who provide a nonprofit's services, run its programs, and raise and manage its funds are the backbone of most nonprofit organizations. Paid or voluntary, they work daily in the organization, very often developing a deep sense of emotional attachment to and ownership of it. Thus their concerns are paramount during merger integration.

Some nonprofits accomplish their work through paid staff, but all nonprofits, to one extent or another, accomplish their work through volunteers. Sometimes the board members are the only unpaid human resources of a nonprofit, but most often volunteers play a much wider role. Volunteers often act as staff. In many nonprofits, the volunteers are, in fact, the only staff to be found. In many others, volunteers work side-by-side with paid staff, offering client services, organizing fundraising events, soliciting donors, managing office workflow . . . the list is endless.

Volunteers often possess a longer institutional memory and have lower turnover than paid staff. Thus they will often have a great investment in the old ways of doing business. They can be tremendous allies in the transition if they are brought on board, or formidable adversaries if they are ignored or alienated.

This chapter is primarily about the role of the staff in merger integration, so our consideration of volunteers will largely be limited to those who play a staff role. We will refer to both paid and unpaid workers collectively as "staff," for ease of reference, only distinguishing volunteers from paid staff when necessary.

The process of integrating staff is challenging. Those responsible must address multiple issues:

- Functions: how each job changes.
- Relationships: how each job now connects with others.
- Roles: changes in power, authority, and position.
- Disrupted expectations: Regardless of how happy or unhappy a worker was with the pre-merger reality of his or her job, at least it was a known entity. The merger changes everything: specific plans, goals, and career expectations may have to be reexamined in light of the new organizational reality.

The work of staff integration will intersect with cultural integration (Chapter 8), management integration (Chapter 9), and human resources integration (Chapter 13). In many ways it is impossible to separate these functions, as they are inherently interconnected. You cannot succeed or fail in one without affecting your progress in the others.

As you think through this chapter, make notes on what some of your organization's desired outcomes and activities would be with respect to staff and volunteer integration. Develop a plan with the integration team and staff, and use the software tool to record it. Exhibit 8: Staff Integration, page 102, and Exhibit 9: Volunteer Integration, page 103, provide ideas for desired outcomes and activities for these areas.

Envisioning the Future

After merger, a well-integrated staff will have clear roles, be accountable for goals, and know how their best efforts impact the mission. In a well-functioning merged organization, staff not only will be effective in the accomplishment of tasks, but also will be cohesive and exhibit camaraderie. They will both perform well and hold together well. They will exhibit the traits and qualities of healthy working teams, which include

- Broad consensus on the mission, vision, and purposes of the organization
- Clearly defined and accepted individual roles, goals, and responsibilities
- Clearly defined and accepted group roles, goals, and responsibilities
- The ability to understand the difference between activity and progress
- The ability to recognize, engage in, and resolve conflict
- An understanding of the nature and limits of authority, responsibility, and accountability
- The possession of emotional intelligence
- A free exchange of information within the system
- The presence of learning systems and processes
- The existence of a positive and healthy humor

Pre-Merger Steps to Successful Integration

In most cases, little "formal" integration of staff can or does happen before the merger becomes a legal reality. In the immediate pre-merger stage, much of the board and executive director's energy will focus on communicating the decision to merge to the various constituent groups, forming an integration team, filling open management positions, and planning for integration. This is all-important and appropriate. At the same time, however, the leadership must be attuned to staff concerns, and communicate as much information as possible about the pending change. During pre-merger it can also be helpful to bring the staff from the merging organizations together for a social event.

> **From the Field . . .**
>
> "Next time around, I'd have a more proactive plan to deal with disaffected volunteers."
>
> — *Chief executive officer of a national health organization that assisted in the consolidation of multiple affiliates*

Post-Merger Steps to Successful Integration

Integrating staff after a merger is far more of an art than a science. As such, there is no definitive "checklist" for how to get it done. Success depends heavily on awareness of what the staff's concerns, feelings, and challenges are, and on communication. Positive progress in other, more "technical" integration areas, such as finance, fundraising, programs, and communication materials, can often lead to improved employee morale and a greater sense of teamwork among individuals from different pre-merger organizations. That said, the organization's leaders can do several things to make staff integration go more smoothly. These are

- Address employee concerns
- Communicate early and often
- Work to align organizational and staff interests
- Clarify new roles
- Engage staff with exercises and experiences
- Celebrate

Let's look at each of these in turn.

Address employee concerns

To transform a post-merger staff group into a well-functioning work team, the organization's leadership needs to understand what people are most concerned about. The list is fairly standard:

1. My job
2. My role
3. My title
4. My boss
5. My team
6. My office
7. My compensation
8. My benefits
9. My career
10. My future

Most of these concerns are common to both paid and volunteer staff. The human resources function can help to alleviate many of them through clear policies, job descriptions, and the like. However, the organization's leadership will need to address the last two concerns in particular, and the integration team has a duty to bring these to the leaders' attention.

The immediate concern that occurs to most people when they hear of an impending merger is job security—number one in the list on the previous page. Since most nonprofit mergers result in few, if any, layoffs, this concern can usually be allayed fairly early on by indicating which jobs, if any, will be eliminated. Numbers two through eight are generally dealt with through the human resources function. Tough situations

may arise if the changes being made feel less-than-optimal for staff, such as might happen if, for example, certain benefits are to be reduced in a trade-off between health care and retirement. If handled sensitively, preferably through one-on-one meetings with supervisors, these issues can usually be satisfactorily resolved.

Numbers nine and ten may need to be addressed over a longer time frame. Career paths in the nonprofit sector are often circuitous at best. Most organizations are relatively flat, often making a move out necessary in order to move up. One benefit of a merger that can be "sold" to employees is that a larger organization may result in additional career opportunities over time.

The fact that the organization is bigger, and may thus offer more career opportunities, can address number seven, but the real question behind the last concern, "my future," is whether the employee or volunteer still has a place in the organization. If someone is a marginal performer, the message you may want to send is no. However, you want to help your best employees and volunteers to see a future for themselves in the organization. Many managers are reluctant to be so explicit, but it can be a real boost to morale (and retention) for staff to hear that they are a valued part of the new organization going forward.

Communicate early and often

As noted in Chapter 5, if you do not keep employees informed and aware of impending changes and transitions, they will make up interpretations of their own, and these will seldom be either accurate or positive. Even when you do a stellar job of keeping people informed—passing along all the latest information from the integration team, posting minutes of important meetings, and so forth—you still have to create mechanisms for clarification and response to questions. As an "insider" to the integration process, what may seem obvious or clear to you may be quite obscure or confusing to a front-line staff member or occasional volunteer. Therefore, you must put in place mechanisms that allow employees to bring their concerns to leadership, ask questions, and question rumors. Exactly how to do this is the topic of Chapter 12, so we will not go into detail here. For now, just know that interactive, two-way communication with staff is critical, and that feedback mechanisms must be both plentiful and effective.

Work to align organizational and staff interests

Organizations often make one of two major mistakes: ignoring the needs, requirements, and perceptions of staff members, or making those same needs, requirements, and perceptions the defining factor in leadership decisions. It is important to balance the needs and concerns of staff, both paid and unpaid, with the needs and requirements of the organization, such as meeting goals and commitments within a balanced budget.

Using suggestions offered earlier, and some that you will read about in Chapter 12, you should be able to get a good handle on what your staff think and feel they need. The next question is how those staff-defined concerns stack up against your sense of the organization's needs. For example, staff may believe very strongly that the great retirement plan offered by the smaller of the pre-merger organizations should be continued and extended to everyone in the new, much larger, merged organization, while you know that doing so would be a budget-buster.

From the Field . . .

"Don't underestimate self-preservation as an important motive for people."

— *Chief operating officer of a national health organization that assisted in the consolidation of multiple affiliates*

How you identify and address such conflicts will be key to the acceptance of the merger by staff. The first step is to identify them. Through your interactive communications with staff, try to identify their most strongly felt needs. Don't try to craft a response to any one of these needs on its own. Instead, when you are reasonably certain that you understand all the big issues, list them, and try to quantify their cost. The cost may be as simple as a dollar figure, or it may be more complex, as when combining a generous holiday and sick-leave policy at one organization with a generous vacation policy at the other would lead to an untenably high number of days off per year.

Once you have totaled the costs, consider how much, in the aggregate, you can afford to spend addressing these concerns. With this number in mind (total dollars, total days off, total hours for training, whatever it is), you are ready to involve the staff in solving the problem.

The key to resolving these difficult conflicts is to come out of the process with a resolution that is both affordable to the organization and acceptable to the staff. Managers who try to work out a fair solution on their own will find that regardless of its patent fairness, it will be poorly received if staff have not been engaged in struggling with the problem themselves. Let them see your lists and your idea of the constraints, and let them work with you to find a balance. Ultimately the decision will be made by management, but usually this collaborative method produces the best thinking on the issue, and a resolution that is acceptable to the vast majority of staff.

Clarify new roles

Everyone's role changes in a merger, even if they are doing the same job. The transitions that occur need to be made specific and clear to the impacted employees. Changes to roles are best communicated individually, at least in the early stages of integration. While each person's role may be quite clear in *your* mind as a leader of the integration process, it is quite possible that it is less than perfectly clear in the mind of, say, the receptionist, who is wondering how to answer the telephone. (With the new name? Both of the old names? Not at all, as these new folks like calls to route directly to their voice mail?)

Roles change in a few basic ways post-merger:

- *Reporting relationships:* Each person may have a different overall role in the reporting structure post-merger. Departments may be restructured, and an individual may have a new boss and responsibility for more, fewer, or a different group of supervisees. Middle managers often experience the greatest shift in this area.

- *Function:* The actual work done by a person may change either slightly or entirely post-merger. A receptionist may become support staff for several managers; a development staffer may take on responsibility for communication.

- *Authority:* As an organization grows, it is not uncommon for people to be asked to take on additional independent authority. Again, this is particularly true for middle managers. Previously, they may have had regular access to a senior manager for advice and confirmation of decisions. That person may now be too distant, or too busy, for such regular contact.

In each of these areas, it is important to tell the affected employee what to expect in the new organization. Greater independence may be a relief, but not if it is perceived simply as neglect. And nothing makes someone more unhappy and confused at work than either having two bosses or being unclear who the boss is.

Some positions will require more immediate clarification than others—but not by much. The chief financial officer will need to know early on when to provide reports on the new organization, and the shelter managers of two merging homeless organizations will need to know from the outset if they are to act as peers, or if one of them now reports to the other. On the other hand, some positions may be able to "fly below the radar" for quite some time. Staff or volunteers who provide services in an isolated location, or whose job does not normally bring them into contact with other staff or volunteers, may be content to wait as long as possible before adapting their behavior in any way. These people, nonetheless, need to receive as much information about the merger as the receptionist who is asking how to answer the phone. Why? Because they are bound to come in contact with vendors, clients, or personnel from other organizations in the community—and possibly even funders—and you want to be sure that they understand both the reasons for the merger and their role in the new order of things. (For more on the need for employees to impart consistent messages to external stakeholders, see Chapter 12.)

Engage staff with exercises and experiences

The work of integration happens every day. However, taking time during staff meetings or a longer staff retreat to focus on the integration process can be a powerful intervention. Below we provide examples of exercises that can be used to facilitate staff integration. Any of them could be the topic of a brief (thirty-to-sixty minute) discussion at a departmental or all-staff meeting.

The ideal size for discussions such as these is six to eight people. If the group is larger, break it into subgroups, being sure to mix staff from both pre-merger organizations. Be sure to establish basic ground rules for the discussion (for example, let each person speak, no put-downs, the right to "pass" for anyone who chooses not to participate). Ideally, a trained facilitator should lead each discussion. Absent this resource, choose discussion leaders (or ask for volunteers) and provide a basic training session on group facilitation in advance.

Why do we do this work? In this exercise, each staff member talks in turn about his or her personal commitment to the mission. The articulation of why this work is important helps accelerate the process of alignment with the new organization and its potentially new—or at least modified—mission. Despite organizational cultural differences, people who work for the same cause probably share strong basic beliefs and motivations.

What is my role? Each staff member discusses his or her role and the connection between that role and the mission of the organization. This allows individuals to test their emerging understanding both of their own role and function in the new organization, and of where that fits into the bigger picture. Staff, having heard others discuss their roles and possibly having helped to define them, may well leave the discussion with a stronger sense of connection to each other.

What kind of future do we have? This topic allows a wide-ranging conversation about the substance, structure, and direction of the new organization. One way to approach this discussion is by asking each person to write a headline about the organization that might appear in a newspaper five years in the future. Then share and discuss headlines. For example, discussion might revolve around the societal transformation that the organization seeks to achieve.

Clarification of values. This discussion brings to the surface the values that each person, and each former organization, holds. After everyone speaks, the leader asks group members to attempt to synthesize their values into one coherent statement that reflects everyone's input. If the group is willing, this list or statement of values can then be presented to the integration team for discussion organization-wide.

Draw the organization. This exercise requires some skill to interpret. Ask each person in the group to draw a picture of the new organization, using images, symbols, metaphor, or other representations. One person may draw an organizational chart; another may draw a town or village. This can be a powerful way to compare the different images and suppositions that staff members have about the organization. Be aware, however, that many people are shy and uncomfortable about their drawing, so this will work best with a visually oriented, comfortable group.

Charting our history. The staffs of each pre-merger organization make a presentation to each other. They meet first in groups according to their previous affiliation, and decide which elements of their history are most significant and useful for the other group to know. Set a limit of ten items. This exercise can capture the traditions, accomplishments, and setbacks that are the most important elements of the former organizations' fabrics. After the presentations and discussion, you can (time allowing) follow up with the next exercise.

Fishbowl with leadership. In this exercise, which can be quite powerful, a facilitator and the organization's leader sit down in front of a staff group and discuss the nuts and bolts of the transition and the leader's deepest hopes for the future. The two are surrounded by the staff, who do not comment or intervene in the discussion. Later the entire staff debrief what they heard the leader say. It's a bit like watching live theatre.

Celebrate

If you had any doubts before reading this book, you are probably convinced now: integration is a lot of work! It is also, lest we forget, a monumental achievement. To acknowledge both of these facts, a variety of large and small celebrations are in order.

- *Community celebration:* This is the "official" event to kick off the merger. It is usually sponsored by the board of the merged entity, and it should include invitations to funders, government officials, and other external constituents. The kickoff celebration is a perfect lead-in to greater press coverage, external communication of the message about the merger, and future fundraising efforts. (For more on communication after the merger, see Chapters 5 and 12.)

- *Departmental or work group acknowledgment:* People who are now working together need to make time to acknowledge their accomplishments. After the integration of the financial system is complete, and before tackling the top-to-bottom revision to the budgeting process (and oh, yes, before the auditors arrive next week), take time as a work group or department to have a cup of coffee, go out to lunch, or maybe go for a group walk to clear the cobwebs. This is an opportunity to congratulate each other on what you have accomplished.

- *Farewell:* This small or large party (depending on the internal significance and network of the person leaving) is traditionally thrown by co-workers for anyone who is leaving the organization, for any reason. This is an important opportunity for creating new, shared cultural practices, while acknowledging staff persons who are departing. How did each group previously say good-bye? Make it a post-merger challenge to find a new way to say farewell together.

Challenges and Roadblocks

The challenges that arise as part of the staff integration process are no different than those discussed in Chapters 8 and 9, on cultural and management integration. They are related to the *people* in the organization—their feelings, their worries, their fears, and their natural resistance to change. Do not ignore these things, but instead be on the lookout for them, and address them as quickly and completely as possible. Doing so will help lessen resistance throughout the organization, which will contribute to a much more successful—and pleasant—experience for all.

Be particularly aware, with staff, of the effect that rumors can have on morale. Just one person leaving under "suspicious" (to the staff) circumstances is all it takes to begin eroding whatever positive energy might have built up around the merger. Word spreads quickly in organizations, and word of discontent spreads even faster than good news. If there are layoffs, announce and explain them, and treat the departing individuals well. If people are frustrated or confused, work with them. Remember, too, that a focus on individual concerns must be balanced with a focus on the organization's overall well-being.

From the Field . . .

"Understand that not everyone is going to be happy. Sometimes you have to just push on, understanding that not everybody is going to be thrilled or happy with what you're doing. If you tried to get everybody under the tent in a happy frame of mind, you could take years to get a merger done. So know when to push and know when to lighten up."

— *Chief operating officer of a national health organization that assisted in the consolidation of multiple affiliates*

Summary

A nonprofit could not exist without its staff and volunteers. The integration of staff, like that of culture, is not just a matter of making a to-do list and checking off tasks as you complete them. It is a much more fluid process, and one that has no clear beginning or end. Yes, you need to do specific and important things—clarify roles and responsibilities, realign reporting relationships, communicate changes to human resources policies and practices, establish norms for staff meetings, and so forth—but equally important is the work needed to monitor the pulse of the organization and engage the staff in a way that fosters a positive, forward-thinking, open, and honest culture.

When staff feel understood, acknowledged, and valued, they perform better. And "better" is what you need to achieve successful integration of the rest of the organization—including its programs, communications, finance, fundraising, human resources systems, technology, and facilities. We look at the first of these areas, program integration, in Chapter 11.

Exhibit 8: Staff Integration

Desired Outcomes

The following list includes commonly identified desired outcomes for staff integration. You may want to use this as a starting point for your list.

- A staffing structure that meets the needs of the new organization

- Staff who understand their roles, reporting relationships, and authority

- A unified culture, with everyone in the merged organization feeling valued and heard

- Established feedback mechanisms for employee comments and concerns regarding conflict

- A culture that recognizes and incorporates the best of what each organization brings to the table

Key Activities

The following list, while not exhaustive, includes activities that will need to be accomplished in order to achieve successful integration of staff. You may want to include some or all of these activities in your integration plan.

Positions, Roles, and Compensation

❑ Address job losses with the remaining staff: clarify extent, timing, and impact.

❑ Identify positions still needed within the organization.

❑ Delegate responsibility for filling necessary positions.

❑ Clarify roles for all staff: reporting relationships, function, and authority.

❑ Coordinate with human resources director and staff to address compensation issues.

Culture

❑ Complete a cultural audit for each pre-merger organization.

❑ Identify elements of previous cultures to bring forward, leave behind.

❑ Articulate a desired culture for the new organization.

❑ Plan regular opportunities for the staff to come together and "live" the culture.

❑ Establish a staff team to create new rituals.

Communication

❑ Communicate regularly about the integration progress.

❑ Establish specific feedback mechanisms for staff questions, comments, and concerns.

❑ Establish regular staff meeting times and "must-have" agenda items, including integration exercises.

Cultural Conflict

❑ Train senior staff to consider how culture contributes to conflicts and problems.

Celebration and Acknowledgment

❑ Create and implement methods to recognize staff contributions.

❑ Plan to celebrate milestones and accomplishments at the department and work group level.

❑ Plan a farewell ritual for departing employees.

Exhibit 9: Volunteer Integration

Desired Outcomes

The following list includes commonly identified desired outcomes for volunteer integration. You may want to use this as a starting point for your list.

- A volunteer program structure that meets the needs of the new organization

- Volunteer policies and manual for the new organization

- A plan for recruiting and managing volunteers

Key Activities

The following list, while not exhaustive, includes activities that will need to be accomplished in order to achieve successful integration of volunteers. You may want to include some or all of these activities in your integration plan.

Positions and Roles

❑ Create a mechanism for volunteer involvement in the integration of volunteer programs.

❑ Clarify the volunteer needs of the new organization.

❑ Identify any changes needed in the volunteer program.

❑ Design roles and assignments for volunteers in the new organization.

❑ Create job descriptions for volunteer positions.

❑ Develop a volunteer recruitment plan.

Policies and Procedures

❑ Create a volunteer policies manual for the new organization.

❑ Develop a volunteer orientation and training manual and process.

❑ Establish policies for volunteer supervision, evaluation, and recognition.

Communication

❑ Establish a plan for communicating with volunteers about the integration process and how it will impact them.

CHAPTER 11

Program Integration

Within the context of a merger, *program integration* is the process of bringing together distinct programs from separate organizations within the newly merged structure. It includes the melding of some programs and the development, to a varying degree, of linkages between and among other programs. Program integration may also include closing a program (or finding it another home) because it no longer fits the mission or strategy of the merged organization.

When integrating programs, the organization must understand not only the services offered by the pre-merger organizations, but also how those programs fit within the context of the greater community, including the work of other nonprofits. Program integration affects not only the clients and customers served by particular programs, but also the larger community of public, private, and nonprofit organizations that engage in similar work or have related interests. Organizations that have been sources of referrals to the affected programs, contractors, vendors, and funders are all possible external constituents for a nonprofit's programs. Internally, of course, employees and volunteers who work in the organization's programs have a strong interest in any changes that emerge through the integration process.

As you think through this chapter, make notes on what some of your organization's desired outcomes and activities would be with respect to program integration. Develop a plan with the integration team and staff, and use the software tool to record it. Exhibit 10: Program Integration, page 112, provides a suggested list of desired outcomes and activities.

Envisioning the Future

A successful program integration process will eliminate—or at least reduce—competition and conflict between programs of formerly competing organizations. Sometimes the programs themselves may overlap, and thus need direct integration. Other times services are not directly competitive with one another, but the organizations have competed for dollars or public attention. For example, if the merging organizations operated in the same geographic area, they may see themselves as competitors even though their programs are, in reality, complementary. Perceived competition, whether for clients, media coverage, or donors, may have created a climate of distrust or even dislike between the program staffs, and it can have as strong an impact on program integration efforts as actual head-to-head competition.

Well-integrated programs have a cohesive staff who use accepted professional processes to resolve the usual creative differences that occur among professionals with varying approaches. In other words, if you have reduced the level of conflict among program staff from the former organizations to what is normal within any healthy organization (recently merged or not), you have probably succeeded in program integration.

Sometimes programs from the merging organizations are complementary (a suburban museum and a downtown gallery). In this case, they will need some level of coordination, but they will operate relatively independently. Other times programs are essentially the same but do not have overlapping regions (two homeless shelters, operating in neighboring communities). In this case, they probably need to develop similar policies and procedures so that the organization is internally consistent. A great deal can also be learned from the different approaches taken by very similar services, if the program staff can overcome the "threat" of having a similar set of experts in their midst. Finally, some programs will need to be partially or fully integrated (two primary health clinics located within blocks of one another). This will be the hardest integration, as the staffs will be consolidated, and even if no positions are eliminated, roles will likely shift, perhaps dramatically. This is particularly true for supervisory and management staff, who may find themselves with a wider, or narrower, span of control.

An organization with well-integrated programs will be seen from the outside as a single, coherent entity, with a clearly defined mission, values, and identity, and with a staff whom a casual outsider could not identify as being affiliated with either of the pre-merger organizations.

Well-integrated programs contribute to and support unified management teams that are able to pursue a coherent strategy and direction, rather than spend precious time protecting turf and intervening in staff squabbles.

Well-integrated program staff use the language of "we" rather than "us and them." They create traditions that are unique to the newly merged organization and include all staff members.

If the merger was inspired at least in part by a hope for growth and innovation, well-integrated programs will make possible the flowering of new ideas, and the eventual creation of new programs, that spring from a blended work group. Staff who are fighting along pre-merger lines, or who feel their interests are not aligned, will have neither the energy nor the creativity necessary for programmatic growth and innovation.

Pre-Merger Steps to Successful Integration

Successfully integrating the programs of merging organizations requires a solid understanding of what programs each organization offered *before* the merger, and what programmatic strengths and weaknesses each brings to the table. Building this type of understanding begins—at least ideally—early in the merger process.

To begin with, any organization considering a merger should identify its programmatic assets and liabilities in light of those of its potential partner. Such an assessment includes identification of the type and size of each organization's programs, the degree of compatibility between them (do the programmatic approaches of the organizations complement each other?), the degree of competition (do the programs provide the same service to similar clientele?), and the client base, staffing, and geographic area covered by the programs. Also consider outcome evaluations, funding outlook, budget history, program reputation, and linkages to other programs, contractors, and referral sources.

This initial assessment should also ask whether the services offered are of unique value to the community or duplicate work done by others. Assessing the value of an organization's programs can help in understanding its place in the community and the value the organization brings to a potential partnership.

Similarly, an assessment of programmatic liabilities helps an organization understand the potential baggage it brings to a partnership. For example, a program that consistently requires financial support from fundraising efforts rather than earned revenue may be an unattractive component to one potential partner. Another potential partner, however—perhaps one that depends on government contracts—may view this as an asset, since it means that after merger the organization will have a track record with both public and private sources of revenue. If a potential partner does view this situation as a liability, it may be necessary either to look for another partner or to strategize corrective actions. The latter could include consideration of new income sources, analysis of the potential for increased efficiency potential, or the development of exit strategies if the program is unable to reach an acceptable level of self-support. Bringing corrective action strategies to the negotiating table shows a potential merger partner that the organization is pragmatic and forward thinking in dealing with program-related issues.

At some point during a successful negotiation process it will become apparent that a merger is likely. At this point, senior program staff should begin to consider new ways of doing business at the program level. Will the merger provide opportunities for significant program growth or redesign or the development of new programs that serve the mission? Although full-fledged program development isn't likely to happen until

From the Field . . .

"You need to be sure people are engaged and are participants. You know, it's awfully hard to be against something you are a part of."

— *Chief executive officer of a national health organization that assisted in the consolidation of multiple affiliates* after the merger actually *has* been agreed to, it is never too soon to consider options and begin thinking creatively.

Here are some specific steps that can be taken toward the end of the negotiation process:

- Begin helping program staff get to know each other. Have staff share presentations on their programs: descriptions, successes, challenges, and so forth. Encourage staff to express their hopes and fears about the potential merger to one another. Identify the programmatic benefits the merger might bring, as well as areas of concern.

- Provide opportunities for staff interaction. Invite the other organization's staff to scheduled events. Provide tours of one another's facilities. These tours may combine staff and board as a way for these two groups to get to know each other. You might sponsor a high-quality professional development activity or training that staff from both parties can attend.

- Perform a simplified cultural audit (see Chapter 8) to determine the cultural compatibility of the organizations. Programs are the real work of any nonprofit, and thus the course of programmatic integration will be heavily influenced by the cultures of the merging organizations. Identify the most important elements of each organization's current culture and begin determining which are valuable and worth carrying forward, and which are best left behind. Spend time considering potential new cultural traditions as well.

Post-Merger Steps to Successful Integration

Both the management structure dedicated to program work and the programs themselves must be integrated after a merger.

Program management integration

Chapter 9 addressed management integration in general. Given the importance of program work in most nonprofits, however, we will summarize the main points here as they relate to program management.

First, determine the skills and competencies needed for effective program management. This includes management for existing programs (and the process of integrating them) as well as for the development of programs that the organization may decide to introduce or expand in the future. Some organizations depend too heavily on existing management staff to oversee new program development at the same time that their energy is necessarily being directed at integrating and managing the existing programs of the merged organization. Keep in mind that a merger often results in a larger, more complex organization, and such an organization may need an additional level of management skill beyond that required at the pre-merger organizations.

Next, assess the current program management personnel and determine if they possess the skills identified as necessary for program management in the merged organization. Ideally, they will, and there will be balanced representation from each of the merging organizations at the program management level post-merger. However, it is important to send a message throughout the organization that balanced representation is not the primary consideration—that senior management will assign the most qualified individual to each position and role. If there is a need to develop new positions for which multiple staff members are qualified, put in place an application process to ensure a fair approach to filling them.

Once you have filled the necessary positions, your program management team should be ready to go. You want to get to this point as quickly as possible. Staff will not be able to attend to the business of integrating the merging organizations if they are unsure of their position within the new structure, or unclear on the organization's leadership.

Program integration

The integration team should include program staff or volunteers (or both) who can help develop recommendations for the successful integration of programs. Choose individuals who have a solid base of experience within their program, and who also have a personality that will help advance the process. Important characteristics of these individuals include openness, the ability to grasp complex systems and models, an eye to the future, and an appropriate sense of both the achievements and limitations of the past.

The integration team, supported by program staff and volunteers from each pre-merger organization, should take responsibility for the following priorities:

- Compare information on each of the merging organizations' programs and culture, if this has not already been done.

- Adopt a clear statement of the purpose, values, and expected culture for the merged organization's programs. Include as many members of the program staff as possible in this process—acceptance of these statements is critical if the integration is to be successful.

- Identify obstacles and issues likely to arise in the program integration process. Assign working groups to tackle specific issues as necessary. For example, a particular program unit may be resistant to the merger, and therefore may need an expanded process and closer management attention to work through its issues. As much as possible, design strategies to deal with such situations ahead of time.

- If you get wind that a popular or crucial program staff person is planning to leave, try to convince that person to stay to help in the integration process. These employees may have been planning to leave or retire, and they might see the merger as an ideal time to make their move, not realizing that other staff could mistake their departure for dissatisfaction with the merger. Ask the employee to stay on for six to twelve months to help with integration. You may find the challenge reinvigorates his or her commitment to the organization.

- Develop a communication strategy for disseminating information on the program integration process to management, staff, and board. (See Chapter 12 for more information on communications.) Within the communication strategy be sure to include everyone who will be impacted by changes in programs. Do not overlook the less obvious constituents; the impact of a merger is likely to be felt more strongly by a significant contractor or referral source than by a colleague organization, for example. Therefore the former's "need to know" will be higher.

- Design the process for integrating each program within the merged organization. Issues to be addressed include the best level of integration for each program, integration of staffing and training, and, if needed, how to close (or transfer to another organization) programs that for business or mission reasons no longer fit within the merged organization. The senior management team, and ultimately the board, is responsible for making decisions on program closure or transfer, and the strategy for doing so. Something to keep in mind as you plan: it is best not to begin the program integration process with a program that you know is going to face difficult personality issues. Wait a few months, until some degree of overall cultural integration has taken place and other programs have been successfully integrated; it will make everyone's life a little easier.

The senior management team must next evaluate the proposed program design, using the new mission statement as an overarching guide. This is especially important for more complex program integration. Whenever possible, seek input on program design from staff, management, board, and potentially outside stakeholders, testing its feasibility.

At this point, the integration team should incorporate the feedback received, finalize recommendations for program design, and present them to management and the board.

Develop an evaluation process to assess program integration as it proceeds. Initially, weekly progress reports should be prepared for the senior management team, identifying areas of success and concern, with corrective action plans for the areas of concern. As integration proceeds, the time frame between progress reports may be lengthened.

Strategic planning can be helpful in clearly establishing programmatic direction and priorities, as well as for defining areas for future program development within the merged organization. Strategic planning should be completed within approximately one year of the merger date.

Challenges and Roadblocks

As is the case in merger negotiations, the primary roadblock issues—autonomy, self-interest, and culture clash—occur with regularity in the program integration process.[18]

Nonprofit organizations are, at the best of times, fiercely independent and staunch defenders of their autonomy. Individual programs often have the same affinity for their autonomy as their parent organizations. To allay concerns, staff must come to believe that merging or integrating their programs does not mean an end to their autonomy, but rather the beginning of a collaborative experience among similar programs within the newly merged organization. Ultimately, the benefits of collaboration will enhance each program as learning grows. Also, staff should be encouraged to take heart—as the

---

[18] For a more in-depth discussion of these issues, see Chapter 4 in *The Nonprofit Mergers Workbook Part I—Considering, Negotiating, and Executing a Merger.*

integration effort progresses and the organization develops greater stability, the newly aligned programs will probably enjoy just as much if not more professional autonomy as they did before the merger. After all, the demands of a larger organization will leave senior staff with even less time to "meddle" in daily operations, the arena most nonprofit program professionals most jealously guard.

The legitimate self-interest (what will happen to my job, my pay, my role?) of the staff and volunteers who operate an organization's programs can help or hinder the integration process, depending on the self-awareness of program staff and managers. A person who is aware of his or her self-interest and is able to place it within the greater context of working toward the best interests of clients and the overall organization will bring to the process the reality of his or her own feelings, beliefs, and desires, without using them to sidetrack integration. The open discussion of self-interest can be used to benefit the integration process and, as a result, avoid some of the negative consequences of self-interest, such as a tendency toward destructive behavior, and even sabotage.

A strong programmatic subculture is an asset to most organizations. It is where the larger organization's corporate culture usually gets played out in daily behavior and activity. It is also the area in which proactive cultural integration can greatly enhance the speed and success of the overall integration effort. Lack of attention to culture at the program level, on the other hand, will almost surely lead to the development of resistance and low morale.

It bears repeating: careful attention to cultural integration within programs is critical to the overall integration process. An inability to blend the cultures of the merging organizations makes it difficult, if not impossible, to effectively merge the organizations into a smoothly operating entity. See Chapter 8 for more on cultural integration.

Summary

The specific tasks of program integration will vary a great deal from merger to merger, depending on the number, type, and focus (geographic and otherwise) of the programs involved. In some cases, programs may need to be partially or full integrated. In other cases, programs will need to be coordinated, but not truly integrated. In all cases, however, the program *staff* must be integrated—they must work together, trust each other, learn from each other, and coordinate with each other to the extent that doing so helps advance the mission of the organization.

The key to knowing what level of integration is most appropriate in a given situation is understanding the purpose, values, structure, strengths, weaknesses, client base, reputation, funding sources, and resource constraints of each program. Never forget, however, that programs are really made up of people; as we have said many times before, it is the people that make or break merger integration. Keep the lessons of previous chapters in mind as you plan for program integration.

The next chapter looks at communication and marketing, both of which can be helpful tools for program integration—and both of which need integration as well.

Exhibit 10: Program Integration

Desired Outcomes

The following list includes commonly identified desired outcomes for program integration. You may want to use this as a starting point for your list.

- An integrated set of programs and services

- An organization chart with an overview of all programs

Key Activities

The following list, while not exhaustive, includes activities that will need to be accomplished in order to achieve successful program integration. You may want to include some or all of these activities in your integration plan.

Pre-Merger Data
- ❏ Gather and compare information on all pre-merger programs.

- ❏ Identify programmatic strengths, weaknesses, assets, and liabilities.

- ❏ Identify any obstacles or issues likely to arise in program integration.

- ❏ Agree on programs that need to be closed or moved to another organization.

Program Management
- ❏ Agree on necessary skills and competencies for program management.

- ❏ Match current (pre-merger) employees to positions where appropriate.

- ❏ Identify program positions that need to be filled.

- ❏ Create a process to fill open positions.

Planning and Recommendations
- ❏ Adopt a statement of the purpose, values, and culture for each program.

- ❏ Assign working groups to address specific issues or programs.

- ❏ Develop a communication strategy for program integration information.

- ❏ Design the process for integrating, closing, or moving each program.

- ❏ Gather input on proposed program design from the senior management team and other stakeholders.

- ❏ Bring recommendations for program design to the senior management team and board.

- ❏ Develop an evaluation process to assess the program integration progress.

Other (organization-specific)
- ❏ To be specified in the planning process

CHAPTER 12

Communication and Marketing Integration

The communication system in an organization facilitates the exchange of ideas and information using a variety of vehicles (print, audio, speech, electronic) and media. These are tailored to the needs of the organization, and also customized to the needs, interests, and concerns of the organization's stakeholders. A communication system is necessarily two way, supporting not only the sending of messages, but also the receiving of them.

Communication must be both internal and external. Internal communications are delivered to those on the "inside" of an organization: board members, staff, and volunteers. The internal communication function interfaces closely with human resources functions. Communication shapes, and is shaped by, the organization's culture.

External communications are delivered to persons and organizations "outside" of the organization. These include funders, donors, clients and customers, the press, community leaders, and collaborating and partnering organizations.

Marketing communications are a subset of all communications. Marketing communications primarily target external audiences, and strive to position the organization positively with these stakeholders. However, they are also directed to internal stakeholders, all of whom have a responsibility to "market" the organization.

There are two aspects to managing communication in the post-merger period—integrating the communication functions and communicating about the integration itself. The latter is almost certainly the more difficult—and sensitive—task of the two, and thus the one we emphasize in this chapter.

As you think through this chapter, make notes on what some of your organization's desired outcomes and activities would be with respect to communication and marketing integration. Develop a plan with the integration team and staff, and use the software tool to record it. Exhibit 12: External Communication and Marketing Integration, page 125, provides a suggested list of desired outcomes and activities.

Envisioning the Future

A well-functioning organization considers communication to be a fundamental management system, encompassing a plan, strategy, accountability for outcomes (through formal and informal evaluation), and education and training. While its role and focus will change over time, the overriding objective of communication in merger integration remains the same: to win stakeholders' understanding of, and support for, the merger, as well as their commitment to the new organization and its mission. Thus the communication system, and the communications it sends and receives, strives to shape the behavior and attitudes that are necessary to ensure the success of the integration process, and ultimately the success of the new organization.

The integration process offers an opportunity to instill, at the outset, best practices for communication in the new organization. Although customized to particular audiences, the fundamental messages conveyed by the communication system should be consistent. While all internal stakeholders (board members, staff, and volunteers) have a communication role (and associated responsibilities and accountabilities), the executive leadership has ultimate responsibility, and should model excellence in communication at all times. This includes demonstrating strong listening skills.

A well-integrated communication system will provide structure and support for both internal and external communication, including an effective marketing function. It will facilitate widespread dissemination of the vision, mission, goals, and activities of the organization in a clear and compelling fashion and, in doing so, will support and enhance fundraising and recruitment efforts.

Pre-Merger Steps to Successful Integration

As in the other chapters of this workbook, our focus here is primarily on the immediate post-merger and integration phases of the merger process. That said, successful integration depends in no small part on there having been clear, honest, two-way communication throughout the negotiation process. Thus, we begin by briefly reviewing things you can do throughout that earlier stage to maximize the effectiveness of your communication planning.

As discussed in Chapter 5, effective communication is an integral component of a successful integration process. Thus communication should be one of the first functions to be integrated. Beginning in the negotiation phase, staff with communication responsibility from each of the merging organizations will need to meet to develop a plan for communication throughout negotiations and into the post-merger phase. One or more of these individuals (preferably one from each organization) should serve on the integration team when it is formed.

During the negotiation phase, each organization should identify all staff responsible for internal and external communication. It can be helpful to make a list of these individuals' names, titles, and communication-related responsibilities (staff/volunteer newsletter, board relationship, intranet and web site design and maintenance). Remember to consider information technology and human resources functions, as these are closely tied to communication, particularly internal communication.

At least one person from each organization (the designated "communication leader") should serve as a staff resource to the negotiations committee. These individuals should report back to their respective organizations throughout the process, and channel information from their organizations back to the negotiations committee.

Internal communication

Each communication leader should meet regularly with all staff in his or her organization that have communication-related responsibilities. These meetings provide an opportunity to report on the progress of negotiations, to discuss issues and concerns that have surfaced with stakeholders and develop strategies for addressing these, and to track progress on activities related to the communication plan.

Messages

One of the tasks of the negotiations committee and supporting communication staff will be to craft the messages that should be disseminated regarding, first, the merger negotiations and, later, the integration process. The core message answers the why question: Why is this merger being considered? What problem will the merger solve, and what opportunities will the merger make possible? What would be the negative consequence if the merger didn't occur? Why merge these two (or more) organizations? You should be able to base your answers, at least in part, on the work you did during the assessment phase to articulate the motivators, desired outcomes, critical issues, and usable skills and assets of each partner. (For more on this, see Chapters 2 and 3 in *The Nonprofit Mergers Workbook Part I*.)

Equally important is the ability of both the negotiations committee and the supporting communication staff to address questions about any of the potential partners' weaknesses (such as negative publicity) and any stakeholders' objections to the merger. One of the guiding principles of effective communication is honesty, which is critical to establishing the trust needed to make the integration process successful down the road. Thus you must be aware of any organizational weaknesses or "soft spots" from the beginning, and consider how you will honestly react to questions or concerns that are raised about them.

The negotiations committee also develops and articulates the vision and mission of the to-be-merged organizations. While the board and executive leadership of the new organization might need to refine these statements after the merger, it is important to clarify the primary elements during the negotiation process, and to make sure that everyone involved can explain and champion them. The mission is the centerpiece of organizational communication. All activities and communications should be evaluated in the context of the vision and mission.

Responding to inquiries

Not all stakeholders will be contacted during the negotiation phase. The approach with some (for example, the media) may be to wait until a decision to merge has been made and approved by both boards, and then to contact them with the official announcement. However, information leaks do occur, and stakeholders may ask what's going on. Be forthright; withholding information only causes bad feelings and rumors. To prepare for these instances, develop a standby response that provides minimal, essential information and makes clear that decisions are not yet final. It can also (depending on the audience) make clear that staff will be informed of any decisions first.

While everyone on the negotiations committee, on the boards, and in senior management at either organization should be familiar with and able to articulate the standby statement, it is best if each organization identifies one or two key spokespersons during the negotiation phase. Contacts from stakeholders should be forwarded to these individuals as much as possible. They should be prepped with the standby statement.

Announcing the merger

As soon as both boards have approved the merger you will want to announce the decision publicly. Doing so effectively actually takes a significant amount of planning. Begin by thinking about *how* you will announce the merger to all key stakeholders. Consider the timing of these announcements carefully. Ideally, the news will be delivered almost simultaneously to all key stakeholders. Inform the board and top management first, however, and provide the tools they need as spokespersons to answer the questions and address the concerns of their key constituencies.

Paid staff and volunteers should be informed before all external parties. Typically, the key concerns of staff are job security and related issues; human resources concerns loom large. Thus, the human resources and internal communication functions, if not carried out by the same staff, must coordinate very closely.

You may also wish to draft a press release to announce the merger, hold a press conference, or do both. If so, think carefully about content and timing. Designate an individual or working group to draft the message, and define a process for getting it approved (by the new board and executive director, for example) and finalized. While planning for such a release, consider also whether to tie any major events to the announcement, or whether these will come later, to mark milestones in the post-merger integration process.

The matrix in Worksheet 5: Planning for the Announcement, page 219, will help you begin planning for announcement activities.

While announcing the merger might feel like the first action to take once the decision to merge has been made, if at all possible begin by putting your post-merger leadership team in place. The less time it takes to select and put in place the (possibly new) executive director and integration team, the better. Even if the merger won't *legally* take effect for some weeks, or even months, the "executive director-elect" and integration team can begin putting together an integration plan, assembling staff, and dealing with the many people issues that are likely to arise in the short term. From now on, all communication work should be guided by whatever leadership structure you have chosen to oversee the merged organization and the integration process.

The rest of the chapter takes you through the steps necessary to create the communication component of the integration plan. Please refer to Chapter 5 for the theory and rationale behind these activities.

Post-Merger Steps to Successful Integration

Once the merger becomes a reality, the focus shifts to communication about human resources–related issues as well as the integration process itself. Communication staff should work closely with human resources staff to develop communications related to benefits, retirement, severance, incentives, and so forth. They should also communicate regularly with both internal and external stakeholders about the progress of integration and any changes those stakeholders may notice or experience.

Communication-related tasks

There are other communication-related tasks to attend to as well.

Integrate the communication and marketing functions. Each of the merging organizations will have had some system of managing communication and marketing prior to the merger. Your goal is first to understand the existing systems, and then to create a new system that combines (and improves on) the best elements of each. If you did not identify the names, titles, and responsibilities of all staff responsible for internal and external communications within each pre-merger organization during the negotiation phase, do so now. Then think about how this will translate to the new organization. Will there be a communication department or a marketing department? Or perhaps just a director of communications and a director of marketing? Will there be dedicated communication and marketing staff, or will staff in other departments (information technology, human resources, fundraising) share the various responsibilities? The executive director, working within the boundaries (typically budgetary) set by the board, should work with relevant management staff to articulate communication and marketing roles and responsibilities for the new organization, and how these fit into the larger organization.

Establish guiding principles for communication. Post-merger communications are likely to be more consistent and successful if those creating them have a set of guiding principles to follow. It can be both useful and reassuring to begin the integration process by articulating what these will be. Guiding principles are, in a sense, value statements, and a commitment to strive for high standards in communication. Some examples might be "All communications will be courteous and respectful." "Any staffing changes will be communicated to staff prior to external parties." "Sharing of information will be encouraged." "People will have the information they need to get their jobs done and to make informed decisions."

Use Worksheet 6: Guiding Principles for Communication, page 221, to help you articulate principles for communication in your organization.

Draft a talking-points document and designate a spokesperson. Many common questions arise once a merger is announced. The new organization's leadership, along with the integration team, should take time in advance to think about answers. These answers—called "talking points" in communication jargon—furnish everyone in the organization with a common understanding of the basics, which they can share with others. Talking points should be clear, concise, compelling, and easily understood. Use Worksheet 7: Talking Points, page 223, to develop talking points for your newly merged organization. Once you are done, make sure everyone has a copy and feels comfortable drawing on it when talking about the merger. While official inquiries (for example, from the press) should be referred to a designated spokesperson for the organization, there will be many unofficial inquiries, and staff at all levels of the organization are likely both to ask and be asked at least some of the questions on the list.

Maintain a questions-and-answers document. While a talking-points document is a useful way to lay out the basics, there are bound to be more questions—and more complex questions—asked at various points in the integration process. Creating and maintaining several questions-and-answers (Q&A) documents—one for staff and another for external stakeholders, for example—can help board members, the executive, managers, and other designated speakers prepare for such questions and ensure consistency in the responses. These should be living documents, evolving over time as new questions—and answers—arise. They can be posted on the organization's web site, available in hard copy at each of the organization's sites, distributed via mail or e-mail, included in marketing packets, and so forth.

The internal Q&A document should address questions about benefits, salaries, management, and other systems, as well as present information on how to respond to questions from external parties. External stakeholders will have a different set of concerns. They will likely want or need to know about changes to programs, location of services, and funding goals. The documents will likely overlap, which is fine as long as one does not contradict another. Exhibit 11: What Will Stakeholders Ask about the Merger?, page 119, lists questions that arise most frequently when a merger is announced. You may want to address these in your Q&A documents.

Make sure you designate the person or persons who will be responsible for maintaining and updating the Q&A documents.

Consider a newsletter. Many of the nonprofit leaders we interviewed mentioned the value of a newsletter during the merger integration process. Newsletters are a great way to keep people informed, as well as to high-

---

From the Field . . .

"Our executive director focused a lot on the administrative aspects of this merger, and . . . he overlooked the importance of spending one-on-one and face-to-face time with people that were complete strangers to him a few months ago. And there just wasn't enough trust in the tank to be able to take care of that absence of the executive director out there in the field. So when the executive director stayed inside the office, there was just more and more mistrust built. I would recommend that the executive director really look to balance his or her time between the inside and outside."

— *President of the board of*
a merged youth service
organization

light successes and accomplishments in the integration process. You may want to send out two newsletters, one to internal stakeholders, and one to external stakeholders.

Talk with staff. As helpful as the aforementioned documents can be, they are no substitute for in-person communication within the organization. The leaders need to talk with staff, share information verbally, and be available to answer questions—just walking around and being *present* can assuage staff fears.

One good way to communicate in-person with larger groups of staff is to hold periodic town hall meetings. Depending on organization size and location, these meetings can either involve "everybody" or be broken down into geographic or other groups.

The elements of a successful town hall meeting are fairly straightforward (see the sidebar Elements of a Successful Town Hall Meeting, page 120). To encourage participation and avoid resentment, state the topic clearly in the invitation, schedule the meeting on work time rather than employees' own time, and keep the meeting short, preferably about an hour and definitely not more than ninety minutes. At the meeting itself, the executive director should lead the discussion. Remember that this is *not* a forum for an endless string of unrelated announcements. ("Since I have you all here, let me first take a moment to describe some changes to our procedures when taking kids on bus trips.")

Exhibit 11: What Will Stakeholders Ask about the Merger?

Use these questions to start crafting the messages that you will deliver to your internal and external stakeholders.

Staff

- Will I lose my job?
- If so, what will I receive in exchange (severance, benefits)?
- What will my pay and benefits be under the new organization?
- If I stay, what will my new role and responsibilities be?
- Will we have to change how we do things?
- How can I get more information?

Funders and donors

- How will the new organization differ from the one that I have supported in the past?
- Will the new organization pursue a mission consistent with my funding priorities?
- Will my funds continue to support the services and programs for which they were designated?
- Will any current grants or restricted endowments continue to be used for the intended purpose?
- Will the organization still be named after my grandfather?

Clients and customers

- Will you still provide the services that I use? Will they cost the same?
- How will your programs change?

The media

- How will the merger impact the community and the organizations' staff?
- What's the headline?

Stay focused on the announced topic. ("We're here to discuss the new mission and strategic direction we are embracing through this merger.") The executive director's comments should be limited to a statement of any decisions that have been made in regard to the discussion topic, and any questions on which the leadership needs input. Beyond that, make the meeting an open forum for staff questions and comments on the announced topic. When an off-topic question arises, do one of two things: If it is simple, answer it quickly and remind the group of the topic. If it is more complex and providing an answer would detract from the focus of the meeting, write it on a flip chart or white board reserved for this purpose and promise to respond via e-mail or at a subsequent meeting—and then be sure to do so.

Create, update, and capitalize on the organization's web site. More and more nonprofits are developing web sites to support their communication efforts. In fact, having a web site is almost required for legitimacy in this day and age. If neither organization comes to the merger with a web site, now is the time to develop one. If both do, identify and incorporate the best elements of each into a new site for the merged organization. As much as possible, make sure that the web site isn't just an online brochure: make it interactive and update it regularly. Designing a top-notch web site is not easy. Like all marketing materials, the "look and feel" is as important as the content. Get help from a professional if you don't have the necessary expertise in-house.

Collect and utilize feedback on the integration process. Chapter 5 emphasized the importance of two-way communication. All stakeholders will have feedback, and, if anyone feels their concerns or feelings are being ignored, you will hear about it, one way or another. You will fare much better if you take a proactive approach and acknowledge and address concerns before they become real problems.

In the first few months of the integration process, follow up weekly with key stakeholders. The integration team will need to decide early on who will be responsible for such check-ins, how they will be done, and how the feedback will be brought back to the larger group and incorporated into future communication and planning. Some methods of obtaining feedback should be done on an ongoing basis (one-on-one meetings, group meetings, "walking around," having an open door policy). Other mechanisms are best used infrequently (surveys, focus groups). Still others can be "always on" in the background (suggestion boxes, a hotline).

Worksheet 8: Feedback Mechanisms, page 225, provides a chart to lay out how and how often you will collect feedback from stakeholder groups.

Plan for celebration. Celebration is an important part of the integration process. Bringing staff together around shared successes is an excellent way to build that ever-desirable sense of "us" within the organization. It also reinforces the value of teamwork, progress toward integration, and the merger itself.

Elements of a Successful Town Hall Meeting

Periodic "town hall meetings" are a great way to talk with and listen to larger groups of stakeholders. Here are the basics for making these meetings work:

- State the topic in the invitation.
- Schedule it during work time.
- Keep it under ninety minutes.
- Stick to one topic per meeting and politely guide participants to stay on topic.
- Avoid speeches; the executive should keep a low profile.
- Answer questions directly and honestly.

What are some "quick successes" you can recognize in the integration process? How will you acknowledge these? How will the past be honored at these celebrations? Will you also announce these to the press? These questions go beyond the scope of the communication function as it is most narrowly defined, but they are an important element of a merger communication campaign. Celebrations communicate success much more vividly than any memo, article, or web site can.

Internal communication: No rest for the weary!

If you have thought through and acted on all the suggestions above, you probably have a fairly good plan in place for communicating with your board, staff, and volunteers. Let's assume you handled the announcement phase with aplomb; distributed a talking-points document to help everyone understand and articulate the facts of—and the case for—the merger; distributed an internal Q&A document addressing board, staff, and volunteer concerns and questions; put in place multiple mechanisms for sharing information with and collecting feedback from these groups; and set specific short-term goals and milestones that can and will be celebrated in the first months of the merger.

What else is there to do? Communicate more. Check in again. And listen—always listen. In our interviews with leaders of merged organizations, one of the most oft-cited success factors was frequent communication with staff, and one of the most common regrets was not communicating enough. Here are some of the more telling statements:

- "In any implementation of a merger, you cannot reassure enough, you cannot over-communicate enough."—*Post-merger executive director of an HIV/ AIDS service organization*

- "You cannot, in my opinion, over-communicate once you get started."—*Chief operating officer of a national health organization that assisted in the consolidation of multiple affiliates*

- "If it weren't so damned important, it would be laughable about how much you have to bend over backward and repeat yourself and go the extra mile to communicate, or someone thinks it's being done behind their back."—*Chief executive officer of a national health organization that assisted in the consolidation of multiple affiliates*

- "If I had to do it over again, I would probably have staff meetings every other week and let them ask whatever they wanted."—*Post-merger executive director of a nonprofit serving victims of domestic violence and sexual assault*

From the Field . . .

"The staff knows that I want their opinions. I sit and I listen to them. They see that there are opportunities within the organization and that they're valued as part of the organization—that they are encouraged as part of the organization and that I'm accessible to them and I don't hide in an ivory tower. As the leader of the organization I have never separated myself. I have always been with them."

— *Post-merger executive director of a nonprofit serving victims of domestic violence and sexual assault on what helped make her organization's merger successful*

External communication: Create a marketing strategy

While a full-blown marketing plan is best done after (or as part of) a strategic planning process, now is the time to begin articulating a marketing strategy, and to develop new marketing materials. Ideally, you began thinking about these in the announcement phase. Now, they need to be finalized.

In thinking through your marketing strategy, consider the unique value your organization brings to its customers and community, the niche it fills in society, and its value statements. Also consider what you want its image and brand identity to be, what the audiences will be for your communications, and what messages will most effectively reach and impact those audiences.

Next think about what type of marketing materials will best serve your goals. Marketing materials are the vehicles through which you communicate your messages to your stakeholders, and each of the merging organizations will bring related preferences, strengths, weaknesses, and resources to the table. Take time to articulate what these are, and see which of them will work within the merged organization and which will not, either in their current form or at all.

Marketing Materials to be Updated

❑ Letterhead
❑ Business cards
❑ Web site
❑ E-mail
❑ Signage
❑ Posters
❑ Advertising
❑ Trade show materials
❑ Press releases
❑ Annual report
❑ Brochures
❑ Flyers
❑ Proposal language
❑ Presentations

For more detailed guidance on creating a marketing plan and marketing materials, you might want to consult one of the more popular texts on the subject. Gary Stern's *Marketing Workbook for Nonprofit Organizations Volume I: Develop the Plan* and *Marketing Workbook for Nonprofit Organizations Volume II: Mobilize People for Marketing Success* are both excellent resources, as is *Strategic Communications for Nonprofit Organizations: Seven Steps to Creating a Successful Plan* by Janel M. Radtke.

Train the staff and board. Everyone is responsible for communication and marketing, and consistency of the message is important. Train all staff and board members on the messages you wish to impart about the merger, the integration process, and the new organization; and on available marketing tools and resources.

Collect and utilize feedback on your communication and marketing efforts. Just as you must collect feedback on the integration process, it is a good idea to also collect feedback on the effectiveness of your overall communication and marketing efforts. This is an ongoing requirement for nonprofits; the need isn't limited to the integration period. You can use the same basic tools and methods described earlier. The key is to be continually aware of the effectiveness of your communication efforts, both internal and external, and to keep them "fresh," relevant, and compelling.

Challenges and Roadblocks

One of the most common roadblocks that surfaces throughout a merger process, and one we have addressed several times already, is self-interest. The concern over what happens to "my job, my pay, my role, my *importance*" is real, and valid. It can also serve as an unwanted filter on communications about the merger. If people are nervous, uncertain, or afraid, they will naturally listen specifically for information that is relevant to their concerns—often regardless of the source. They may misinterpret what they hear, they may *not* hear what you believe you communicated, and they may contribute—even unintentionally—to the spread of misinformation. Those leading the integration effort, and specifically the communication aspects, must be very clear in their communications and vigilant in seeking feedback. Make sure that what you *intend* to communicate is actually what is "heard."

Being prepared for questions from the public—donors, the media, members of the community—is another challenge after a merger. The chapter talked about creating talking-points and questions-and-answers documents. Make sure you do this as soon as possible following the decision to merge, and make sure you distribute these to *everyone* in your organization. Questions can come to anyone, at any time—and are bound to come sooner than you expect. Many merging organizations have been unpleasantly surprised to find that not everyone on the staff or board is as "in the know" as they should be—and that those who aren't share information just as liberally as those who are.

From the Field...

"God gave you two ears and one mouth—use them in that proportion."

— *Old proverb*

Summary

Communication during a merger process is tough: it is almost guaranteed that no matter how much you communicate, someone will think it wasn't enough. Here are some common stakeholder complaints after a merger:

- I don't know what is going on.
- No one asked my opinion.
- No one *listened* to my opinion.
- I don't know why we're doing it *this* way.
- I heard some of us were going to lose our jobs through this merger, but I'm still not sure who, or when, or why.
- My neighbor knew that our food program was being cut before I did.
- All we hear about from management is what is going to change after the merger—weren't we doing things well beforehand?
- All of a sudden I get a newsletter from this new organization—what happened to the organization I've supported all these years?
- My favorite program is changing, and it doesn't look like it's for the better.
- What merger? No one told me.

What can you do to ensure that you don't hear any of these comments after your own merger? Communicate, communicate, communicate. Share information twice as often as you think you need to, and put three times as much effort into listening and responding to feedback. Establish and follow a set of guiding principles for communication, and make sure you continually monitor the effectiveness of your communication efforts.

Most importantly, always remember that communication is not just the responsibility of the board and the management team—*all* stakeholders are communicators and potential ambassadors for your organization. Make sure they all have the information and tools they need to be effective in that role.

Exhibit 12: External Communication and Marketing Integration

Desired Outcomes

The following list includes commonly identified desired outcomes for external communication and marketing integration. You may want to use this as a starting point for your list.

- Stakeholders understand why the merger occurred and how it will advance the mission
- Stakeholders understand the changes that will occur as a result of the merger
- Stakeholders feel positive about the merger and support it
- Established two-way communication channels with stakeholders that are characterized by honesty, accuracy, and timeliness
- A sound marketing-communication plan, created by a coordinated marketing-communication function, that is successfully implemented and monitored on an ongoing basis

Key Activities

The following list, while not exhaustive, includes activities that will need to be accomplished in order to both communicate about the merger and achieve successful integration of the communication function. You may want to include some or all of these activities in your integration plan.

Announcing the Merger
- ❑ Identify stakeholders and the information interests and needs of each stakeholder group.
- ❑ Determine the format and timing of announcement(s).
- ❑ Determine the content of announcement(s).
- ❑ Draft, secure approval for, and finalize messages.
- ❑ Establish and publicize stakeholder feedback channels.

Communicating about Integration
- ❑ Establish guiding principles for communication.
- ❑ Draft a talking-points document.
- ❑ Designate one or more spokesperson(s).
- ❑ Create necessary Q&A documents.
- ❑ Design and plan a distribution schedule for an integration newsletter.
- ❑ Designate a person or team responsible for regular staff check-ins.
- ❑ Convene town hall meeting(s) with staff.
- ❑ Create or update web site.
- ❑ Plan for and implement feedback mechanisms for all marketing-communication efforts.

Integrating the Communication Function
- ❑ Identify all pre-merger communication staff and resources.
- ❑ Design marketing and communication functions in the new organization.
- ❑ Define an overall marketing strategy.
- ❑ Identify required and desired marketing materials.
- ❑ Draft initial marketing plan.
- ❑ Train staff and board both on messages and tools/resources.

CHAPTER 13

Systems Integration

A variety of systems need integration after a merger, including finance, fundraising, human resources, technology, and facilities. The actual work that needs to be done in these areas tends to be a bit more straightforward than in the areas addressed in earlier chapters. There will still be challenges, of course, especially given the natural tendency of people to express their generalized anxiety as if it were the result of some specific choice or difficulty.

This chapter addresses each of the integration areas listed above, following the same format as earlier chapters. Our treatment is somewhat more brief, however, and our Steps to Successful Integration more succinct, reflecting the fact that the biggest challenges in integration really do come from people issues and not the technical requirements of integration.

As you think through this chapter, make notes on what some of your organization's desired outcomes and activities would be with respect to systems integration. Develop a plan for each systems area with the integration team and staff, and use the software tool to record your plans.

Finance

Financial integration begins during the due diligence process, which should have been conducted during the negotiation phase. After merger it includes integration of all financial records and systems, including accounting, budgeting, payroll, purchasing, and inventory tracking. Exhibit 13: Financial Integration, page 133, provides ideas for desired outcomes and activities for this area of your integration plan.

Envisioning the future

A well-integrated organization will take the best financial practices from the pre-merger entities and combine them or replace them with new and improved ideas, tools, and systems. The financial leaders in each merging organization must step back and assess what has worked well, and what not so well, for their organizations, and commit to moving forward with flexibility and an open mind. Aided by effective planning and strong financial expertise, the new organization has the opportunity to craft an appropriate and optimal financial management and reporting system with the capacity to evolve and expand after the merger.

Pre-merger steps to successful integration

The groundwork for financial integration is laid during the due diligence process, which typically occurs during the final stretch of negotiations. Due diligence is the process by which confidential legal and financial information is exchanged, reviewed, and appraised by the parties before a merger or other legally binding agreement is finalized. The essence of the due diligence process is an effort to make everyone on the negotiations committee—and, by extension, everyone on both boards—as aware as a prudent board member can be of any liabilities the other party may bring to the table. The intent is to have all committee members understand the financial condition of both organizations and to create a "no-surprises" situation so that when, for example, six months after a merger's effective date, a balloon payment on a loan comes due, no one can claim that the matter was hidden.

There are other reasons to review financial information during the negotiation phase. Often the decisions that potential partners need to make are informed by financial considerations:

- If we merge with this organization, are we going to be taking on debts or obligations we cannot handle? If this is so, perhaps some form of partnership short of a full merger is appropriate.
- Does our potential partner have the resources to continue to support our joint programs for the long term?
- How much money could we save by combining all of our administrative or back-office functions?
- How do the organizations' salaries compare, and can the merged organization afford to bring all employees up to comparable salary levels?
- How much overlap is there in our donor bases, and is this likely to present a problem for future joint fundraising?
- Will a merger impact restrictions placed on grant funds? Do any of the restrictions mention changes to the corporate structure of the organization? Are there funds restricted for use in certain geographic areas, and, if so, will the merged organization still be able to deploy those funds in that geographic area?

It is crucial that organizations perform solid due diligence before agreeing to a merger, reviewing—at a minimum—the following information to assess the financial health of the potential partner:

- Financial comparisons, including statement of financial position and statement of activities, year-to-date budget-to-actual reports, ratio analysis, and trend analysis
- Human resources compensation comparison
- Donor comparison

The organizations should also analyze the anticipated financial health of the organization and its programs *after* restructuring is complete. This includes developing projections for combined financial statements and organizational and program budgets, incorporating potential costs and savings associated with the merger.

The first step in making such projections is to bring together the most recent budgets from each partner. List all of the information in one spreadsheet, using one column per organization, and add the numbers from each partner together in a third column. This will provide a *rough* idea of how the budget would have looked if the organizations had been one in that last budget period, with no changes to their structure or operations. Essentially, this is one plus one equals two. From there, the combined budget can be refined to reflect what would be different if the organizations were merged. For example, in a two-party merger the combined salaries number would be somewhat lower than the total of the pre-merger salaries due to the elimination of the extra executive director salary, but might then be adjusted upward due to the need to equalize other salary figures between the organizations. Think carefully about what some of the more subtle effects of the merger might be; it can be easy to overlook things at this stage.

The same type of exercise can be performed with the budgets each organization has prepared for the next year—bring them together on one worksheet, add the columns together, and see what the combined budget would look like without any changes in either organization. Then, adjust the totals up or down to reflect what would change under a merger scenario. Note that nonprofits occasionally stray quite far from their budgets, and some put more effort into making their budgets realistic (reflective of reality) than others. Always test the reasonableness of an organization's budget by comparing it with year-to-date financial statements.

Once the merger recommendation has been approved by both boards, the timing of financial integration can be tricky. Financial records cannot be consolidated until the merger has been legally effected. However, the merging organizations want to be ready to switch to the new consolidated financial system as soon as possible after the legal nod is received. The more planning and preparation that can be done before the legal merger, the better. Because of this, we include that planning here as pre-merger activity. You are certainly not doomed if you do not get through this list before the legal merger, however!

From the Field . . .

"It's more than one plus one equals two."

— *Executive director of a merged HIV/AIDS service organization*

"Part of what you're doing is you're going to make mistakes. You have to have enough money to make mistakes—and every mistake is a $50,000 mistake."

— *Executive director of a merged nonprofit training, consulting, and research organization*

The integration team is ultimately responsible for financial integration. It is wise to designate a working group to focus exclusively on financial issues, however. This group should include the top financial people from each organization. It might also include the treasurers of the pre-merger and post-merger boards, as well as the executive director, chief financial officer or chief operating officer, and controller or accountant for each organization. It may also be necessary to bring in a consultant or financial expert to assist with the review and recommendation process, particularly if the organizations are very large or unusually complex.

The first step will be to establish a timeline for the integration of all financial systems, ensuring in the process that the necessary budgetary resources are in place or being sought to cover this one-time cost. While the legal process of merger is under way, the financial-point people on the integration team should attend to the following tasks, identifying the short-, medium-, and long-term actions needed:

- Determine the fiscal calendar year of the new organization.
- Work on and tighten the consolidated budget (building on the first iteration, created during the due diligence process). Don't forget to include the costs associated with the integration process itself.
- Clarify how the merged organization will continue to honor the limitations of any restricted funding brought to the merger by the parties.
- Compare the current budgeting processes of each organization—who is involved, timing of the process, format of presentation—so that an integrated system can be developed.
- Compare the pre-merger financial statements of the organizations and address inconsistencies in budgets and actual experience.
- Review and identify inconsistencies between the charts of accounts of each merging organization; adopt a unified chart of accounts.
- Examine and compare the accounting system used by each organization, including all subsystems, hardware, software, and internal controls, and determine the features that are desirable for the merged organization. If it is going to be necessary to upgrade the accounting software, begin a search for the right product.
- Review and revise position descriptions for all accounting/finance positions.
- Decide where the combined organization will do its banking.
- Review each organization's investment policies and practices—risk tolerance, investment mix, brokers, and so forth. The new board should choose a single investment and cash management policy for the merged organization.
- Compare the processes used for tracking staff activities—reporting requirements (including applicable government reporting), the handling of billable versus non-billable time, software used, and so forth—and determine the features that are desirable for the combined organization.
- Develop a unified payroll system—either in-house or through an outside service—determining frequency of payments, direct deposit options, and even which checks to use.

- Develop purchasing policies, including authorization processes, and revisit and refine group purchasing agreements as necessary.
- Review maintenance schedules for both organizations' buildings and major equipment—including planned replacement schedules, deferred maintenance issues, and relations with major contractors—and incorporate these into the budgeting process.
- Develop a petty cash policy.
- Decide what kind of financial skills and staff the new organization will need, create a department budget, and prepare to rapidly implement the new staff structure.

Post-merger steps to successful integration

Assuming that you have completed the activities outlined above by the time the merger becomes legal, the following timeline will take you through the rest of the financial integration process.

Immediately (zero to three months):

- Consolidate banking and investment accounts.
- Proceed with the integration of systems as outlined above, using staff, management, and outside consultants or experts as necessary.
- Finalize a new budget and format for financial statements for the merged organization and circulate it to the board.
- Notify funders of the transfer of their funds from one organization to another.
- Notify clients and vendors about any change in billing address or procedures.
- Prepare any special financial analyses needed to support decision processes with regard to systems integration, program development, and so forth.

By the end of six months:

- If necessary, contract for a "short-year" audit to close out the merging organizations' previous fiscal years.
- Provide a training session for board and staff on the new financial reports.
- Complete the finance/accounting policies and procedures manual.

Ongoing integration:

- Over time, continue revising the budget for the merged organization, based on the work of the integration team, any strategic planning done by the new board, and the results of management team and systems integration planning.
- Continue regular check-ins with staff and management to ensure that financial systems integration is proceeding as planned, and is meeting the needs of the merged organization.
- At the close of each fiscal year, commission an annual audit.

Challenges and roadblocks

The most significant roadblocks to financial integration often lie not in the execution itself, but in addressing the political and cultural implications of the decisions that are made. Individuals who are secure in their understanding of their own organization's accounting program, time-tracking system, purchasing procedures, and so forth, may be very uneasy at the prospect of having to switch to a new system that, for a time at least, they will not know or understand nearly as well. Management should watch for signs of tension that if not addressed could lead to resistance and decreased morale. Assure financial staff they will get whatever training they need to implement the new systems, and get them involved in the transition. Their input is invaluable, as they understand best how the systems are used on a day-to-day basis.

For the financial staff, the largest challenge will be balancing the need to keep focused on integration tasks while still managing day-to-day financial operations. For obvious reasons, it is crucial that payroll, billing, purchasing, and other financial functions continue without disruption. This may require the hiring of temporary accounting staff who can assist with more basic tasks, allowing core financial staff to focus on the "meatier" integration responsibilities.

Ironically, after the initial crush of work that typically comes with merger implementation, the merged organization may find itself with too many staff in the financial management department. This is one area in which layoffs are common in nonprofit mergers, since the new organization is likely to have overlapping or redundant financial positions if all pre-merger staff are brought on board. If this issue was not addressed during negotiations, it can be a challenging situation to rectify after the merger. The executive director and senior management team will need to determine what staff skills are necessary for the best staffing mix, and then make difficult decisions about letting people go. Those who are laid off should be treated gently and graciously.

From the Field . . .

"After our merger, the management of the money became much more complicated. If there's anything in terms of administrative infrastructure that I wish we had spent more time thinking about, it was the financial management end of it. You absolutely have to assess your accounting department's capacity to take on these new challenges, and you need to almost predict the need rather than wait and assess it post-merger."

— *Executive director of a legal services organization after the merger of his organization with two similar groups.*

Fundraising

Fundraising integration includes combining all sources of contributed income while respecting donor restrictions. It also includes combining all donor databases, management systems, proposal writing processes, and case statements, and the development staff who use them to raise necessary funds. Exhibit 14: Fundraising Integration, page 137, summarizes possible desired outcomes and ideas for this area of your integration plan. The groundwork for integrating the fundraising systems of merging organizations is laid during the due diligence process. The financial information exchanged by the negotiating parties at that point should include their grant histories and donor lists.

Exhibit 13: Financial Integration

Desired Outcomes

The following list includes commonly identified desired outcomes for financial integration. You may want to use this as a starting point for your list.

- A system for accounting that meets the needs of the new organization
- A clear budgeting process that is understood by all
- Appropriate staffing for the finance function in the new organization
- Management staff trained in their roles related to finance department needs

Key Activities

The following list, while not exhaustive, includes activities that need to be accomplished in order to achieve successful financial integration. You may want to include some or all of these activities in your integration plan.

Budgeting and Financial Statements
- ❑ Determine the new organization's fiscal year.
- ❑ Refine the consolidated budget created during negotiations.
- ❑ Adopt a unified budgeting process.
- ❑ Compare pre-merger financial statements; update budget-to-actual information.
- ❑ Adopt a unified format for financial statements; circulate to board and managers.
- ❑ Adopt a unified chart of accounts.
- ❑ Clarify limitations on restricted funds.
- ❑ Review maintenance schedules for buildings and equipment (for budgeting).
- ❑ Contract for partial-year audit to close out pre-merger fiscal years.

Accounting Systems and Procedures
- ❑ Examine and compare pre-merger accounting systems.
- ❑ Define features of a desired accounting system.
- ❑ Select an accounting system.
- ❑ Adopt unified time-tracking processes and systems.
- ❑ Notify clients and vendors of any change to billing address and procedures.

Money Management
- ❑ Consolidate banking and investment accounts.
- ❑ Adopt a single investment and cash management policy.
- ❑ Select or adopt a payroll system.
- ❑ Develop purchasing policies
- ❑ Develop a petty cash policy.
- ❑ Notify funders of transfer of funds to new organization.

Staffing and Structure
- ❑ Define optimal staffing for the finance function.
- ❑ Create a plan for necessary hiring or reallocation of staff resources.
- ❑ Train staff and board on new financial systems and procedures.

Insurance
- ❑ Evaluate the insurance policies of the pre-merger organizations.
- ❑ Secure insurance policies for the new organization.

Envisioning the future

A well-integrated organization will have a fundraising function that clearly serves the mission, vision, and financial requirements of the new entity. Successful fundraising also depends on adept management of the relationships each partner has with its board members, donors, volunteers, staffs, vendors, and prospects. Fundraising integration is highly interwoven with marketing, communication, finance, and technology integration. In all of these areas, the new organization has an opportunity to build on each partner's strengths, tackle any deficiencies, and leverage the relationships that each brings to the table.

Pre-merger steps to successful integration

Collect and share fundraising information from each merging organization during the due diligence process. A comparison of the organizations' sources of funds and donor bases should be completed toward the end of negotiations.

After the boards approve the merger and the executive director and management team have been identified, the fundraising leaders must immediately get to work. Include top fundraising staff on the integration team. These individuals should consult with others involved in fundraising at each of the merging organizations, as well as with staff responsible for technology, finance, marketing, and communication, as needed.

Those responsible for fundraising integration should review and analyze the current fundraising activities, practices, and systems at each merging organization, and make recommendations for integrating these in a way that will ensure the financial success of the new entity. Included in this review should be the following:

- Sources of income from each organization, including a three- to five-year trend analysis.
- Diversification of revenue streams: Is there too much reliance on one or two sources of income? Do the organizations excel in different areas of fundraising (for example, one receives many grants, the other has many loyal individual donors) and, if so, how will that expertise be leveraged by the combined organization?
- Donor databases: How much overlap, if any, is there between the organizations? Give particular attention to relationships with major individual donors, corporations, and foundations. If there is significant overlap among these key contributors, it could be difficult to maintain current funding levels.
- Current commitments in planned giving, grants, and contracts: Are any steady sources of income scheduled or anticipated to stop in the near future?
- Participation from stakeholder groups in the fundraising efforts of each organization, including board members, volunteers, staff, vendors, community leaders, and others.
- Technology: What systems are in place to manage the fundraising function? How will the fundraising and finance systems be linked?

- Staffing: What structure and distribution of responsibilities will work best for the new organization?
- Office needs: What are the space and technology requirements of the fundraising function?
- Policies and procedures: What fundraising policies and procedures are established and practiced in the merging organizations? What will the new organization do?
- Marketing and communications: What coordination needs to happen between marketing, communications, and fundraising to position the new organization to raise the funds necessary for success?
- Case statements: Have a mission and vision been defined for the new organization? Can a case statement be prepared from these?
- Materials: From thank-you cards to brochures, what will you need and what will it cost?
- Budget: What are the resources necessary to successfully integrate the fundraising function and to position the organization for the growth needed to accomplish its mission and vision?

Post-merger steps to successful integration

The analysis described above—which may well continue into the post-merger phase—should result in a set of recommendations for integrating the fundraising activities, practices, and systems of the merging organizations. The integration team should review these recommendations, take into account the funding needs of the newly merged organization, and work with fundraising staff to develop a timeline for implementation. It is important to balance short-term and long-term needs as you move forward. It may seem crucial to solicit funds immediately to cover integration costs; on the other hand, it may be better to devote a month or two to refining the merged organization's case statement and value proposition before approaching funders for large grants.

The initial budget set early in the integration process should guide early fundraising planning. That budget will be refined over time, as additional integration needs are identified and additional decisions about post-merger operations are made. As soon as possible, develop an initial one-year fundraising plan for the new entity. A strategic planning process undertaken during the first year of integration will drive future fundraising goals and strategies.

Challenges and roadblocks

Many of the challenges and roadblocks that arise in fundraising integration will stem from differing philosophical approaches to fundraising. One organization may steer clear of special events, for example, while another sees them as fun and a key strategy in raising funds. In addition, relationships between donors and staff can be special and cherished. It is often difficult to share those relationships, and trying to do so may jeopardize them.

There may be a significant difference in the fundraising cultures of the merging organizations, such as expectations regarding contributions from board members or the level of participation from board members in fundraising efforts. It is very important to clarify those expectations—both to define the role the board will have in fundraising, and to retain each board member's commitment to performing that role.

There may also be challenges integrating the technology that supports the fundraising function. Converting databases is often time-consuming and costly, and may require hiring temporary contract staff. New technology also means retraining staff and providing tech support. Balancing the daily demands of their work with the demands of the integration process will be difficult for fundraising staff and development committee members. Note that many newer fundraising software packages are quite adept at automatically importing and converting data from different software systems. This feature can save much time and trouble.

Daily demands are not likely to lessen after the merger. To the contrary, many merged organizations find it quite challenging to "gear up" and raise the additional funds necessary to support both the merger process itself and the larger, more complex organization that is the likely result. As one post-merger executive director commented, "We used to have to come up with a million and a half bucks a year, and now we have to come up with four million a year. And it's a lot harder. It means you've got to change the way you look at your income stream and the way you go after it."

However you address these challenges and roadblocks, your approach should be grounded in the mission and vision of the new organization, and in a strong commitment to communication. It will be important for staff and volunteers to both understand and be open to new ideas as they work to create a successful new organization.

Human Resources Systems

The primary charter of the *human resources* (HR) function is to promote effectiveness (we do what we do well), cohesiveness (we hold together and relate to each other appropriately), and safety (both physical and emotional well-being) within the organization. To envision a desirable human resources future for the merged organization, you must first develop an appreciation of what human resources involves.

- Philosophy: What are our core values around how people are treated?
- Policies: How do we apply those core values through our personnel policies?
- Procedures: What are the procedures we follow and expect others to follow?
- Programs: What do we offer management and staff in order to fulfill our charter?

From conception through implementation, human resources is a critical partner and resource in the merger. *Human resources integration* includes the merging of separate human resources philosophies, policies, procedures, and programs to best support the new organization's mission. The human resources function is integral to cultural,

Exhibit 14: Fundraising Integration

Desired Outcomes

The following list includes commonly identified desired outcomes for fundraising integration. You may want to use this as a starting point for your list.

- An integrated fund development department that supports the needs of the new organization
- A clear relationship and established processes between the fundraising and marketing/communication departments
- All donors informed about and supportive of the new organization
- A development plan and fundraising calendar for the next fiscal year

Key Activities

The following list, while not exhaustive, includes activities that need to be accomplished in order to achieve successful fundraising integration. You may want to include some or all of these activities in your integration plan.

Pre-Merger Data

- ❏ Review and analyze pre-merger fundraising activities, practices, and systems (including any related membership structures).
- ❏ Review and analyze pre-merger sources of income.
- ❏ Review and analyze pre-merger diversification of revenue streams.
- ❏ Review current commitments in planned giving, grants, and contracts.
- ❏ Review and analyze donor management systems.
- ❏ Review and analyze pre-merger technology for fundraising management.
- ❏ Review pre-merger fundraising staffing.

Systems and Resources

- ❏ Adopt unified policies and procedures around fundraising.
- ❏ Put necessary or appropriate technology in place.
- ❏ Merge donor management systems (including any related membership structures).
- ❏ Create a plan to communicate with current donors.
- ❏ Create integrated gift acknowledgment and recognition processes.
- ❏ Create a revised or updated case statement for the new organization.
- ❏ Establish a fundraising budget for the new organization.
- ❏ Establish an integrated fundraising plan with a fundraising calendar.
- ❏ Clarify how fundraising will coordinate with the marketing/communication function.
- ❏ Coordinate materials needed with the marketing/communication function.

Staffing and Structure

- ❏ Define optimal staffing for the fundraising function.
- ❏ Plan for the necessary hiring or reallocation of staff resources.

Training and Support

- ❏ Train the staff and board on new fundraising systems and procedures.

management, and staff integration, which were discussed in Chapters 8–10. Here, we will address only the systems aspect of human resources integration. Exhibit 16: Human Resources (HR) Integration, page 145, provides a list of suggested desired outcomes and activities for this area of the integration plan.

Envisioning the future

Integrating the human resources systems of two or more organizations requires patience, competence, and clarity. Most human resources systems tend to be idiosyncratic: they form to the specific needs and culture of an organization. Often in the nonprofit world, human resources has evolved out of the finance function, and may have been primarily a record-keeping or paperwork-centered process. A merger is an ideal time to take stock of what each organization's human resources function does and does not offer, and to craft a new and improved system that will serve the merged organization more effectively and efficiently in the future. Such a system would clearly articulate—and take responsibility for—the following:

- Human resources policies (for example, work hours, safety issues, reporting relationships)
- Human resources procedures (timesheets, performance reviews)
- Recruitment processes
- Compensation and benefits systems
- Employee relations
- Performance management and evaluation systems
- Training and development
- Record keeping (ensuring that legally required paperwork is completed and maintained)
- Risk management and safety issues

Pre-merger steps to successful integration

Information on human resources policies and procedures should have, to at least some degree, been exchanged during the negotiation process and due diligence. Pass on whatever information was collected to the integration team as soon as one is established, along with any recommendations the negotiations committee wishes to make with regard to human resources.

Once the decision to merger is made, include at least one senior human resources staff person on the integration team. It may be necessary to bring in an outside human resources consultant if internal expertise is not available.

The first step in human resources integration is to complete a human resources audit for each of the organizations. As seen in Appendix C: Sample Human Resources Audit, page 193, the audit consists of questions covering the eight primary components of the human resources function:

- Roles, head count, and human resources information systems (HRIS)[19]
- Recruitment
- Documentation
- Training, development, and career management
- Compensation and benefits
- Performance measurement and evaluation
- Termination and transition
- Legal issues and personnel policies

The results of the audit will reveal the strengths and weaknesses in each organization's human resources systems, laying important groundwork for the development of a new system for the merged organization.

Once the audit is complete, the integration team, supported as necessary by a working group, should create a plan and set a timeline for human resources systems integration. The plan should cover the following:

- How to address equity issues (among the merging organizations) related to compensation and benefits—salaries, bonus and incentive programs, insurance coverage, retirement plans, vacation, and so forth.
- Resolutions to legal issues that surface as part of the human resources audit and due diligence process, with a goal of minimizing exposure to potential employment relationship claims (for example, wrongful termination, harassment, discrimination).
- New personnel policies, and how to best orient employees to the new policies.
- Human resources "department" staffing: Where will responsibility lie for human resources—in a separate department, or within finance or operations? How many staff will be needed?
- Human resources information system (HRIS): Will it be possible (or necessary) to integrate existing systems, or should you create a new one?
- Documentation processes, including creation of personnel files, forms, templates, and other paperwork.
- Performance management and evaluation systems.
- Policies and processes for risk management and worker safety.

Exhibit 15: Designing a New Human Resources System, page 143, presents questions that you will need to ask yourself in the integration process. It also lists specific tasks that need to be accomplished within the process.

---

[19] HRIS refers to a type of software that is written specifically for human resources management. It might include modules for recruitment, benefits, compensation, and employee records.

Post-merger steps to successful integration

Assuming that you have completed the activities outlined above by the time the merger becomes legal, the following timeline will take you through the rest of the human resources integration process.

Immediately (zero to three months):

- Proceed with the integration of human resources systems as outlined above, using staff, management, and outside consultants or experts as necessary.
- Develop and put in place—on day one of life as a merged organization—a new compensation system (both salary and benefits). Explain it to staff both in groups and individually.
- Prepare any special analyses needed to support decision processes with regard to staffing, severance packages, budgeting, or changes to organizational structure or reporting relationships.

By the end of six months:

- Work with the executive director and management team to decide what staffing changes are still necessary to integrate the organizations. Decide what, if any, layoffs will be needed among current employees, and what severance will be offered to departing staff.
- Develop a new personnel manual for the merged organization and circulate to the board.
- Combine the training and staff development functions of the former organizations.

Following are other tips for human resources integration.

Facilitating employee transitions

A merger involves some kind of transition for almost every staff member. Some will have new duties, others will move their primary workplace, while still others, regrettably, may leave the organization altogether. In a merger, the way people are treated during transition will become the basis for the new organizational culture. In times of change or uncertainty, employees and board members will attach massive significance to the smallest indicator of a shift in the way business is done. In fact, the larger the perception of loss (in wages, benefits, status, career options, or position)—regardless of reality—the more power the perception will have to derail successful integration.

Each of the following policies and benefits can help to facilitate a more positive transition for both the staff and the organization as a whole. However, each has to be clearly articulated and communicated in order to have maximum impact.

- Retention or stay pay: identifying key managers you want or need to retain and providing incentives, often financial, for them to stay through a critical transition time.
- Transition bonus: given if key individuals take on work above and beyond their normal scope during the transition.

- Training and cross-training: if there are significant staffing changes—some positions eliminated and others created—will you train, retrain, or cross-train staff to fit into those new positions, or will you simply lay off existing staff and hire new staff that might be a better "fit" initially? Retraining can provide significant benefit to both the organization and the staff members involved, but it takes a commitment of both time and resources.
- Severance pay: given to laid-off workers.
- Outplacement policy: helping displaced workers find a new job.
- Relocation costs: for those required to move as a result of the merger.
- Employee assistance program (EAP) arrangements: A well-designed employee assistance program is a good investment for any organization; it can reduce absenteeism and attrition, increase productivity, and make managing easier. Having one in place during the integration phase can be of great benefit to employees, who may need the extra support to deal with the changes and any associated stress.

Retaining key staff

The question of retention of key personnel during any significant organizational transition is a critical one. During a merger, when so much uncertainty abounds, it becomes even more important to identify and retain key individuals who will assist in the negotiation and integration processes, bring confidence and competence to the tasks at hand, and help build the new organization into its envisioned capacity.

There are three elements to retaining key talent: identify, communicate, and motivate.

First, identify the talent you want to retain—those staff members who you believe bring the skills, attitude, credibility, integrity, and capacity to the challenges at hand. Identifying key talent has to be done with great intention. You should know not only whom you want to retain, but also why the organization needs them, and how they will be integral in moving forward in the merger process and beyond.

Second, communicate to these staff members that they are critical and that you desire to retain them during and after the transition. Often, the message that you see them as valuable and want them to stay can be a significant step in the process of retention. Find out about their concerns and what they hope to experience and gain personally through the transition.

Third, find out what motivates them, which may include

- Security: assurance that they will have a job now and in the foreseeable future.
- Status: a new title or inclusion in the senior management team of the merged organization.
- Money: "stay pay," a performance bonus, or a raise.
- Growth opportunities: potential for promotion to higher positions, career development, and/or training in new skills.

Finally, come to an agreement with mutually defined expectations for the periods before, during, and after merger implementation.

There is no blanket approach to talent retention during transition. However, a good rule of thumb is to create an environment and a relationship that make the best people want to stay. Don't promise what you can't deliver, keep your word, and be clear and direct to all employees.

Some specifics on volunteer management

The recommendations given thus far apply, for the most part, to both staff and volunteer integration. In addition, however, any organization that depends on volunteers will need to be explicit in planning how to integrate the volunteer management function.

Many authorities in the area of volunteer management advocate developing human resources policies for unpaid staff that mirror those for paid staff. This would mean policies or processes for unpaid staff that parallel whatever human resources policies or processes the organization creates in the areas of employee retention, communication, recruitment, performance management, and rewards.

Here are specific questions to ask when planning the integration of the volunteer or unpaid staff workforce:

- What volunteer program policies currently exist?
- How are volunteer positions currently designed?
- How are staff-volunteer relations currently managed?
- What recruitment efforts are used to bring in new talent?
- How are volunteers oriented and trained?
- How are records kept on volunteers?
- How are volunteers evaluated?
- How are volunteers recognized?
- How do we engage and communicate with our volunteers during the integration process?

The executive director needs to decide where the responsibility for volunteers will reside. This could be assigned to a dedicated volunteer manager, within human resources, or distributed to the individual program directors. Whoever is responsible for volunteer integration must work closely with the integration team to ensure that volunteers are not "left out" of the process.

A merger presents an opportunity to intentionally grow and develop an organization's volunteer management process, and in doing so take advantage of a valuable asset of the new organization.

Exhibit 15: Designing a New Human Resources System

What questions need to be asked?	What work needs to be done?
I: Recruitment and Screening	
What positions will exist? When will the merging entities freeze positions and hiring? How and when will files be integrated and archived? What legal and transitional issues need to be settled?	Develop policies and procedures on: • Job analysis and job descriptions • Personnel planning and forecasting • Recruitment • Applications and reference checking • Employee background check and testing • Interviewing and selection • Offer letters • File creation
II: Termination	
Are we an at-will employer, or must we terminate only for cause? How will we handle job closure, resignation, and termination? What kind of severance packages will we offer? How will we inform employees of their termination? What kind of exit interview process will we have?	Understand legal obligations and all relevant legal issues, including the laws regarding protected classes. Keep detailed documentation to support all decisions, actions, and reactions.
III: Compensation and Benefits	
What will employees be paid in the new organization? How do we ensure that employees feel the benefits offered by the new organization provide equal, if not greater, benefit to them? How will we address transition-related compensation issues? When will insurance programs be shifted?	Do a total compensation analysis, and make recommendations to management. Develop a basic compensation system, paying attention to: • Internal and external equity • Benefits management • Legislated benefits (state disability insurance, unemployment, other) • Non-legislated benefits (health, dental, life/accidental death and dismemberment insurance, disability, retirement plan, educational assistance, flex programs, other) • Paid time off (holidays, vacation, sick leave, personal days) Establish an employee assistance program(EAP).

Exhibit 15: Designing a New Human Resources System (continued)

What questions need to be asked?	What work needs to be done?
IV: Appraisal and Career Management	
What will our performance appraisal system look like? What does our culture believe about accountability? What has been effective and not effective in the past? How will we assist employees with career management?	Compare existing performance appraisal systems. Establish and disseminate policies on: • Performance appraisal • Coaching and corrective action • Goal setting and planning • Mentoring • Career management and life planning
V: Training and Development	
Where will responsibility for learning lie in this new organization?	Develop an orientation and training program, including: • Orientation to the organization • Orientation to the position • Technical training • Management development
VI: Employee Relations	
Who will have primary responsibility for employee relations in the organization? Where do employees go to address grievance issues during the transition? What will be communicated to employees, and when, about the partnership and the transition? How will we address retention issues and reduce turnover?	Establish and disseminate policies on: • Scheduling and hours • Service awards • Recognition programs • Employee feedback • Work environment • Conflict resolution and grievance • Collective bargaining agreements
VII: Volunteer Relations	
Where does volunteer management reside in the new organization? What will the policies be around volunteer recruitment, training, retention, and recognition? What will be communicated to volunteers, and when, about the merger and the transition? How will volunteer concerns be addressed? How will we ensure that volunteers feel connected and included in the new organization?	Establish a structure for volunteer management. Develop policies around recruitment, training, retention, and recognition of volunteers. Establish communication channels and feedback mechanisms specific to volunteers.

Exhibit 16: Human Resources (HR) Integration

Desired Outcomes

The following list includes commonly identified desired outcomes for human resources integration. You may want to use this as a starting point for your list.

- Integrated human resources policies, including updated employment and hiring policies, workplace standards and practices, and compensation and benefits policies for the new organization

- Integrated human resources systems

Key Activities

The following list, while not exhaustive, includes many of the activities that need to be accomplished in order to achieve successful human resources integration. You may want to include some or all of these activities in your integration plan.

Pre-Merger Data

❑ Complete a human resources audit for each pre-merger organization.

❑ Review pre-merger human resources staffing.

Policies and Procedures

❑ Develop and put in place a new compensation and benefits system.

❑ Arrange meetings with staff (group, individual) to explain the compensation system.

❑ Create and disseminate new personnel policies.

❑ Create and disseminate a personnel manual.

❑ Develop a human resources information system.

❑ Integrate pre-merger personnel files.

❑ Develop performance management and evaluation systems.

❑ Develop policies and processes for risk management and worker safety.

❑ Develop policies and processes for addressing grievances.

Staffing and Structure

❑ Define optimal staffing for the human resources function.

❑ Plan for the necessary hiring or reallocation of staff resources.

❑ Review all layoff decisions and policies; ensure smooth transitions.

Training and Support

❑ Train staff on new human resources systems and procedures.

❑ Develop systems and resources for ongoing staff training and development.

Union Considerations

❑ If any of the merging organizations are unionized, steps will need to be taken to address this. Union considerations should be included in the planning process as appropriate, preferably from the very beginning.

Challenges and roadblocks

In the worst case, human resources integration can be an attempt to blend two poorly functioning systems, replicating their inadequacy. Preferably, a new, better system will be created. The ideal is not simply a good paper system (policies and procedures, files and forms), but a human resources system that is a strategic part of the organization. Many small nonprofits do not have the resources or internal expertise, however, to create a high-functioning human resources system. These groups should rely on outside assistance.

The biggest roadblock to human resources integration, aside from a lack of human resources expertise, is likely to be resistance to change. Organizations may recognize that problems exist with their current systems, yet still retain a sense of ownership and defensiveness. Even with more effective options available, people often prefer the familiar.

The transition to new systems, and the way people are treated during that transition, will be strong determinants of the new organizational culture. It is very important that this transition be handled deftly, with open, honest lines of communication to everyone who is affected. Using policies and benefits described in the section Facilitating Employee Transitions, page 140, can help make the process more palatable as well.

Technology

Technology integration includes both the integration of the systems themselves—the hardware, software, and processes that support an organization's success—and the training of all staff on how to use and take full advantage of the new organization's technical resources. Exhibit 18: Information Technology (IT) Integration, page 149, lists desired outcomes and activities that you might want to incorporate into this area of your integration plan.

Envisioning the future

Successful integration of technology results in the following:

Hardware

- Common platforms throughout most or all of the organization (for example, PC versus Mac)
- Compatible phone, e-mail, and other systems
- All employees on the same network (if one is used)
- An updated inventory of all computer and telecommunications hardware owned or leased by the organization, including all relevant technical specifications, maintenance schedules, and contracts

Software

- Fully merged administrative databases, including client databases, contact management databases, development databases, and human resources databases
- All employees on the same e-mail system, with common format e-mail addresses
- Full distribution of chosen software applications (word processing, spreadsheets, databases)
- Creation of any standard document templates or formats for word processing, spreadsheets, and databases, to ensure that documents have a standard look
- One web site for the merged organization

Training

- All employees trained on and comfortable with all hardware, software, and systems they use in their jobs
- Available ongoing training

Support

- A clearly identified technical support person, team, or vendor and a "path" for each employee to follow when they need technical support

Pre-merger steps to successful integration

As soon as possible after the decision to merge has been made and approved, a technology audit should be performed. The goal here is similar to that of a human resources audit: to understand what each organization has, how it does things, and what its technological strengths and weaknesses are. Appendix D: Sample Technology Audit, page 201, lists the questions that need to be answered.

Post-merger steps to successful integration

Have at least one person with technological expertise serve on the integration team. Technology staff from each of the pre-merger organizations will need to work with, and support, this person. Depending on the size of the organization, a separate technology work group may be created to report to the integration team. Together these individuals review the results of the technology audit and identify the technological needs of the merged organization. Because every department depends on technology to some extent—even if only to make and receive phone calls and messages—every department needs to be examined. Consider holding focus groups within the organization to discuss how each function or department uses technology, and how technology could help each do its work more effectively. While large technological leaps may need to wait until after a strategic planning process, it is never too early to begin improving the systems on which an organization depends.

Once the integration team (or technology work group) has a good handle on what the new organization will need and what resources each partner brings, it can recommend how to upgrade and integrate hardware, software, and systems for training and support. After further evaluating the recommendations in light of other integration costs and demands, the integration team should clarify the budget for technology integration and have staff directly responsible for the work make a detailed plan and timeline that reflects that budget. Refining these recommendations and prioritizing them will be an ongoing process, informed by budgetary constraints.

While you, of course, will want to complete the integration of technology as soon as possible, it isn't possible to do everything immediately. Your first priority should be to make sure that everyone in the merged organization can communicate with everyone else, and that whatever mechanisms will be used for communication during the integration process—phone systems, voice mail, e-mail—are in place. No matter how sophisticated and cool someone's new computer is, they won't be happy if they didn't know that it was coming, or if they didn't hear about the training session held yesterday on how to use it.

Challenges and roadblocks

The choice of which hardware or software to use is often more about politics than practicalities. If the chief executive officer likes Mac computers, for example, it is likely the organization will use Macs. Likewise, if the more influential of the merging organizations has always used a particular accounting package, that is very often the package chosen for the merged organization. Playing follow the leader is not necessarily the best way to make these decisions. Remember also that when two organizations merge, they create something bigger. It's important to ask: does either current system meet the new organization's needs? It may be that neither of the systems used by the previous organizations is suitable for the new, larger entity. Try to approach technology integration with a goal of finding the best possible solution, no matter how new or different it might seem.

That said, it is often difficult to persuade people to move to new and unfamiliar systems or software applications—even for things as basic as e-mail. Resistance is normal. The feeling of competence—a huge component of morale in the workplace—can be severely diminished if you take away familiar tools and replace them with ones that seem foreign. Early and often, explain which technology will change, when it will change, and why the change will benefit the organization's mission. Most importantly, make sure that training on any new systems or software is available *immediately*, and that everyone knows where to go for help when needed.

Switching platforms or software cannot happen in such a way that it disrupts the ongoing work of the organization. The merging of client databases, for example, needs to be done at a particular point in time, not gradually—you should not be using two different "live" versions at the same time.

Last but by no means least, it is easy to underestimate the amount of time and effort that will be required for training and transition management. It is also easy to underestimate the cost. Keep close tabs on both your timeline and your budget, and revisit them often.

Exhibit 18: Information Technology (IT) Integration

Desired Outcomes

The following list includes commonly identified desired outcomes for information technology integration. You may want to use this as a starting point for your list.

- Information systems that meet the needs of the new organization
- Compatible hardware and software throughout the organization
- A technology plan to address ongoing needs of the new organization

Key Activities

The following list, while not exhaustive, includes activities that need to be accomplished in order to achieve successful information technology integration. You may want to include some or all of these activities in your integration plan.

Pre-Merger Data

❑ Complete a technology audit for each pre-merger organization.

❑ Review pre-merger information technology staffing.

❑ Hold focus group meetings to gather input on technology needs and potential.

❑ Identify the technology needs of the new organization.

❑ Review the web sites of the pre-merger organizations (if appropriate) and create a plan for integration.

Systems and Resources

❑ Draft recommendations for the integration of hardware, software, and systems.

❑ Gather feedback on recommendations.

❑ Finalize the plan for integration of hardware, software, and systems.

Staffing and Structure

❑ Define optimal staffing for the information technology function.

❑ Plan for the necessary hiring or reallocation of staff resources.

Training and Support

❑ Develop and publicize training on any new hardware, software, and systems.

❑ Develop and publicize technical support options for all staff and volunteers.

❑ Ensure feedback mechanisms are in place for ongoing technical support needs.

Facilities

Facilities integration is the process of analyzing needs and resources, and developing a plan to best use available space and facilities. This may entail the following:

- Reduction or consolidation of space and facilities
- Sale of unneeded facilities or renegotiation of leases on unneeded facilities
- Purchase or lease of new facilities
- Remodeling or reconfiguration of facilities
- Relocation of departments, programs, and people

Exhibit 21: Facilities Integration, page 155, provides a list of possible desired outcomes and activities for this area of your integration plan.

Envisioning the future

A well-crafted plan for facilities integration ensures the best use of space, allows the organization to meet its space needs, and ensures appropriate access to services by clients and other stakeholders. It allows you to more successfully co-locate integrated programs and functions, and facilitate linkages among staff who previously worked in separate organizations. Organizations with well-planned facilities are better able to anticipate future administrative and programmatic space needs. A well-thought-out plan for facilities integration also supports your organization's goals for cultural integration and internal communication.

Finally, for most nonprofits, facilities are the largest fixed expense aside from personnel. You need to be sure you are getting the most for your money.

Pre-merger steps to successful integration

As the decision to merge approaches, organizations with a complex physical infrastructure will find it useful to prepare a facilities audit, or overview of their facilities. The audit will jump-start the process of considering options for space use after the merger takes place. Many organizations are deeply committed to their facilities, even if the space is inadequate or in need of significant upgrading. The sooner staff can start to consider new options, the easier it will be to move beyond historic allegiances and look to potential changes that can provide more appropriate space. An audit document should list all facilities each organization owns or uses, and identify the following facts about each facility:

- Location
- Size
- Usage
- Condition
- Ownership
- Mortgage or lease details
- Any other information that should be considered when planning for facilities integration

Exhibit 19: Sample Facilities Audit, page 151, shows part of an audit document for two merging organizations.

Exhibit 19: Sample Facilities Audit

	Organization A	Organization B
Facility ID	Facility 1 of 2	Facility 1 of 4
Location	124 Market St., Smithville, CA	421 3rd St., Smithville, CA
Size	10,000 square feet	5,000 square feet
Usage	Administration, finance, HR, program intake and services (counseling)	Administration, finance, and development
Condition	Excellent—new building meets current needs well	Adequate—needs cosmetic repair, i.e., paint, carpeting, and general decorating
Ownership	ABC Leasing Co.	Owned by Nonprofit ABC. CDBG grant helped upgrade foundation and HVAC. Must maintain facility use or repay.
Mortgage or Lease Details	Lease—$1.05 per square foot, 5 years remaining on lease— 3% increase per year	Mortgage—$30,000—8 years remaining on 30-year mortgage at 7.75%
Additional Information	No space available in current facility. Space is available within the complex, however. Economy has brought down lease rates and increased availability. Owner is amenable to negotiation.	One-third of building is vacant. Could lease out to tenant or consider moving in other functions.

Post-merger steps to successful integration

Those members of the integration team charged with leading the facilities integration effort must be able to gain input from—and work with—staff responsible for programs, finance, human resources, and administration. They need to pragmatically consider the needs of clients, staff, visitors, and outside stakeholders. They also need to consider both the immediate and longer-term space needs of the merged organization.

The first step in this process should be a facilities audit, if one was not done during the negotiation process.

The next step is to determine the current and intermediate space needs of the merged organization in terms of

- Size and location
- Inter- and intradepartment and program communication needs
- Consolidation potential
- Growth and expansion potential
- Cultural integration potential
- Any other information that seems relevant

Exhibit 20: Sample Inventory of Current and Intermediate Space Needs, page 153, shows a sample inventory of space needs for two merging organizations.

With this information in hand, the integration team can begin outlining options for the space needs of the merged organization. Again, these options need to be developed and assessed in coordination with the integration of finance, human resources, and programs.

For the example shown in Exhibit 20, one set of recommendations might be as follows:

> Move the program functions of Organization A into the primary facility of Organization B. Consolidate the development departments of the merging organizations and move that function into facility A, along with all other administrative functions. If moving program functions out of facility A does not provide enough administrative space, we will need to lease additional space within the complex. This may offer an opportunity to renegotiate our current lease on more favorable terms. We also need to upgrade facility B so that program staff see that their space needs are being given the same consideration as that of administration, and are of equal quality.

Bring the options and recommendations that emerge from this process to the executive director and the full integration team for discussion and approval. Depending on the scope and cost of the recommendations, approval from the board might also be necessary. Once approved, the facilities integration plan can be folded into the overall integration plan. As with all sections of the plan, review it regularly and update as necessary.

Challenges and roadblocks

Several challenges and potential roadblocks may impact the facilities integration process. Some are very facilities-specific. Leases, for example, may or may not be close to the renewal date at the time of merger. You may want to leave one facility for another, but not be able to do so without a penalty. On the other hand, a merger might provide an excellent opportunity to renegotiate a lease. Challenge your organization to be open-minded when considering options, and take advantage of the change to try to improve the organization's situation.

Deferred maintenance is another challenge for many merging organizations. One or both may have facilities that are in poor condition due to deferred maintenance, and the merged entity needs to be prepared to do the necessary upgrades, or at least to be aware of what is needed.

Sometimes a newly merged organization will decide that a particular facility is no longer appropriate for its mission or programs, and wish to sell it. In some situations this might be a problem, as when, for example, a major donor provided the facility and it is believed that the sale would offend the donor. Be sensitive in your communications with such a donor, and work with the donor to envision how the change would truly benefit the mission of the organization.

Exhibit 20: Sample Inventory of Current and Intermediate Space Needs

	Organization A	Organization B
Size and Location	Need additional space. Staff are cramped in current facilities. Location is great for administration—right downtown—close to everything. Location not ideal for program—clients are mostly from out of area.	Currently have too much space. Could increase the number of staff in this location. Ideal location for program functions as many clients live within close proximity.
Inter- and Intra-department/ program communication needs	Administration, finance, and HR communicate well in this facility. Development department is off-site. Needs to be brought into administrative facility. Program intake function is not near client base.	Administration, finance, and development communicate well within this facility. Program functions are not located here and would benefit from this location.
Consolidation potential	Would have to move out program functions in order to consolidate other departments in this facility	Room to consolidate some functions within this facility
Growth and expansion potential	Could expand only by leasing additional space within the complex	Expansion possible within the current facility—one-third of space currently unused
Cultural integration potential	Should consider moving development department into administrative offices. Currently these departments are not interacting very well—too much physical distance between them. They are culturally separate with poor communication.	Communication among program staff could be enhanced by moving from various sites into this facility if administrative functions could be consolidated elsewhere
Additional information	Recommendations for consolidation of the development departments of Organizations A & B have been made. Combined staff of 8 will be reduced to 6.	Merged programs of the new organization will need to be housed together in order to enhance communication and integration of program cultures

Other challenges involve culture and trust. For example, one organization may be reluctant to give up or move its offices because it perceives such a change as disruptive to how business has traditionally been conducted. Departments may need to be separated in the newly merged organization, splitting up long-standing office relationships and changing well-established patterns of communication.

Staff may be concerned that they are not going to be treated equally in the provision of facilities. When there is a merger of organizations of disparate size or power, staff of the smaller organization need to be assured that all staff will be treated equitably. This does not mean that facilities are all equal, but that the assignment of staff to facilities is based on the best interests of the organization as a whole, and not on preferential treatment for staff from a particular pre-merger organization.

Staff, as well as external constituents, may also be concerned about any decision that moves a program from proximity or easy access to its clients. Or an organization that moves staff from a suburban to an inner-city location may find that some staff are uncomfortable with this change. In all cases, open discussion, a focus on the mission-related reasons for the move, and attendance to the staff's and constituents' legitimate needs are the key to resolving these issues.

Summary

As with all aspects of integration, successful systems integration depends on careful analysis of an organization's needs and desired outcomes, and careful planning. The sooner you can begin this planning, the better. With each "system"—finance, fundraising, human resources, technology, and facilities—there are things you can do as soon as the decision to merge is made that will increase your chances of facilitating a smooth transition.

That said, it is never too late to start—or to get "back on track." If you find yourself stuck in some area after the merger, go back to the recommendations in this chapter and think through what steps you might have skipped, or what could help you jump-start your process again. Beware the temptation to move full speed ahead with whatever your new systems are going to be. Truly understanding each organization's strengths and weaknesses, and the merged organization's desired outcomes, will help ensure that your new systems work best for everyone, for the long haul.

Exhibit 21: Facilities Integration

Desired Outcomes
The following list includes commonly identified desired outcomes for facilities integration. You may want to use this as a starting point for your list.

- Facilities that meet the space needs of the new organization
- A facilities plan that outlines growth needs over the next five years

Key Activities
The following list, while not exhaustive, includes activities that need to be accomplished in order to achieve successful facilities integration. You may want to include some or all of these activities in your integration plan.

Pre-Merger Data
❑ Complete a facilities audit for each pre-merger organization.
❑ Determine current and intermediate space needs.

Planning
❑ Gather input on projected space needs for the merged organization from staff, clients, and other stakeholders.
❑ Outline options for addressing space needs.
❑ Bring recommendations to the executive director, integration team, and board as appropriate.
❑ Finalize the plan and budget for meeting space needs.
❑ Ensure that longer-term space considerations are included in future strategic planning.

Other (organization-specific)
❑ To be specified in the planning process

Conclusion

We have now come to the end of our integration planning guide, and a few observations are in order.

First, congratulations if you have created a plan to guide your integration efforts. As we noted earlier, our research and experience show that the existence of such a plan is a major factor in the successful integration of two or more nonprofits. It is not so much that a fully realized plan—much less one created according to our recommended approach—is necessary to success. Rather, what is key is the process of planning, of thinking through the challenges you will face in advance, and of bringing people together to work on possible solutions. Thus, your efforts in working through the tasks outlined in this guide, even if they do not result in a full-blown plan, will bring you a long way toward the ultimate goal nonetheless. This is because the ultimate goal of planning for merger integration is not the plan you create, but the newly merged organizations you transform.

We highlighted the challenges of integration on many fronts—systems, people, and culture in particular. But, as we repeatedly emphasized, your leadership, and that of your colleagues, is the crucial variable in your merger's success. If you act graciously toward people coming from a different organization and culture, mindfully as you assemble your board and staff teams, and inspirationally as you leave behind old patterns in favor of newly created and shared ones, you will bring your people into a better future, both for them and for the clients and causes you serve.

It is likely, given the economic and political pressures nonprofits labor under, that there will continue to be opportunities for you to experience mergers in the future. That is, once you have completed this round of integration—or maybe even before that point—you may find yourself faced with an opportunity to do it all again! While this thought may send shivers down your spine at the moment, please consider two important facts.

First, as you will probably continue to be confronted with merger possibilities, remember that these opportunities may allow you to advance your mission even further. You can take such merger opportunities or leave them, but you can't avoid seeing them as they arise.

Second, having gone through the current merger and integration experience, you will be in a much better position to succeed on the next merger. Practice does, in fact, help; and, while every merger situation is different, with unique dynamics and people, you have probably learned enough from this guide to recognize the similarities. So consider your apprenticeship at merger integration as more than a necessary piece of work to complete. Consider it to be an additional skill or another tool in your personal and organizational tool box, ready to be pulled out and used when needed.

Remember also that the processes and dynamics of merger integration are simply an extreme form of the change issues you face on a regular basis as a nonprofit leader. Struggling with these issues here, where so much is at stake and so many depend on (and watch) you, will make you more effective with managing the next nonmerger-related challenge. It could be a major staff transition as a long-term leader retires, or an industry sea change that requires rethinking the way you provide or finance your programs or services. Whatever the challenge, you will face it with greater confidence and skills for having successfully negotiated the difficulties of merger integration.

Finally, we invite you to let us know how your merger integration is going, and whether this guide has been helpful. We depend on your feedback for tips on future research, improvements to our consulting practices, and revisions to *The Nonprofit Mergers Workbook Part I* and to this guide itself. Please send any feedback to info@lapiana.org.

Sample Integration Plans

Sample Integration Plan
Organized by Activity Area and Target Date

Board

January 2004

Ongoing	Start Date	Target Date	Activity	Lead	Team	Complete?
		1/14/04	Establish a board integration committee	(Bd Pres) Jules Hoffner		☐
		1/17/04	Identify desired outcomes for board integration	(Bd Pres) Jules Hoffner		☐
		1/17/04	(Plan and convene FIRST JOINT BOARD MEETING)	(Bd Pres) Jules Hoffner	Susan	☐
		1/17/04	Establish schedule for future board meetings	(Bd Pres) Jules Hoffner		☐

February 2004

Ongoing	Start Date	Target Date	Activity	Lead	Team	Complete?
		2/20/04	Review each board's prior practices, responsibilities, job descriptions	(Bd Mem) David Ryan	Tomas	☐
		2/20/04	Establish a committee structure and job descriptions for the new board	(Bd Pres) Jules Hoffner	David, Kathryn	☐

March 2004

Ongoing	Start Date	Target Date	Activity	Lead	Team	Complete?
		3/1/04	Survey board members re: interests, strengths	(Bd Pres) Jules Hoffner		☐
		3/15/04	Assess board composition; determine needed skills/characteristics	(Bd Mem) Jackie Lousilla	Kathryn	☐
		3/15/04	Finalize board committee assignments	(Bd Pres) Jules Hoffner		☐
		3/31/04	Articulate communication practices for the board, and with the executive director	(Bd Mem) Susan Yi	Kathryn	☐
		3/31/04	Create a fund development plan to meet short-term needs	(Bd Treas) Rob Wyland	Jackie, Will, DD	☐
		3/31/04	Approve a budget for the merged organization	(Bd Pres) Jules Hoffner	Rob	☐
	1/17/04	3/31/04	Plan a retreat for members of the new board	(Bd Pres) Jules Hoffner	Susan, David, Will	☐

April 2004

Ongoing	Start Date	Target Date	Activity	Lead	Team	Complete?
		4/15/04	Provide training to all members regarding their role as ambassador	(Consultant) Sean Fisher	Jules	☐
		4/15/04	Provide training to all members regarding fundraising responsibilities	(Bd Treas) Rob Wyland	Sean Fisher (assist)	☐
		4/30/04	Develop a board-member recruitment plan	(Bd Mem) Jackie Lousilla	Kathryn, Will	☐

May 2004

Ongoing	Start Date	Target Date	Activity	Lead	Team	Complete?
☐	4/1/04	5/30/04	Create a fundraising plan for the merged organization	(Bd Treas) Rob Wyland	Jackie, Will, DD	☐

June 2004

Ongoing	Start Date	Target Date	Activity	Lead	Team	Complete?
☐	3/1/04	6/30/04	Develop an orientation program for incoming members	(Bd Mem) Susan Yi	Rob, Will, Tomas	☐
☐	3/1/04	6/30/04	Develop a board handbook	(Bd Mem) David Ryan	Kathryn	☐

July 2004

Ongoing	Start Date	Target Date	Activity	Lead	Team	Complete?
☐	7/1/04	7/30/04	Ensure that all current members have been through orientation	(Bd Mem) Susan Yi		☐

October 2004

Ongoing	Start Date	Target Date	Activity	Lead	Team	Complete?
☐	9/1/04	10/30/04	Create and implement a board self-assessment process	(Bd Mem) Jackie Lousilla	Jules	☐

December 2004

Ongoing	Start Date	Target Date	Activity	Lead	Team	Complete?
☐	4/15/04	12/31/04	Work with management to establish an evaluation process for the organization		ED	☐
☐	6/1/04	12/31/04	Develop and pursue a strategic planning process	(Bd Pres) Jules Hoffner	ED	☐

Communication / Marketing

January 2004

Ongoing	Start Date	Target Date	Activity	Lead	Team	Complete?
☐		1/15/04	Identify all pre-merger communication staff and resources	(Mktg Dir) Michael Doyer	Marketing staff	☐
☐		1/30/04	Design marketing and communication functions in new organization	(Mktg Dir) Michael Doyer	ED	☐

February 2004

Ongoing	Start Date	Target Date	Activity	Lead	Team	Complete?
		2/15/04	Draft initial marketing plan	(Mktg Dir) Michael Doyer	Marketing staff	☐
		2/15/04	Define an overall marketing strategy	(Mktg Dir) Michael Doyer	Marketing staff	☐
		2/15/04	Identify required/desired marketing materials	(Mktg Dir) Michael Doyer	Marketing staff	☐
		2/28/04	Draft a talking-points document	(Mktg Dir) Michael Doyer	ED	☐
		2/28/04	Designate a spokesperson(s)	(ED) Liza Neuman		☐
		2/28/04	Establish guiding principles for communication	(Mktg Dir) Michael Doyer		☐

March 2004

Ongoing	Start Date	Target Date	Activity	Lead	Team	Complete?
		3/15/04	Create necessary Q&A documents	(Mktg Dir) Michael Doyer		☐
		3/20/04	Draft, secure approval for, and finalize messages	(Mktg Dir) Michael Doyer	Marketing staff	☐

April 2004

Ongoing	Start Date	Target Date	Activity	Lead	Team	Complete?
		4/30/04	Design and plan distribution schedule for an integration newsletter	(Mktg Dir) Michael Doyer		☐

May 2004

Ongoing	Start Date	Target Date	Activity	Lead	Team	Complete?
		5/30/04	Create and/or update web site	(Mktg Dir) Michael Doyer	IT Director	☐

Evaluation

Ongoing	Start Date	Target Date	Activity	Lead	Team	Complete?
☑			Review integration plan and accomplishment of activities	(ED) Liza Neuman	Team	☐

March 2004

Ongoing	Start Date	Target Date	Activity	Lead	Team	Complete?
		3/31/04	Conduct check-in meeting with senior management team	(ED) Liza Neuman		☐

Facilities

February 2004

Ongoing	Start Date	Target Date	Activity	Lead	Team	Complete?
☐	1/1/04	2/1/04	Gather input on space needs from staff, clients, other relevant stakeholders	(Consultant) Sean Fisher		☐
☐		2/15/04	Determine current and intermediate space needs	(Consultant) Sean Fisher	ED, HR Dir, CFO, David Ryan	☐

March 2004

Ongoing	Start Date	Target Date	Activity	Lead	Team	Complete?
☐		3/1/04	Complete a facilities audit for each pre-merger org.	(Consultant) Sean Fisher	ED, CFO, David Ryan	☐
☐		3/15/04	Bring facilities recommendations to ED, Integration Team, and board as appropriate	(Consultant) Sean Fisher		☐
☐		3/30/04	Finalize plan and budget for meeting space needs	(Consultant) Sean Fisher		☐

Finance

December 2003

Ongoing	Start Date	Target Date	Activity	Lead	Team	Complete?
☐		12/15/03	Determine the new organization's fiscal year	(ED) Liza Neuman	Board Treasurer, CFO	☐
☐		12/15/03	Review maintenance schedules for buildings, equipment (for budgeting)	(CFO) Marcus Jade		☐

January 2004

Ongoing	Start Date	Target Date	Activity	Lead	Team	Complete?
☐		1/15/04	Define optimal staffing for finance function	(CFO) Marcus Jade	HR	☐
☐		1/15/04	Select/adopt a payroll system	(CFO) Marcus Jade	ED	☐
☐		1/15/04	Plan for necessary hiring/reallocation of staff resources	(CFO) Marcus Jade	HR	☐
☐		1/15/04	Examine/compare pre-merger accounting systems	(CFO) Marcus Jade		☐
☐	1/1/04	1/15/04	Refine the consolidated budget created during negotiations	(CFO) Marcus Jade	ED, Board Treasurer	☐
☐		1/20/04	Define features of a desired accounting system	(CFO) Marcus Jade		☐
☐		1/30/04	Consolidate banking and investment accounts	(CFO) Marcus Jade		☐
☐		1/30/04	Select accounting system	(CFO) Marcus Jade		☐
☐		1/30/04	Develop a petty cash policy	(CFO) Marcus Jade	Finance	☐
☐		1/30/04	Develop purchasing policies	(CFO) Marcus Jade	Finance	☐
☐		1/30/04	Adopt a unified format for financial statements; circulate to board	(CFO) Marcus Jade	ED, Board Treasurer	☐

February 2004

Ongoing	Start Date	Target Date	Activity	Lead	Team	Complete?
☐		2/15/04	Train staff/board on new financial systems/procedures	(CFO) Marcus Jade	Board	☐
☐		2/28/04	Notify clients and vendors of any change to billing address/procedures	(CFO) Marcus Jade	Finance	☐

Fundraising

Ongoing	Start Date	Target Date	Activity	Lead	Team	Complete?
☑			Train staff/board on new fundraising systems/procedures	(Dir Dev) Calvin Wright	IT	☐

February 2003

Ongoing	Start Date	Target Date	Activity	Lead	Team	Complete?
☐		2/28/03	Make recommendations for new databases and donor systems to board	(Dir Dev) Calvin Wright		☐

January 2004

Ongoing	Start Date	Target Date	Activity	Lead	Team	Complete?
☐		1/1/04	Review/analyze technology used for fundraising management	(Dir Dev) Calvin Wright	IT	☐
☐		1/15/04	Review pre-merger fundraising staffing	(Dir Dev) Calvin Wright	ED	☐
☐		1/15/04	Create plan to communicate with current donors	(Dir Dev) Calvin Wright	ED, Board	☐
☐		1/30/04	Define optimal staffing for fundraising function	(Dir Dev) Calvin Wright	ED	☐

February 2004

Ongoing	Start Date	Target Date	Activity	Lead	Team	Complete?
☐		2/15/04	Plan for necessary hiring/reallocation of staff resources	(Dir Dev) Calvin Wright	ED, HR	☐
☐		2/15/04	Review/analyze donor databases	(Dir Dev) Calvin Wright	IT	☐
☐		2/15/04	Assess level/types of pre-merger participation in fundraising efforts	(Bd Pres) Jules Hoffner	Calvin, ED	☐

March 2004

Ongoing	Start Date	Target Date	Activity	Lead	Team	Complete?
☐		3/1/04	Create integrated gift acknowledgment and recognition processes	(Dir Dev) Calvin Wright	Development staff	☐

May 2004

Ongoing	Start Date	Target Date	Activity	Lead	Team	Complete?
☐		5/10/04	Create updated case statement for the new organization	(Dir Dev) Calvin Wright	ED	☐ ☐
☐		5/10/04	Establish a fundraising budget for the new organization	(Dir Dev) Calvin Wright	Board fundraising committee	
☐	4/1/03	5/10/04	Establish an integrated fundraising plan with fundraising calendar	(Dir Dev) Calvin Wright	Development staff	☐
☐		5/30/04	Adopt unified policies and procedures for fundraising	(Dir Dev) Calvin Wright	ED, Board	☐
☐		5/30/04	Finalize and adopt fundraising plan	(Bd Pres) Jules Hoffner	ED, Board	☐

Human Resources (HR)

January 2004

Ongoing	Start Date	Target Date	Activity	Lead	Team	Complete?
☐		1/15/04	Review all layoff decisions and policies; ensure smooth transitions	(HR Dir) Bill Harris	ED	☐
☐		1/30/04	Complete an HR audit for each pre-merger organization	(HR Dir) Bill Harris		☐

February 2004

Ongoing	Start Date	Target Date	Activity	Lead	Team	Complete?
☐		2/15/04	Develop systems/resources for ongoing staff training and development	(HR Dir) Bill Harris	HR staff	☐
☐		2/15/04	Integrate pre-merger personnel files	(HR Dir) Bill Harris		☐
☐		2/15/04	Define optimal staffing for HR function	(HR Dir) Bill Harris		☐

March 2004

Ongoing	Start Date	Target Date	Activity	Lead	Team	Complete?
☐		3/1/04	Train staff on new HR systems/procedures	(HR Dir) Bill Harris	HR staff	☐
☐		3/1/04	Create and disseminate new personnel policies	(HR Dir) Bill Harris	HR staff	☐
☐		3/1/04	Develop performance management and evaluation systems	(HR Dir) Bill Harris		☐
☐		3/1/04	Develop and put in place a new compensation and benefits system	(HR Dir) Bill Harris	ED	☐
☐		3/15/04	Arrange meetings with staff (group, individual) to explain compensation system	(HR Dir) Bill Harris	HR staff	☐

Information Technology (IT)

January 2004

Ongoing	Start Date	Target Date	Activity	Lead	Team	Complete?
☐		1/15/04	Ensure that all staff can immediately communicate via phone, e-mail	(IT Dir) Haley Grant	IT staff	☐
☐		1/30/04	Identify the technology needs of the new organization	(IT Dir) Haley Grant	IT staff	☐
☐		1/30/04	Arrange focus groups to gather input on technology needs/potential	(IT Dir) Haley Grant	IT staff	☐
☐		1/30/04	Review pre-merger IT staffing	(IT Dir) Haley Grant	IT staff	☐

February 2004

Ongoing	Start Date	Target Date	Activity	Lead	Team	Complete?
☐		2/15/04	Define optimal staffing for IT function	(IT Dir) Haley Grant	ED	☐
☐		2/15/04	Draft recommendations for integration of hardware, software, systems	(IT Dir) Haley Grant		☐
☐		2/25/04	Gather feedback on recommendations	(IT Dir) Haley Grant		☐
☐		2/28/04	Plan for necessary hiring/reallocation of staff resources	(IT Dir) Haley Grant	Ed, HR Dir	☐

March 2004

Ongoing	Start Date	Target Date	Activity	Lead	Team	Complete?
☐		3/5/04	Finalize plan for integration of hardware, software, systems	(IT Dir) Haley Grant		☐
☐		3/30/04	Develop and publicize training on any new hardware, software, systems	(IT Dir) Haley Grant	IT staff	☐
☐		3/30/04	Ensure feedback mechanisms are in place for ongoing tech support needs	(IT Dir) Haley Grant		☐

Management/Senior Management Team (SMT)

January 2004

Ongoing	Start Date	Target Date	Activity	Lead	Team	Complete?
☐		1/1/04	Establish a regular SMT meeting time and list of "must-have" agenda items	(ED) Liza Neuman	SMT	☐
☐		1/15/04	Articulate the integration-related duties and responsibilities of the SMT	(HR Dir) Bill Harris	SMT	☐
☐		1/15/04	Articulate the general duties and responsibilities of the SMT	(HR Dir) Bill Harris	SMT	☐
☐		1/15/04	Define a desired managerial culture for the new organization	(ED) Liza Neuman	SMT	☐

Ongoing	Start Date	Target Date	Activity	Lead	Team	Complete?
☐	1/1/04	1/15/04	Identify specific work required to achieve desired managerial culture	(ED) Liza Neuman	SMT	☐
☐		1/30/04	Create process to monitor the integration plan	(ED) Liza Neuman	Integration Team	☐
☐		1/30/04	Articulate processes, policies, and procedures around conflict resolution	(HR Dir) Bill Harris	SMT	☐

February 2004

Ongoing	Start Date	Target Date	Activity	Lead	Team	Complete?
☐	1/1/04	2/1/04	Identify management positions needed in the merged organization	(HR Dir) Bill Harris		☐
☐		2/15/04	Develop a recruitment plan for any remaining senior management positions	(HR Dir) Bill Harris		☐
☐		2/15/04	Create process to fill open positions	(HR Dir) Bill Harris		☐
☐	1/1/04	2/28/04	ED work with each manager to create a personal development and training plan	(ED) Liza Neuman		☐

March 2004

Ongoing	Start Date	Target Date	Activity	Lead	Team	Complete?
☐		3/15/04	Have ED create own development plan in partnership with board	(ED) Liza Neuman	Board	☐
☐		3/30/04	Create a development and training plan for each manager	(ED) Liza Neuman	SMT	☐
☐		3/30/04	Work with Integration Team to evaluate integration progress (ongoing)	(ED) Liza Neuman	Integration Team	☐

Overall

Ongoing	Start Date	Target Date	Activity	Lead	Team	Complete?
☑	1/7/04		Coordinate Integration Team activities with the Board Integration Committee	(Chair, Int Team) Maya Coughlin	Team	☐

January 2004

Ongoing	Start Date	Target Date	Activity	Lead	Team	Complete?
☐	1/3/04	1/15/04	(Plan, convene FIRST MEETING OF INT TEAM)	(Chair, Int Team) Maya Coughlin		☐
☐	1/15/04	1/22/04	Clarify the team's role, goals, channels of communication	(Chair, Int Team) Maya Coughlin	ED, Int Team	☐
☐	1/15/04	1/22/04	Decide how to create the first draft of an integration plan	(ED) Liza Neuman	Maya, Int Team	☐
☐	1/15/04	1/29/04	Designate "sub-teams" or working groups for key integration areas	(Chair, Int Team) Maya Coughlin	ED, Int Team	☐ ☐

February 2004

Ongoing	Start Date	Target Date	Activity	Lead	Team	Complete?
☐	1/15/04	2/5/04	Articulate desired outcomes for each integration area	(Chair, Int Team) Maya Coughlin	ED, all senior managers	☐
☐	1/15/04	2/5/04	Design process for gathering and incorporating feedback on the plan	(HR Dir) Bill Harris	Maya, Marty	☐
☐	1/15/04	2/5/04	Design process for making the integration plan a "living document"	(HR Dir) Bill Harris	Maya, Marty	☐
☐	1/15/04	2/13/04	Generate first draft of an integration plan	(Chair, Int Team) Maya Coughlin	Ken, Marty, Int Team	☐
☐	1/15/04	2/20/04	Distribute first draft of integration plan to management, staff for "fleshing out"	(Chair, Int Team) Maya Coughlin	ED, Bill	☐

Program

January 2004

Ongoing	Start Date	Target Date	Activity	Lead	Team	Complete?
☐		1/15/04	Gather and compare information on all pre-merger programs	(Prog Dir) Natalie Casper	Sarah	☐
☐		1/15/04	Identify any obstacles/issues likely to arise in program integration	(Prog Dir) Natalie Casper	Sarah	☐
☐		1/15/04	Identify necessary skills and competencies for program management	(ED) Liza Neuman	SMT	☐
☐		1/30/04	Identify positions that need to be filled	(Prog Dir) Natalie Casper		☐
☐		1/30/04	Identify any programs needing to be closed or moved elsewhere	(Prog Dir) Natalie Casper	Sarah, ED	☐
☐		1/30/04	Identify programmatic strengths, weaknesses, assets and liabilities	(Prog Dir) Natalie Casper	Sarah, ED	☐
☐		1/30/04	Match current (pre-merger) employees to positions where appropriate	(ED) Liza Neuman	Natalie	☐

February 2004

Ongoing	Start Date	Target Date	Activity	Lead	Team	Complete?
☐		2/10/04	Gather input on proposed program design from SMT and other stakeholders	(Prog Dir) Natalie Casper	Sarah, SMT	☐
☐		2/15/04	Design the process for integrating, closing, or moving each program	(Prog Dir) Natalie Casper		☐
☐		2/15/04	Incorporate feedback on program design	(Prog Dir) Natalie Casper	Sarah	☐
☐		2/15/04	Create process to fill open positions	(Prog Dir) Natalie Casper	HR Director	☐
☐		2/25/04	Finalize recommendations for program design	(Prog Dir) Natalie Casper	Sarah, ED	☐

Staff

January 2004

Ongoing	Start Date	Target Date	Activity	Lead	Team	Complete?
☐		1/1/04	Identify positions still needed within the organization	(HR Dir) Bill Harris	ED	☐
☐		1/1/04	Address job losses with remaining staff: clarify extent, timing, impact	(ED) Liza Neuman	HR Director	☐
☐		1/15/04	Plan a farewell ritual for departing employees	(HR Dir) Bill Harris	ED	☐
☐		1/15/04	Establish specific feedback mechanisms for staff questions/comments/concerns	(HR Dir) Bill Harris	ED	☐
☐		1/15/04	Identify one or more integration exercises that can be done at staff meetings	(HR Dir) Bill Harris		☐
☐		1/15/04	Establish regular staff meeting times and "must-have" agenda items	(ED) Liza Neuman		☐
☐		1/15/04	Delegate responsibility for filling necessary positions	(ED) Liza Neuman		☐
☐		1/15/04	Clarify roles for all staff: reporting relationships, function, authority	(HR Dir) Bill Harris		☐
☐		1/30/04	Identify opportunities to be explicit in acknowledging staff contributions	(HR Dir) Bill Harris	ED	☐

February 2004

Ongoing	Start Date	Target Date	Activity	Lead	Team	Complete?
☐		2/1/04	Institute a plan to celebrate milestones, accomplishments at the department/work group level	(HR Dir) Bill Harris	Program Dir.	☐

December 2004

Ongoing	Start Date	Target Date	Activity	Lead	Team	Complete?
☑	1/1/04	12/30/04	Communicate regularly about integration progress	(ED) Liza Neuman	SMT	☐

Volunteers

December 2003

Ongoing	Start Date	Target Date	Activity	Lead	Team	Complete?
☐		12/31/03	Create mechanism for volunteer involvement in integration process of volunteer programs	(Vol Coor) Alex Hayes		☐
☐		12/31/03	Establish plan for communicating with volunteers about integration process and how changes will impact them	(Vol Coor) Alex Hayes		☐

January 2004

Ongoing	Start Date	Target Date	Activity	Lead	Team	Complete?
❑		1/30/04	Clarify the volunteer needs of the new organization	(Vol Coor) Alex Hayes		❑
❑		1/30/04	Identify any changes needed in the volunteer program	(Vol Coor) Alex Hayes		❑

February 2004

Ongoing	Start Date	Target Date	Activity	Lead	Team	Complete?
❑		2/15/04	Design roles and assignments for volunteers in the new organization	(Vol Coor) Alex Hayes		❑
❑		2/15/04	Create job descriptions for volunteer positions	(Vol Coor) Alex Hayes		❑
❑		2/15/04	Clarify roles for all volunteers: reporting relationships, function, authority	(Vol Coor) Alex Hayes		❑
❑		2/28/04	Establish policies for volunteer supervision, evaluation, and recognition	(Vol Coor) Alex Hayes		❑

March 2004

Ongoing	Start Date	Target Date	Activity	Lead	Team	Complete?
❑		3/15/04	Develop a volunteer recruitment plan	(Vol Coor) Alex Hayes		❑
❑		3/30/04	Create volunteer policies manual for the new organization	(Vol Coor) Alex Hayes		❑

April 2004

Ongoing	Start Date	Target Date	Activity	Lead	Team	Complete?
❑		4/30/04	Develop a volunteer orientation and training manual/process	(Vol Coor) Alex Hayes		❑

Sample Integration Plan
Organized by Target Date and Activity Area

Evaluation

Ongoing	Start Date	Target Date	Activity	Lead	Team	Complete?
☑			Review integration plan and accomplishment of activities	(ED) Liza Neuman		☐

Fundraising

Ongoing	Start Date	Target Date	Activity	Lead	Team	Complete?
☑			Train staff/board on new fundraising systems/procedures	(Dir Dev) Calvin Wright	IT	☐

Overall

Ongoing	Start Date	Target Date	Activity	Lead	Team	Complete?
☑		1/7/04	Coordinate Integration Team activities with the Board Integration Committee	(Chair, Int Team) Maya Coughlin		☐

February 2003

Fundraising

Ongoing	Start Date	Target Date	Activity	Lead	Team	Complete?
☐		2/28/03	Make recommendations for new databases and donor systems to board	(Dir Dev) Calvin Wright		☐

December 2003

Finance

Ongoing	Start Date	Target Date	Activity	Lead	Team	Complete?
☐		12/15/03	Determine the new organization's fiscal year	(ED) Liza Neuman		☐
☐		12/15/03	Review maintenance schedules for buildings, equipment (for budgeting)	(CFO) Marcus Jade	Board Treasurer, CFO	☐

Volunteers

Ongoing	Start Date	Target Date	Activity	Lead	Team	Complete?
☐		12/31/03	Establish plan for communicating with volunteers about integration process and how changes will impact them	(Vol Coor) Alex Hayes		☐
☐		12/31/03	Create mechanism for volunteer involvement in integration process of volunteer programs	(Vol Coor) Alex Hayes		☐

January 2004

Board

Ongoing	Start Date	Target Date	Activity	Lead	Team	Complete?
☐		1/14/04	Establish a board integration committee	(Bd Pres) Jules Hoffner		☐
☐		1/17/04	Establish schedule for future board meetings	(Bd Pres) Jules Hoffner		☐
☐		1/17/04	(Plan and convene FIRST JOINT BOARD MEETING)	(Bd Pres) Jules Hoffner	Susan	☐
☐		1/17/04	Identify desired outcomes for board integration	(Bd Pres) Jules Hoffner		☐

Communication / Marketing

Ongoing	Start Date	Target Date	Activity	Lead	Team	Complete?
☐		1/15/04	Identify all pre-merger communication staff and resources	(Mktg Dir) Michael Doyer	Marketing staff	☐
☐		1/30/04	Design marketing and communication functions in new organization	(Mktg Dir) Michael Doyer	ED	☐

Finance

Ongoing	Start Date	Target Date	Activity	Lead	Team	Complete?
☐		1/15/04	Define optimal staffing for finance function	(CFO) Marcus Jade	HR	☐
☐		1/15/04	Select/adopt a payroll system	(CFO) Marcus Jade	ED	☐
☐		1/15/04	Plan for necessary hiring/reallocation of staff resources	(CFO) Marcus Jade	HR	☐
☐		1/15/04	Examine and compare pre-merger accounting systems	(CFO) Marcus Jade		☐
☐	1/1/04	1/15/04	Refine the consolidated budget created during negotiations	(CFO) Marcus Jade	ED, Board Treasure	☐
☐		1/20/04	Define features of a desired accounting system	(CFO) Marcus Jade		☐
☐		1/30/04	Adopt a unified format for financial statements; circulate to board	(CFO) Marcus Jade	ED, Board Treasurer	☐
☐		1/30/04	Select accounting system	(CFO) Marcus Jade		☐
☐		1/30/04	Consolidate banking and investment accounts	(CFO) Marcus Jade		☐
☐		1/30/04	Develop a petty cash policy	(CFO) Marcus Jade	Finance	☐
☐		1/30/04	Develop purchasing policies	(CFO) Marcus Jade	Finance	☐

Fundraising

Ongoing	Start Date	Target Date	Activity	Lead	Team	Complete?
☐		1/1/04	Review/analyze technology used for fundraising management	(Dir Dev) Calvin Wright	IT	☐
☐		1/15/04	Review pre-merger fundraising staffing	(Dir Dev) Calvin Wright	ED	☐
☐		1/15/04	Create plan to communicate with current donors	(Dir Dev) Calvin Wright	ED, Board	☐
☐		1/30/04	Define optimal staffing for fundraising function	(Dir Dev) Calvin Wright	ED	☐

Human Resources (HR)

Ongoing	Start Date	Target Date	Activity	Lead	Team	Complete?
☐		1/15/04	Review all layoff decisions and policies; ensure smooth transitions	(HR Dir) Bill Harris	ED	☐
☐		1/30/04	Complete an HR audit for each pre-merger organization	(HR Dir) Bill Harris		☐

Information Technology

Ongoing	Start Date	Target Date	Activity	Lead	Team	Complete?
☐		1/15/04	Ensure that all staff can immediately communicate via phone, e-mail	(IT Dir) Haley Grant	IT staff	☐
☐		1/30/04	Review pre-merger IT staffing	(IT Dir) Haley Grant	IT staff	☐
☐		1/30/04	Arrange focus groups to gather input on technology needs/potential	(IT Dir) Haley Grant	IT staff	☐
☐		1/30/04	Identify the technology needs of the new organization	(IT Dir) Haley Grant	IT staff	☐

Management/Senior Mangement Team (SMT)

Ongoing	Start Date	Target Date	Activity	Lead	Team	Complete?
☐		1/1/04	Establish a regular SMT meeting time and list of "must-have" agenda items	(ED) Liza Neuman	SMT	☐
☐		1/15/04	Articulate the general duties and responsibilities of the SMT	(HR Dir) Bill Harris	SMT	☐
☐		1/15/04	Articulate the integration-related duties and responsibilities of the SMT	(HR Dir) Bill Harris	SMT	☐
☐		1/15/04	Define a desired managerial culture for the new organization	(ED) Liza Neuman	SMT	☐
☐		1/15/04	Identify specific work required to achieve desired managerial culture	(ED) Liza Neuman	SMT	☐
☐		1/30/04	Create process to monitor the integration plan	(ED) Liza Neuman	Integration Team	☐
☐		1/30/04	Articulate processes, policies, and procedures around conflict resolution	(HR Dir) Bill Harris	SMT	☐

Overall

Ongoing	Start Date	Target Date	Activity	Lead	Team	Complete?
☐	1/3/04	1/15/04	(Plan, convene FIRST MEETING OF INT TEAM)	(Chair, Int Team) Maya Coughlin		☐
☐	1/15/04	1/22/04	Clarify the team's role, goals, channels of communication	(Chair, Int Team) Maya Coughlin	ED, Int Team	☐
☐	1/15/04	1/22/04	Decide how to create the first draft of an integration plan	(ED) Liza Neuman	Maya, Int Team	☐
☐	1/15/04	1/29/04	Designate "sub-teams" or working groups for key integration areas	(Chair, Int Team) Maya Coughlin	ED, Int Team	☐

Program

Ongoing	Start Date	Target Date	Activity	Lead	Team	Complete?
☐		1/15/04	Gather and compare information on all pre-merger programs	(Prog Dir) Natalie Casper	Sarah	☐
☐		1/15/04	Identify necessary skills and competencies for program management	(ED) Liza Neuman	SMT	☐
☐		1/15/04	Identify any obstacles/issues likely to arise in program integration	(Prog Dir) Natalie Casper	Sarah	☐
☐		1/30/04	Identify any programs needing to be closed or moved elsewhere	(Prog Dir) Natalie Casper	Sarah, ED	☐
☐		1/30/04	Match current (pre-merger) employees to positions where appropriate	(ED) Liza Neuman	Natalie	☐
☐		1/30/04	Identify programmatic strengths, weaknesses, assets and liabilities	(Prog Dir) Natalie Casper	Sarah, ED	☐
☐		1/30/04	Identify positions that need to be filled	(Prog Dir) Natalie Casper		☐

Staff

Ongoing	Start Date	Target Date	Activity	Lead	Team	Complete?
☐		1/1/04	Address job losses with remaining staff: clarify extent, timing, impact	(ED) Liza Neuman	HR Director	☐
☐		1/1/04	Identify positions still needed within the organization	(HR Dir) Bill Harris	ED	☐
☐		1/15/04	Establish specific feedback mechanisms for staff questions/comments/concerns	(HR Dir) Bill Harris	ED	☐
☐		1/15/04	Clarify roles for all staff: reporting relationships, function, authority	(HR Dir) Bill Harris		☐
☐		1/15/04	Delegate responsibility for filling necessary positions	(ED) Liza Neuman		☐
☐		1/15/04	Establish regular staff meeting times and "must-have" agenda items	(ED) Liza Neuman		☐

Ongoing	Start Date	Target Date	Activity	Lead	Team	Complete?
		1/15/04	Plan a farewell ritual for departing employees	(HR Dir) Bill Harris	ED	☐
		1/15/04	Identify one or more integration exercises that can be done at staff meetings	(HR Dir) Bill Harris	ED	☐
		1/30/04	Identify opportunities to be explicit in acknowledging staff contributions	(HR Dir) Bill Harris	ED	☐

Volunteers

Ongoing	Start Date	Target Date	Activity	Lead	Team	Complete?
		1/30/04	Clarify the volunteer needs of the new organization	(Vol Coor) Alex Hayes		☐
		1/30/04	Identify any changes needed in the volunteer program	(Vol Coor) Alex Hayes		☐

February 2004

Board

Ongoing	Start Date	Target Date	Activity	Lead	Team	Complete?
		2/20/04	Establish a committee structure and job descriptions for the new board	(Bd Pres) Jules Hoffner	David, Kathryn	☐
		2/20/04	Review each board's prior practices, responsibilities, job descriptions	(Bd Mem) David Ryan	Tomas	☐

Communication / Marketing

Ongoing	Start Date	Target Date	Activity	Lead	Team	Complete?
		2/15/04	Define an overall marketing strategy	(Mktg Dir) Michael Doyer	Marketing staff	☐
		2/15/04	Draft initial marketing plan	(Mktg Dir) Michael Doyer	Marketing staff	☐
		2/15/04	Identify required/desired marketing materials	(Mktg Dir) Michael Doyer	Marketing staff	☐
		2/28/04	Draft a talking-points document	(Mktg Dir) Michael Doyer		☐
		2/28/04	Establish guiding principles for communication	(Mktg Dir) Michael Doyer	ED	☐
		2/28/04	Designate a spokesperson(s)	(ED) Liza Neuman		☐

Facilities

Ongoing	Start Date	Target Date	Activity	Lead	Team	Complete?
	1/1/04	2/1/04	Gather input on space needs from staff, clients, other relevant stakeholders	(Consultant) Sean Fisher		☐
		2/15/04	Determine current and intermediate space needs	(Consultant) Sean Fisher	ED, HR Dir, CFO, David Ryan	☐

Finance

Ongoing	Start Date	Target Date	Activity	Lead	Team	Complete?
☐		2/15/04	Train staff/board on new financial systems/procedures	(CFO) Marcus Jade	Board	☐
☐		2/28/04	Notify clients and vendors of any change to billing address/procedures	(CFO) Marcus Jade	Finance	☐

Fundraising

Ongoing	Start Date	Target Date	Activity	Lead	Team	Complete?
☐		2/15/04	Assess level/types of pre-merger participation in fundraising efforts	(Bd Pres) Jules Hoffner	Calvin, ED	☐
☐		2/15/04	Plan for necessary hiring/reallocation of staff resources	(Dir Dev) Calvin Wright	ED, HR	☐
☐		2/15/04	Review/analyze donor databases	(Dir Dev) Calvin Wright	IT	☐

Human Resources (HR)

Ongoing	Start Date	Target Date	Activity	Lead	Team	Complete?
☐		2/15/04	Define optimal staffing for HR function	(HR Dir) Bill Harris		☐
☐		2/15/04	Integrate pre-merger personnel files.	(HR Dir) Bill Harris		☐
☐		2/15/04	Develop systems/resources for ongoing staff training and development	(HR Dir) Bill Harris	HR staff	☐

Information Technology

Ongoing	Start Date	Target Date	Activity	Lead	Team	Complete?
☐		2/15/04	Draft recommendations for integration of hardware, software, systems	(IT Dir) Haley Grant		☐
☐		2/15/04	Define optimal staffing for IT function	(IT Dir) Haley Grant	ED	☐
☐		2/25/04	Gather feedback on recommendations	(IT Dir) Haley Grant		☐
☐		2/28/04	Plan for necessary hiring/reallocation of staff resources	(IT Dir) Haley Grant	Ed, HR Dir	☐

Management/Senior Management Team (SMT)

Ongoing	Start Date	Target Date	Activity	Lead	Team	Complete?
☐	1/1/04	2/1/04	Identify management positions needed in the merged organization	(HR Dir) Bill Harris		☐
☐		2/15/04	Create process to fill open positions	(HR Dir) Bill Harris		☐
☐		2/15/04	Develop a recruitment plan for any remaining senior management positions	(HR Dir) Bill Harris		☐
☐	1/1/04	2/28/04	Have ED work with each manager to create a personal development and training plan	(ED) Liza Neuman		☐

Overall

Ongoing	Start Date	Target Date	Activity	Lead	Team	Complete?
☐	1/15/04	2/5/04	Articulate desired outcomes for each integration area	(Chair, Int Team) Maya Coughlin	ED, all senior managers	☐
☐	1/15/04	2/5/04	Design process for making the integration plan a "living document"	(HR Dir) Bill Harris	Maya, Marty	☐
☐	1/15/04	2/5/04	Design process for gathering and incorporating feedback on the plan	(HR Dir) Bill Harris	Maya, Marty	☐
☐	1/15/04	2/13/04	Generate first draft of an integration plan	(Chair, Int Team) Maya Coughlin	Ken, Marty, Int Team	☐
☐	1/15/04	2/20/04	Distribute first draft of integration plan to management, staff for "fleshing out"	(Chair, Int Team) Maya Coughlin	ED, Bill	☐

Program

Ongoing	Start Date	Target Date	Activity	Lead	Team	Complete?
☐		2/10/04	Gather input on proposed program design from SMT and other stakeholders	(Prog Dir) Natalie Casper	Sarah, SMT	☐
☐		2/15/04	Design the process for integrating, closing, or moving each program	(Prog Dir) Natalie Casper		☐
☐		2/15/04	Incorporate feedback on program design	(Prog Dir) Natalie Casper	Sarah	☐
☐		2/15/04	Create process to fill open positions	(Prog Dir) Natalie Casper	HR Director	☐
☐		2/25/04	Finalize recommendations for program design	(Prog Dir) Natalie Casper	Sarah, ED	☐

Staff

Ongoing	Start Date	Target Date	Activity	Lead	Team	Complete?
☐		2/1/04	Institute a plan to celebrate milestones, accomplishments at the department/work group level	(HR Dir) Bill Harris	Program Director	☐

Volunteers

Ongoing	Start Date	Target Date	Activity	Lead	Team	Complete?
☐		2/15/04	Create job descriptions for volunteer positions	(Vol Coor) Alex Hayes		☐
☐		2/15/04	Clarify roles for all volunteers: reporting relationships, function, authority	(Vol Coor) Alex Hayes		☐
☐		2/15/04	Design roles and assignments for volunteers in the new organization	(Vol Coor) Alex Hayes		☐
☐		2/28/04	Establish policies for volunteer supervision, evaluation, and recognition	(Vol Coor) Alex Hayes		☐

March 2004

Board

Ongoing	Start Date	Target Date	Activity	Lead	Team	Complete?
		3/1/04	Survey board members re: interests, strengths	(Bd Pres) Jules Hoffner		☐
		3/15/04	Assess board composition; determine needed skills/ characteristics	(Bd Mem) Jackie Lousilla	Kathryn	☐
		3/15/04	Finalize board committee assignments	(Bd Pres) Jules Hoffner		☐
		3/31/04	Create a fund development plan to meet short-term needs	(Bd Treas) Rob Wyland	Jackie, Will, DD	☐
		3/31/04	Approve a budget for the merged organization	(Bd Pres) Jules Hoffner	Rob	☐
		3/31/04	Articulate communication practices for the board, and with the ED	(Bd Mem) Susan Yi	Kathryn	☐
	1/17/04	3/31/04	Plan a retreat for members of the new board	(Bd Pres) Jules Hoffner	Susan, David, Will	☐

Communication / Marketing

Ongoing	Start Date	Target Date	Activity	Lead	Team	Complete?
		3/15/04	Create necessary Q&A documents	(Mktg Dir) Michael Doyer		☐
		3/20/04	Draft, secure approval for, and finalize messages	(Mktg Dir) Michael Doyer	Marketing staff	☐

Evaluation

Ongoing	Start Date	Target Date	Activity	Lead	Team	Complete?
		3/31/04	Conduct check-in meeting with senior management team	(ED) Liza Neuman		☐

Facilities

Ongoing	Start Date	Target Date	Activity	Lead	Team	Complete?
		3/1/04	Complete a facilities audit for each pre-merger organization	(Consultant) Sean Fisher	ED, CFO, David Ryan	☐
		3/15/04	Bring facilities recommendations to ED, Integration Team, and board as appropriate	(Consultant) Sean Fisher		☐
		3/30/04	Finalize plan and budget for meeting space needs	(Consultant) Sean Fisher		☐

Fundraising

Ongoing	Start Date	Target Date	Activity	Lead	Team	Complete?
		3/1/04	Create integrated gift acknowledgment and recognition processes	(Dir Dev) Calvin Wright	Development staff	☐

Human Resources (HR)

Ongoing	Start Date	Target Date	Activity	Lead	Team	Complete?
☐		3/1/04	Develop and put in place a new compensation and benefits system	(HR Dir) Bill Harris	ED	☐
☐		3/1/04	Train staff on new HR systems/procedures	(HR Dir) Bill Harris	HR staff	☐
☐		3/1/04	Create and disseminate new personnel policies	(HR Dir) Bill Harris	HR staff	☐
☐		3/1/04	Develop performance management and evaluation systems	(HR Dir) Bill Harris		☐
☐		3/15/04	Arrange meetings with staff (group, individual) to explain compensation system	(HR Dir) Bill Harris	HR staff	☐

Information Technology

Ongoing	Start Date	Target Date	Activity	Lead	Team	Complete?
☐		3/5/04	Finalize plan for integration of hardware, software, systems	(IT Dir) Haley Grant		☐
☐		3/30/04	Develop and publicize training on any new hardware, software, systems	(IT Dir) Haley Grant	IT staff	☐
☐		3/30/04	Ensure feedback mechanisms are in place for ongoing tech support needs	(IT Dir) Haley Grant		☐

Management/Senior Management Team (SMT)

Ongoing	Start Date	Target Date	Activity	Lead	Team	Complete?
☐		3/15/04	Have ED create own development plan in partnership with board	(ED) Liza Neuman	Board	☐
☐		3/30/04	Create a development and training plan for each manager	(ED) Liza Neuman	SMT	☐
☐		3/30/04	Work with Integration Team to evaluate integration progress (ongoing)	(ED) Liza Neuman	Integration Team	☐

Volunteers

Ongoing	Start Date	Target Date	Activity	Lead	Team	Complete?
☐		3/15/04	Develop a volunteer recruitment plan	(Vol Coor) Alex Hayes		☐
☐		3/30/04	Create volunteer policies manual for the new organization	(Vol Coor) Alex Hayes		☐

April 2004

Board

Ongoing	Start Date	Target Date	Activity	Lead	Team	Complete?
☐		4/15/04	Provide training to all members regarding their role as ambassador	(Consultant) Sean Fisher	Jules	☐
☐		4/15/04	Provide training to all members regarding fundraising responsibilities	(Bd Treas) Rob Wyland	Sean Fisher (assist)	☐
☐		4/30/04	Develop a board-member recruitment plan	(Bd Mem) Jackie Lousilla	Kathryn, Will	☐

Communication / Marketing

Ongoing	Start Date	Target Date	Activity	Lead	Team	Complete?
☐		4/30/04	Design and plan distribution schedule for an integration newsletter	(Mktg Dir) Michael Doyer		☐

Volunteers

Ongoing	Start Date	Target Date	Activity	Lead	Team	Complete?
☐		4/30/04	Develop a volunteer orientation and training manual/process	(Vol Coor) Alex Hayes		☐

May 2004

Board

Ongoing	Start Date	Target Date	Activity	Lead	Team	Complete?
☐	4/1/04	5/30/04	Create a fundraising plan for the merged organization	(Bd Treas) Rob Wyland	Jackie, Will, DD	☐

Communication / Marketing

Ongoing	Start Date	Target Date	Activity	Lead	Team	Complete?
☐		5/30/04	Create and/or update web site	(Mktg Dir) Michael Doyer	IT Director	☐

Fundraising

Ongoing	Start Date	Target Date	Activity	Lead	Team	Complete?
☐		5/10/04	Establish a fundraising budget for the new organization	(Dir Dev) Calvin Wright	Board fundraising committee	☐
☐		5/10/04	Create updated case statement for the new organization	(Dir Dev) Calvin Wright	ED	☐
☐	4/1/03	5/10/04	Establish an integrated fundraising plan with fundraising calendar	(Dir Dev) Calvin Wright	Development staff	☐
☐		5/30/04	Finalize and adopt fundraising plan	(Bd Pres) Jules Hoffner	ED, Board	☐
☐		5/30/04	Adopt unified policies and procedures for fundraising	(Dir Dev) Calvin Wright	ED, Board	☐

June 2004

Board

Ongoing	Start Date	Target Date	Activity	Lead	Team	Complete?
□	3/1/04	6/30/04	Develop an orientation program for incoming members	(Bd Mem) Susan Yi	Rob, Will, Tomas	□
□	3/1/04	6/30/04	Develop a board handbook	(Bd Mem) David Ryan	Kathryn	□

July 2004

Board

Ongoing	Start Date	Target Date	Activity	Lead	Team	Complete?
□	7/1/04	7/30/04	Ensure that all current members have been through orientation	(Bd Mem) Susan Yi		□

October 2004

Board

Ongoing	Start Date	Target Date	Activity	Lead	Team	Complete?
□	9/1/04	10/30/04	Create and implement a board self-assessment process	(Bd Mem) Jackie Lousilla	Jules	□

December 2004

Board

Ongoing	Start Date	Target Date	Activity	Lead	Team	Complete?
□	4/15/04	12/31/04	Work with management to establish an evaluation process for the organization	ED		□
□	6/1/04	12/31/04	Develop and pursue a strategic planning process	(Bd Pres) Jules Hoffner	ED	□

Staff

Ongoing	Start Date	Target Date	Activity	Lead	Team	Complete?
☑	1/1/04	12/30/04	Communicate regularly about integration progress	(ED) Liza Neuman	SMT	□

Pre- and Post-Merger Organizational Profile

Editors note: This profile is also included on pages 153–61 of The Nonprofit Mergers Workbook Part I, *published by Amherst H. Wilder Foundation, copyright 2000 David La Piana.*

L a Piana Associates, Inc. uses the following instrument to assess the starting point for merger participants. The same instrument is then used again after the merger is implemented in order to determine some of the outcomes of the process. You may find it useful to conduct your own pre- and post-merger surveys to gather outcome information for management, the board, or funders.

An electronic version of this profile (along with the audits in Appendices C–D and the worksheets) can be found on the CD enclosed with this book. They can also be downloaded off the publisher's web site by using the URL found on page 6.

These materials are intended for use in the same way as photocopies, but they are in a form that allows you to type in your responses and reformat the material to fit your merger. Please do not download the material unless you or your organization has purchased this book.

Pre- and Post-Merger Organizational Profile

Fill in this sheet for each participating organization at the beginning of a project, and one for the resulting organization at the conclusion of the project. Continue with evaluations at designated intervals thereafter.

Identifying information

Organization name _____

Mission _____

_____

_____

(Considering) partnering with

_____

_____

Subsector   ❑ health   ❑ human services   ❑ environment   ❑ arts

❑ advocacy   ❑ education   ❑ other_____

Geography/Catchment area _____

Date founded_____   **Budget size** _____

Number of staff (FT, PT, and FTE) _____

_____

Primary motivation for strategic restructuring

_____

_____

Source of funds for the strategic restructuring effort

Self	_____ %	(amt:_____)
Local government	_____ %	(amt:_____)
Foundation/Corporate	_____ %	(amt:_____)
Other	_____ %	(amt:_____)
Unfunded need	_____ %	(amt:_____)

Financial indicators

Year			
Total Budget			
Fund Balance amount:			
as a percentage of total assets:			
Current Ratio current assets ÷ current liabilities			
Quick Ratio [cash + marketable securities + accounts receivable] ÷ current liabilities			
Days of Working Capital ([current assets − current liabilities] ÷ [total operating expense − depreciation expense]) x 365			
Days of Cash on Hand ([cash + marketable securities] ÷ [total operating expense − depreciation expense]) x 365			
Net Operating Income revenue excess or deficiency ÷ expenses			
Net Operating Ratio net operating income ÷ total operating income			
Dollars spent on administration and overhead amount (include all nonprogram costs):			
as a percentage of total assets:			
Funding Mix (indicate % of each type) Government:			
Foundation:			
Corporate:			
Individual donors:			
Earned income:			
Was an audit done?			

Are there written financial and administrative policies and procedures for this organization? ❏ Yes ❏ No

Human resources indicators

	Year			
Annual percentage turnover	Management staff:			
	Line staff:			
Average annual pay raise (percentage)	Management staff:			
	Line staff:			

Benefits offered

❑ Health insurance for employees

❑ Dental insurance for employees

❑ Health insurance for employees' dependents

❑ Dental insurance for employees' dependents

❑ Long-term disability insurance

❑ Life insurance

❑ Accidental death and dismemberment insurance

❑ Vision insurance

❑ Vacation time

❑ Flexible schedule

❑ Child care for employees' dependents

❑ 403(b) (or other) retirement savings plan (no employer contributions)

❑ Employer contributions to a 403(b) (or other) retirement savings plan

❑ Other:_____

❑ Other:_____

❑ Other: _____

❑ Other: _____

❑ Other: _____

Staff development policies (training, career development, etc.)

_____

_____

_____

_____

Are personnel policies and guidelines written down in any kind of formal document or manual?

_____

Do all employees get a copy of this manual? _____

Language Capacity (as related to service delivery)

Program or Service (break out if desired)	Language	Number of people offering services in this language (FTE)

Average years of job-relevant experience _____

Use of Volunteers Year			
Number of Individual (nonboard) Volunteers			
Total Volunteer Hours Contributed			

Governance Indicators

Year			
Number of board members			
Annual percentage turnover of board members			
Number of meetings held annually			
Average attendance at board meetings			

Is there an assessment of the board's performance? _____

_____

_____

Is there a "board book" or other written set of guidelines for board members? _____

_____

Are minutes recorded and kept for each meeting? _____

_____

What offices are filled at the current time?
❏ President   ❏ VP   ❏ Secretary   ❏ Treasurer   ❏ Other (_____)

What standing committees exist? _____

_____

_____

Do you have an advisory board? ❏ Yes ❏ No   If yes, how large (# of members)? _____

How often does it meet? _____

_____

What other advisory bodies exist (if any)? _____

_____

_____

_____

Fundraising Indicators

Year			
Number of fundraising staff (FTE)			
Cost of fundraising			
Number of major donors *(Major donor = contributes > $ _____)*			
Percent of board members donating money			
Total board contributions			

Does the agency have a written fundraising plan? _____

What types of fundraising does the organization do?

- ❏ Direct mail
- ❏ Personal solicitation
- ❏ Solicitation of planned gifts
- ❏ Special events
- ❏ Grant proposals
- ❏ Entrepreneurial ventures (selling client-made products, thrift store, etc.)
- ❏ Cause-related marketing arrangements with for-profit companies
- ❏ Other (please specify): _____

_____

_____

_____

_____

_____

_____

_____

_____

_____

Programmatic Indicators

Number of programs___ Program Name	Number of people served	Definition of a service unit	Total service units

Demographics: What types of people do you serve? Indicate using percentages in the blanks below.

Age	Annual Income	Ethnicity	Gender	Sexual Orientation
____ < 5	____ Poverty level or below	____ Caucasian	____ Male	____ Straight
____ 5 – 12	____ Low income	____ African American	____ Female	____ Gay
____ 13 – 18	____ Medium income	____ Asian American	____ Transgender	____ Lesbian
____ 19 – 21	____ High income	____ Hispanic / Latino		____ Bisexual
____ 22 – 30		____ Native American		
____ 31 – 50		____ Pacific Islander		
____ 51 – 65		____ European		
____ > 65		____ Other: _____		
		____ Other: _____		
		____ Other: _____		
		____ Other: _____		

Do you keep track of how many client/patron complaints you get?   ❑ Yes   ❑ No

If yes, how many do you get per month (average)? _____

Do you keep track of client/patron turnover?   ❑ Yes   ❑ No

If yes, what is your turnover like now? _____

How do you measure success as an organization? _____

Do you use a scale? If so, what is it? _____

What is your current score on this measure? _____

Government Contract Performance Rating (if applicable): _____

The above questions may not apply to all organizations. If this organization does work that cannot fairly be described or evaluated through the programmatic questions above, please write notes below that would be relevant. (For example, an arts organization might list size of collections, number of patrons/year, number of performances/year, growth in ticket sales, and so forth.)

Sample Human Resources Audit

The human resources (HR) audit[20] is a process of examining policies, procedures, documentation, systems, and practices with respect to an organization's human resources functions. The purpose of using the audit for merger integration is to reveal the strengths and weaknesses in each nonprofit's human resources system, and any issues needing resolution. The audit works best when the focus is on analyzing and improving the human resources function in the merged organization.

The audit itself is a diagnostic tool, not a prescriptive instrument. It will help you identify what you are missing or need to improve, but it can't tell you what to do to address these issues. It is most useful when an organization is ready to act on the findings, and to fully develop its human resources function in support of the organization's mission and objectives.

Who should conduct the audit?

The working group conducting the audit should represent a cross-section of the organization's staff, including line staff, middle and upper management, and those responsible for human resources functions.

How should it be conducted?

The audit process consists of a series of questions covering the eight primary components of the human resources function:

1. Roles, head count, and human resources information systems (HRIS)[21]
2. Recruitment

---

[20]Prepared by Bill Coy, senior associate for human resources consultation, La Piana Associates, Inc.

[21]HRIS refers to a type of software that is written specifically for human resources management. It might include modules for recruitment, benefits, compensation, and employee records.

3. Documentation
4. Training, development, and career management
5. Compensation and benefits
6. Performance management and evaluation
7. Termination and transition
8. Legal issues and personnel policies

The team collects information to answer the human resources audit questions in each of these categories. The focus is on how these activities and tasks are *actually* performed in the organization. The first step is to collect all the pertinent information. The process of getting information, in and of itself, can be quite instructive.

How are needed improvements identified?

Once information is gathered, the audit team reviews each major section and notes disparities between paper (what we *think* or *say* we do) and practice (what we *actually* do, as revealed by the answers to the audit questions). This can then be compared to best practice (what we *should* do to best support our organization's mission).

A cautionary note: Finding out what is insufficient and inadequate is the first step toward improvement. If deficiencies are identified, it is important to take steps to correct those deficiencies. Organizations should take that first step only when they are ready to act on the findings, and to make necessary improvements in their human resource skills, processes, and systems.

How is follow-up and correction done?

Improving the human resources system takes some time. A work plan—with a timeline, accountability, and deliverables—should be created after the team reviews the completed audit and identifies areas where improvement is needed. Follow-up and review should be a regular management function, performed on an ongoing basis.

Questions?

If you have any questions about the use of the human resources audit, or if you would like assistance in performing the audit and creating workable human resources solutions for your organization, contact Bill Coy at coy@lapiana.org or 510-325-1900.

For more information on La Piana Associates' human resources services and other consulting services, visit our web site at www.lapiana.org/consulting.

LA PIANA ASSOCIATES, INC.

The Human Resources Audit

Roles, Head Count, and Human Resources Information Systems (HRIS)

- How many employees are currently on staff?
- How many employees are
  – Regular
  – Probationary
  – Temporary
  – Full-time
  – Part-time
  – Exempt
  – Non-exempt
- What is the definition of a part-time employee? (What is the maximum number of hours an employee can work to be considered part-time?)
- What is the minimum number of hours an employee has to work to be considered full-time?
- How long is the probationary period?
- Are employees aware of their status?
- How long can an employee be temporary?
- How many employees have supervisory responsibility?
- Are there currently up-to-date job descriptions for all employees? If not, which ones don't have descriptions?
- Are independent contractors used? If so, how many are being used? And for what functions?
- What tests are used to ensure appropriate classification of independent contractors?
- Have employees been classified properly in terms of being exempt or non-exempt?

Recruitment

- How much growth has there been in the workforce in the last five years?
- What are some of your organization's future needs for personnel?
- What are the procedures for hiring in your organization?
- What recruitment sources are used? (Advertisements, referrals from other agencies, personal contacts, other?)
- Are current employees considered for promotion or lateral position changes?
- Who does the preliminary screening of candidates?

- Who selects candidates for interviews?
- Is training provided for those who conduct interviews?
- How is the recruitment, screening, and selection process documented?
- What interview process is used (for example, individual, sequential, panel)?
- Who holds final authority to hire?
- Who checks references?
- How are the reference checks documented?
- Who makes the offer of employment?
- Where is the hiring paperwork generated?
- Who negotiates compensation packages?
- List the practices you believe are unique to your organization.
- What is the turnover rate (percent of employees leaving each year) in your organization? Has this changed over time?
- Who gives references for former employees?

Documentation

- Where and with whom are the personnel files currently held?
- What documents are held in personnel files?
- How are the following documented by your organization?
  - Hiring: application, interviewing, and reference checks
  - Compensation and benefits
  - Promotions, terminations, layoffs, and retirements
  - Paid time off
  - Training
  - Discipline
  - Work history
  - Work assignments
  - Significant accomplishments
  - Emergency contact information
  - Performance evaluation and performance management
  - Termination
- How long are files held and where are they stored after employees leave?
- How well do Human Resources and Finance work together?
- Is a payroll service used and, if so, which one?
- Does the payroll service provide all governmental employment filings?
- Are managers and employees given training about personnel files, including policies and procedures for accessing them?
- How is paid time off documented?
- When requests for information are made to your organization, who fills the request?
- Is a human resources information system (HRIS) being used and, if so, which one?

Training, Development, and Career Management

- Who is responsible for new employee orientation?
- What are the elements of the new employee orientation program?
- Where and to whom do new employees go when they have questions about your organization or their jobs?
- Is there a formal training program for employees and managers? If so, please describe it.
- What training and development initiatives have occurred in your organization?
- How are managers and supervisors trained and prepared for their roles?
- What is the average length of time an employee stays with your organization? Does this vary by position type?
- How much does your organization spend annually (in total and per employee) on employee training and development? Does this vary by position type?

Compensation and Benefits

Basic Compensation Questions

- Is there a formal compensation program?
- How are wages set?
- Are formal salary ranges set?
- If formal salary ranges are set, are they made public to employees?
- How are jobs rated?
- How frequently are jobs reevaluated or updated?
- Are any salary surveys used? If so, which ones?
- Are pay ranges revised as a result of these surveys? How frequently?
- Who in your organization (what position) administers the compensation program?
- Are cost of living adjustments (COLA) given and, if so, what is the basis for the adjustment?
- Are merit increases given and, if so, are they integrated with performance evaluation?
- Is there a bonus system and, if so, how is it structured?
- How are the compensation program and total compensation package communicated to employees?
- What are the "cultural issues" or beliefs related to compensation in your organization?
- How is employee communication regarding compensation and benefits delivered in your organization?

Health and Welfare Benefits

- Describe the health insurance program provided by your organization.
- Are dependents covered and, if so, in part or in full?

- Are domestic partners covered?
- What are the eligibility requirements for health insurance and other benefits?
- Which of the following health and wellness benefits are offered, and what are the limits and requirements for coverage?
  - Dental
  - Vision
  - Disability
  - Employee assistance program
  - Life insurance
  - Other wellness benefits
  - Flex benefit plan
  - Other benefits

Pension and Retirement

- What is the pension or retirement plan?
- What is the vesting period?
- Can employees contribute?
- Can pretax dollars be put into some form of deferment plan?

Paid Time Off

- What holidays are paid and who is eligible for them?
- Is there a paid time-off system, or is paid time off split between vacation and sick leave? If the policy is straight paid time off, what are the rates of accrual and caps?
- What is the vacation schedule, and how is it earned?
- What is the eligibility requirement for vacation?
- Is there a cap to limit the amount of vacation accrued?
- Are employees permitted to substitute sick leave for vacation?
- How is unused accrued vacation treated?
- Can employees contribute sick leave to other employees and, if so, what are the limits?

Performance Management and Evaluation

- Describe the past and current performance appraisal system in your organization.
- If a performance appraisal instrument is used, attach a copy. (If the instrument differs by position, please attach all instruments.)
- What type of process is used (360 degree, supervisor only, peer evaluation, outcome)?
- What type of training is used in relationship to performance evaluation?
- What is the role of the supervisor or manager in performance appraisal?
- What is the primary purpose of performance management in your organization?
- How often and consistently is the process used?

Termination and Transition

- Is your organization an "at-will" employer?
- What other causes or conditions of termination of employment exist?
- What procedures are used for
  - Termination for cause
  - Job closure
  - Resignation
- What level of approval is needed before a termination can occur?
- Is there any formal checklist or legal review prior to termination?
- Are exit interviews performed for all employees who leave?
- What documentation is required for all employee transitions?
- How are references handled in your organization?
- Who is responsible for internal communications regarding difficult terminations, either for cause or due to layoffs? Who communicates the termination to other employees?

Legal Issues and Personnel Policies

- To your knowledge, are all employees appropriately classified?
- What personnel policies are currently being used? (Attach a copy.)
- When was the last time these policies were reviewed and updated?
- Is there a disparity between policies and practices?
- Who has organizational responsibility for legal or employment questions?
- Is harassment training regularly provided?
- How are employee grievances dealt with?

Sample Technology Audit

The goal of a technology audit is to understand what each organization has, how it does things, and what its technological strengths and weaknesses are. For each merging organization, ask:

Hardware

- What platforms are used (PC, Mac, both)?
- Is there a network? If so, what type, and how is it managed?
- Do employees have desktops, laptops, laptops with docking stations, or some combination? How many of each are there, and what are the basic characteristics? (for example, twelve Pentium 4 desktops with 128 MB of memory, six still under warranty for one more year . . .)
- Do employees have PDAs (Palm Pilots)? If so, what type and how many? Do all employees receive them and, if not, what criteria are used to determine who does?
- What printers are owned? Leased? If leased, what are the terms?
- What copy machines are owned? Leased? If leased, what are the terms?
- Are there any scanners? If so, what type?
- What telephone system is used? Is there a contract for phone service/support?
- What other hardware is owned or leased?
- What are the outstanding hardware needs?
- How do staff access the Internet?

Software

- Do employees use a particular office "suite" (Microsoft Office, WordPerfect Office)? If so, what version?
- What "off-the-shelf" software (brand and version) is used for the following: word processing, spreadsheets, presentations, calendar/contact management, database creation/maintenance, accounting, desktop publishing, web authoring, e-mail, virus protection, and so forth.
- Do staff use any customized software? If so, what is it? How was it created and how is it maintained and updated?
- What databases are used (for fundraising, client tracking, contact management, human resources)?
- Do staff use any standard document templates (for letters, memos, reports)?
- What kind of web site does the organization have? How and how often is it updated? Does the organization have its own domain name? Does it own rights to more than one domain name?

Training

- What, if any, technical training is offered to new employees? Volunteers?
- What ongoing training opportunities are offered to employees? Volunteers?
- Have any particular training needs been identified?

Support

- Is there an internal technical support person, team, or department?
- What external resources do staff call on for technical support? What are the costs and conditions for this?
- Are there any service contracts not outlined above?
- Does everyone in the organization know whom to contact in the event of technical problems?

Resources

Adolph, Gerry, et al. *Merger Integration: Delivering On a Promise.* McLean, VA: Booz-Allen & Hamilton, 2001.

Ainspan, Nathan D., and David Bell. *Employee Communications During Mergers.* New York: The Conference Board, 2000. 1270-00-RR.

Arsenault, Jane. *Forging Nonprofit Alliances: A Comprehensive Guide to Enhancing Your Mission through Joint Ventures and Partnerships, Management Service Organizations, Parent Corporations, and Mergers.* San Francisco: Jossey-Bass, 1998.

Ashkenas, Ronald N., and Suzanne C. Francis. "Integration Managers: Special Leaders for Special Times." *Harvard Business Review* 78, no. 6 (November/ December 2000): 108+.

Austin, James. *The Collaboration Challenge: How Nonprofits and Businesses Succeed through Strategic Alliances.* San Francisco: Jossey-Bass, 2000.

Bailey, Darlyne, and Kelly McNally Koney. *Strategic Alliances among Health and Human Services Organizations.* Thousand Oaks, CA: Sage Publications, 2000.

Bernstein, Philip. *Best Practices of Effective Nonprofit Organizations: A Practitioner's Guide.* New York: The Foundation Center, 1997.

Bridges, William. *Managing Transitions: Making the Most of Change.* Cambridge, MA: Perseus Books, 1991.

Charan, Ram. "Conquering a Culture of Indecision." *Harvard Business Review* 79, no. 2 (March/April 2001): 75+.

Clutterbuck, David. *Linking Communication Competence to Business Success: A Challenge for Communicators.* San Francisco: International Association of Business Communicators (IABC) Research Foundation, 2001.

Conger, Jay. "The Necessary Art of Persuasion." *Harvard Business Review* 76, no. 3 (May/June 1998): 84–95.

D'Aprix, Roger. *Communicating for Change: Connecting the Workplace with the Marketplace.* San Francisco: Jossey-Bass, 1996.

Davenport, Thomas O. "The Integration Challenge." *Management Review* (January 1998): 25–28.

Drucker, Peter F. *Managing the Non-Profit Organization: Principles and Practices.* New York: HarperBusiness, 1990.

Feldman, Mark L., and Michael F. Spratt. *Five Frogs on a Log.* New York: HarperBusiness, 1999.

Ferronato, Sherry. "Nonprofit Mergers: The Perils and the Possibilities." *CharityVillage NewsWeek*, February 1, 1999.

Galpin, Timothy, and Mark Herndon. *The Complete Guide to Mergers and Acquisitions: Process Tools to Support M&A Integration at Every Level.* San Francisco: Jossey-Bass, 2000.

Golensky, Martha, and Gerald L. Deruiter. "Merger as a Strategic Response to Government Contracting Pressures: A Case Study." *Nonprofit Management and Leadership* 10, no. 2 (Winter 1999): 137–52.

Griffith, Victoria. "The People Factor in Post-Merger Integration." *Strategy + Business.* Booz-Allen & Hamilton, Third Quarter 2000.

Heenan, David A., and Warren Bennis. *Co-Leaders: The Power of Great Partnerships.* San Francisco: Jossey-Bass, 1999.

Hesselbein, Frances, and Rob Johnston, eds. *On Leading Change.* San Francisco: Jossey-Bass, 2002.

Hewitt Associates. *M&A Forum Executive Summary: The Role of HR in Mergers, Acquisitions, and Reorganization.* Lincolnshire, IL: Hewitt Associates, 2001.

International Association of Business Communicators. *The Complete Guide to Integrated Change Communication: Best Practices for Major Announcements.* San Francisco: International Association of Business Communicators, 2000. 01-CB085.

Kotter, John. "Leading Change: Why Transformation Efforts Fail." *Harvard Business Review* 73, no. 2 (March/April 1995): 59+.

Kramer, Robert J. *Post-Merger Organization Handbook.* New York: The Conference Board, 1999. 1241-99-RR.

La Piana, David. *The Nonprofit Mergers Workbook Part I—Considering, Negotiating, and Executing a Merger.* Saint Paul: Amherst H. Wilder Foundation, 2000.

Larkin, Sandar, and T. J. Larkin. *Communicating Change: Winning Employee Support for New Business Goals.* New York: McGraw-Hill, 1994.

Lucenko, Kristina. *Implementing a Post-Merger Integration.* New York: The Conference Board, 1999. 1257-99-CH.

Lundquist, Edward. "Smooth Transitions: When You're Communicating Organizational Changes, Job No. 1 is Allaying Employees' Fears." *Communication World* 19, no. 3 (April/May 2002): 24+.

Lynch, Robert Porter. *Business Alliances Guide: The Hidden Competitive Weapon.* New York: John Wiley & Sons, 1993.

Marks, Mitchell Lee, and Philip H. Mirvis. *Joining Forces: Making One Plus One Equal Three in Mergers, Acquisitions, and Alliances.* San Francisco: Jossey-Bass, 1997.

McCormick, Dan H. *Nonprofit Mergers: The Power of Successful Partnerships.* New York: Aspen Publishers, 2000.

McLaughlin, Thomas A. *Nonprofit Mergers and Alliances: A Strategic Planning Guide.* New York: John Wiley & Sons, 1998.

Radtke, Janel M. *Strategic Communications for Nonprofit Organizations: Seven Steps to Creating a Successful Plan.* New York: John Wiley & Sons, 1998.

Schien, Larry. *Post-Merger Integration: A Human Resources Perspective.* New York: The Conference Board, 2000. 1278-00-RR.

Stern, Gary J. *Marketing Workbook for Nonprofit Organizations Volume I: Develop the Plan.* Saint Paul, MN: Amherst H. Wilder Foundation, 2001.

———. *Marketing Workbook for Nonprofit Organizations Volume II: Mobilize People for Marketing Success.* Saint Paul, MN: Amherst H. Wilder Foundation, 1997.

Tillman, Audris, and Sophia A. Muirhead. *The Impact of Mergers and Acquisitions on Corporate Citizenship.* New York: The Conference Board, 2000. 1272-00-RR.

Welch, Nancy, and Mark Goldstein. *Communicating for Change: Ideas from Contemporary Research.* San Francisco: International Association of Business Communicators (IABC) Research Foundation. 01-FN010.

Whalen, Patricia. "Correcting Common Misconceptions about Communicating During Mergers & Acquisitions." *Communication World* 19, no. 3 (April/May 2002): 6+.

―――. *How Communication Drives Merger Success.* San Francisco: International Association of Business Communicators (IABC) Research Foundation, 2001. 01-FN013.

White, Tracy. "Supporting Change: How Communicators at Scotiabank Turned Ideas into Action." *Communication World* 19, no. 3 (April/May 2002): 22+.

Yankey, John A., Barbara Wester Jacobus, and Kelly McNally Koney. *Merging Nonprofit Organizations: The Art and Science of the Deal.* Cleveland: Mandel Center for Nonprofit Organizations, 2001.

Worksheets

Electronic versions of these worksheets (as well as the Pre- and Post-Merger Assessment Tool and the audits in Appendices B–D) can be found on the CD enclosed with this book. They can also be downloaded off the publisher's web site by using the URL found on page 6.

These materials are intended for use in the same way as photocopies, but they are in a form that allows you to type in your responses and reformat the material to fit your merger. Please do not download the material unless you or your organization has purchased this book.

List the "big-picture" outcomes your merging or newly merged organization aims to achieve through this merger. Use this list to measure your progress throughout the next weeks, months, and even years of organizational integration.

Note: The ten outcomes listed below are attributes of a healthy, strong, and well-integrated organization—the type of organization you seek to create through your merger integration process. These should be among the outcomes you list.

Some Common Outcome Targets

1. A cohesive governing body capable of leading the merged entity forward in a unified manner.
2. A single executive director who is supported by the board and staff.
3. A merged vision statement and mission statement expressed in a sound strategic plan that is supported by the entire organization.
4. A clear management structure representing the best skills of the pre-merger management teams.
5. An evolving, integrated organizational culture that staff feel connected to.
6. A sound, realistic budget and budget-monitoring system.
7. A unified human resources management system, including a single set of personnel policies and a unified and equitable compensation system.
8. A method for measuring the success and outcomes of the organization's efforts.
9. A coordinated set of high-quality, effective programs aligned with the new organization's mission.
10. A combined information system that meets management's needs.

What other outcomes are you committed to achieving?

_____

_____

_____

_____

_____

_____

_____

_____

_____

_____

Characteristic/Practice	Is this true for either or both pre-merger organizations? (Yes/No)	Do we want it to be true for the merged organization? (Yes/No)	Is this a priority issue? (Rank A, B, C)
Selection & Composition			
The board is composed of persons vitally interested in the work of the organization.			
The board is representative of the diverse community we serve (race, age, gender, sexual orientation, other?).			
There is a balance of new and experienced board members to guarantee both continuity and new thinking.			
Board members have the right combination of skills (fundraising, management, fiscal, legal) necessary to carry out the board's work.			
There is a limit to the number of consecutive terms a member can serve (no life terms).			
The organization has a pool of potential board members identified for future service.			
The organization develops future board members through the use of volunteers on committees.			
There is space on the board for new board members to join the newly merged organization.			
Orientation & Training			
There is a statement of agreement outlining the duties and responsibilities of board members that all board members sign.			
The board understands its legal liability.			
The organization supplies a board manual to all board members that includes, but isn't limited to, descriptions of current programs, a list of board members, budget and funding information, bylaws, and personnel policies.			

Characteristic/Practice	Is this true for either or both pre-merger organizations? (Yes/No)	Do we want it to be true for the merged organization? (Yes/No)	Is this a priority issue? (Rank A, B, C)
Orientation & Training (continued)			
The organization makes certain that all board members understand the conflict of interest policy and confidentiality statement (if applicable).			
The organization makes training opportunities available to board members to increase skills related to their board responsibilities.			
The organization provides an orientation for new board members.			
There is a plan to expose board members to the range of programs, activities, sites, and services of the newly merged organization.			
The board has a mentoring or other similar process to help new board members get to know the the ropes and understand how to fit in.			
Structure & Organization of the Board			
The board has a simple, concise set of bylaws that describes the duties of board members and officers, as well as the procedures by which the board conducts its business.			
The board has a mechanism (such as an executive committee) for handling matters that must be addressed between meetings.			
The board elects a chairperson to provide leadership and coordinate the ongoing work of the board and its committees.			

Characteristic/Practice	Is this true for either or both pre-merger organizations? (Yes/No)	Do we want it to be true for the merged organization? (Yes/No)	Is this a priority issue? (Rank A, B, C)
Structure & Organization of the Board (continued)			
The board has the appropriate active committees (for example, fundraising, personnel, nominating/ board development, long-range planning) with specific assignments and responsibilities.			
Committee assignments are reviewed and evaluated periodically.			
Working relations between the board chair and the executive director are strong and productive.			
Board and staff members are clear about their respective duties and responsibilities.			
Working relations between the staff and board are characterized by mutual respect and rapport.			
The Board at Work			
There are regularly scheduled board meetings at least four times a year.			
Meetings begin and end on time per an agreed-on schedule.			
There is adequate preparation and distribution of material including agendas and study documents in advance of board meetings.			
Board meetings are characterized by open discussion, creative thinking, and active participation by all.			
Board meetings deal primarily with policy formulation; program, financial, and long-range planning; financial review; and evaluating the work of the organization.			

Published by the Amherst H. Wilder Foundation   Copyright © 2004 La Piana Associates, Inc.

Characteristic/Practice	Is this true for either or both pre-merger organizations? (Yes/No)	Do we want it to be true for the merged organization? (Yes/No)	Is this a priority issue? (Rank A, B, C)
The Board at Work (continued)			
Minutes of board and committee meetings are written and circulated to the members.			
Committees are active and complete assigned tasks in a timely manner.			
The board is aware of matters of community, state, and nationwide concern within our field of advocacy.			
Individual members of the board accept and carry out assignments within the area of their talents, expertise, and/or interest.			
Board members make a generous financial contribution (self-defined) to the organization on an annual basis.			
All board members are involved in some aspect of fundraising for the organization.			
The board conducts an annual review of its own organization and work.			
New leadership is emerging consistently from the board and its committees.			

Distribute this survey to staff, volunteers, board members, and other key constituents from each of the merging organizations. Follow up with a few focus groups and a limited number of interviews with long-term members of each organizational community. Collect and compile the results from each of these processes, and use them to initiate a series of discussions on the culture you want in the merged organization.

To build a new organization, it is important to better understand the cultures of the organizations that are merging. Describe your own experience of the following factors in your organization's culture before the merger. This information will be used anonymously to assemble a picture of what people valued most about their organizations going into the merger.

Name of (pre-merger) organization: _____

Heroes: Who are the organization's founders, supporters, and advocates; those people who have shaped the organization through their own contributions, vision, and leadership? _____

_____

_____

_____

Values: What values, beliefs, traits, and qualities does the organization hold most dear?_____

_____

_____

_____

Verses: What "words of wisdom" or quotes relay a sense of the organization's values, or of how things really work in the organization?_____

_____

_____

_____

Traditions: What recurring events or activities bring people in the organization together? Which of these do you appreciate the most? _____

_____

_____

_____

Turmoil: What conflicts or issues have polarized or confused the organization over the years?_____

_____

_____

_____

Stories: What incidents or events are especially significant to the organization? _____

_____

_____

_____

_____

Victories: What are some of the organization's finest moments? What successes and achievements are people in the organization most proud of? _____

_____

_____

_____

_____

Losses: What prominent failures or events caused people in the organization to experience grief together?_____

_____

_____

_____

Self-perception: What is the "identity" of the organization? As a group, how do members of the organization perceive it? _____

_____

_____

_____

_____

Incompatible managerial cultures can hinder a merger. Clarity about managerial culture will lead to less conflict and a more intentional creation of a new way to manage and lead.

Rate the managerial culture of your pre-merger organization on the following scales. Then, along with the executive director of the newly merged entity and other members of the management team, discuss what the team would like the managerial culture of the merged organization to be, and what types of actions and structures would support that culture. A key outcome of this process is to create a managerial mindset that is both intentional and appropriate to the organization.

Emphasis on results   **Emphasis on methods**

| 1 | 2 | 3 | 4 | 5 | 6 | 7 | 8 | 9 | 10 |

Information is shared   **Information is withheld**

| 1 | 2 | 3 | 4 | 5 | 6 | 7 | 8 | 9 | 10 |

Affirmation is explicit   **Affirmation is implicit**

| 1 | 2 | 3 | 4 | 5 | 6 | 7 | 8 | 9 | 10 |

Correction is for education   **Correction is punitive**

| 1 | 2 | 3 | 4 | 5 | 6 | 7 | 8 | 9 | 10 |

Connections are clear and integrated   **Functions tend to be independent**

| 1 | 2 | 3 | 4 | 5 | 6 | 7 | 8 | 9 | 10 |

Learning is integrated into the work   **Learning is spontaneous**

| 1 | 2 | 3 | 4 | 5 | 6 | 7 | 8 | 9 | 10 |

Published by the Amherst H. Wilder Foundation   Copyright © 2004 La Piana Associates, Inc.

Communication is valued and encouraged   *Communication is haphazard*

1   2   3   4   5   6   7   8   9   10

Accountability is valued   *Creativity and initiative are valued*

1   2   3   4   5   6   7   8   9   10

Management views impact   *Management views intention*

1   2   3   4   5   6   7   8   9   10

Diversity of opinion is valued   *Conformance with the group is valued*

1   2   3   4   5   6   7   8   9   10

Listed below are the key stakeholders for a typical organization. For each group, identify the stakeholders' information interests and needs, potential concerns and questions, who will contact them about the merger decision, how they will be contacted, when they will be contacted, what information they will be given, and what supplementary materials (if any) they will receive. The people responsible for contacting the stakeholder should also be responsible for capturing any questions and concerns that come up, documenting these, and channeling them back to the integration team for evaluation and response.

Stakeholder	Infor-mation interests/ needs	Specific concerns/ questions	**Who will contact?** *Key stakehold-ers should be contacted by board member or executive director*	**How contacted?** *In-person contact is pre-ferred; tele-phone is next best option*	**When?** *Board first, then manage-ment, then staff before all others*	**What informa-tion? What messages?**
Management						
Staff						
Volunteers						
Clients / customers						
Funders / donors						
Community leaders						
Members of the press						
Collaborators / partners						
Government agencies						
Other:						
Other:						
Other:						
Other:						

What guiding principles will the new organization adopt for communication during the integration process, and beyond? Use the information in Chapter 5 to help you think through your priorities.

Some examples might be "All communications will be courteous and respectful." "Any staffing changes will be communicated to staff prior to external parties." "Communication will be collaborative." "Sharing of information will be encouraged." "People will have the information they need to get their jobs done and to make informed decisions."

Write your organization's guiding principles below. Make your list concise, concrete, and manageable; ideally, you will identify no more than ten principles.

1. _____
   _____

2. _____
   _____

3. _____
   _____

4. _____
   _____

5. _____
   _____

6. _____
   _____

7. _____
   _____

8. _____
   _____

9. _____
   _____

10. _____
    _____

Listed below are important talking points for a newly merged organization. Record your responses in the spaces provided, and then work on refining them. Be both honest and enthusiastic in your answers—the talking points are an ideal place to convey the excitement and promise of your merger.

Lead statement: _____

_____

_____

The rationale for the merger or (brief) case statement: _____

_____

_____

The vision and mission of the merged organization: _____

_____

_____

The value each merging organization brings to the table: _____

_____

_____

The population served by the new organization: _____

_____

_____

How the community will benefit from the merger: _____

_____

_____

The strengths of the new organization: _____

_____

_____

_____

The changes that are anticipated (to the extent they are known): _____

_____

_____

How changes will be handled (in accordance with guiding principles): _____

_____

_____

What will not change (to the extent that this is known): _____

_____

_____

When further decisions will be made: _____

_____

_____

Whom to contact (where to go) for more information:

Name: _____

Title: _____

Phone number: _____

E-mail address: _____

Web site: _____

How will you obtain feedback regarding the effectiveness of the integration progress, and the concerns or questions that your various stakeholders might still have? For each stakeholder group in the chart below, indicate how you will learn of their questions, comments, and concerns. Indicate how often you will solicit feedback from each group, and who will be responsible for collecting that feedback and reporting it back to the integration team.

Stakeholder	Method(s) of Collecting Feedback (surveys, focus groups, one-on-one or group meetings, telephone "hotline," telephone calls, e-mail communication, chat rooms, electronic bulletin boards, suggestion boxes, etc.)	Frequency of Collection	Responsible Person
Board members			
Management			
Staff			
Volunteers			
Clients and customers			
Funders and donors			
Community leaders			
Members of the press			
Collaborators			
Government agencies			
Others (define)			

Published by the Amherst H. Wilder Foundation

Index

Charts are indicated by *c*.
Lists are indicated by *l*.

More results-oriented books from the
Amherst H. Wilder Foundation

Resolving Conflict in Nonprofit Organizations
The Leader's Guide to Finding Constructive Solutions
by Marion Peters Angelica

Helps you identify conflict, decide whether to intervene, uncover and deal with the true issues, and design and conduct a conflict resolution process. Includes exercises to learn and practice conflict resolution skills, guidance on handling unique conflicts such as harassment and discrimination, and when (and where) to seek outside help with litigation, arbitration, and mediation.

192 pages, softcover   Item # 069164

Strategic Planning Workbook for Nonprofit Organizations, Revised and Updated
by Bryan Barry

Chart a wise course for your nonprofit's future. This time-tested workbook gives you practical step-by-step guidance, real-life examples, one nonprofit's complete strategic plan, and easy-to-use worksheets.

144 pages, softcover   Item # 069075

Marketing & Fundraising

The Wilder Nonprofit Field Guide to
Conducting Successful Focus Groups
by Judith Sharken Simon

Shows how to collect valuable information without a lot of money or special expertise. Using this proven technique, you'll get essential opinions and feedback to help you check out your assumptions, do better strategic planning, improve services or products, and more.

80 pages, softcover   Item # 069199

Coping with Cutbacks:
The Nonprofit Guide to Success When Times Are Tight
by Emil Angelica and Vincent Hyman

Shows you practical ways to involve business, government, and other nonprofits to solve problems together. Also includes 185 cutback strategies you can put to use right away.

128 pages, softcover   Item # 069091

The Wilder Nonprofit Field Guide to
Fundraising on the Internet
by Gary M. Grobman, Gary B. Grant, and Steve Roller

Your quick road map to using the Internet for fundraising. Shows you how to attract new donors, troll for grants, get listed on sites that assist donors, and learn more about the art of fundraising. Includes detailed reviews of 77 web sites useful to fundraisers, including foundations, charities, prospect research sites, and sites that assist donors.

64 pages, softcover   Item # 069180

Marketing Workbook for Nonprofit Organizations Volume I: Develop the Plan
by Gary J. Stern

Don't just wish for results—get them! Here's how to create a straightforward, usable marketing plan. Includes the six Ps of Marketing, how to use them effectively, a sample marketing plan, tips on using the Internet, and worksheets.

208 pages, softcover   Item # 069253

Marketing Workbook for Nonprofit Organizations Volume II: Mobilize People for Marketing Success
by Gary J. Stern

Put together a successful promotional campaign based on the most persuasive tool of all: personal contact. Learn how to mobilize your entire organization, its staff, volunteers, and supporters in a focused, one-to-one marketing campaign.

192 pages, softcover   Item # 069105

Venture Forth! The Essential Guide to Starting a Moneymaking Business in Your Nonprofit Organization
by Rolfe Larson

The most complete guide on nonprofit business development. Building on the experience of dozens of organizations, this handbook gives you a time-tested approach for finding, testing, and launching a successful nonprofit business venture.

272 pages, softcover   Item # 069245

Collaboration

Collaboration Handbook
Creating, Sustaining, and Enjoying the Journey
by Michael Winer and Karen Ray

Shows you how to get a collaboration going, set goals, determine everyone's roles, create an action plan, and evaluate the results. Includes a case study of one collaboration from start to finish, helpful tips on how to avoid pitfalls, and worksheets to keep everyone on track.

192 pages, softcover   Item # 069032

Collaboration: What Makes It Work, 2nd Ed.
by Paul Mattessich, PhD, Marta Murray-Close, BA, and Barbara Monsey, MPH

An in-depth review of current collaboration research. Major findings are summarized, critical conclusions are drawn, and twenty key factors influencing successful collaborations are identified. Includes The Wilder Collaboration Factors Inventory, which groups can use to assess their collaboration.

104 pages, softcover   Item # 069326

The Nimble Collaboration
Fine-Tuning Your Collaboration for Lasting Success
by Karen Ray

Shows you ways to make your existing collaboration more responsive, flexible, and productive. Provides three key strategies to help your collaboration respond quickly to changing environments and participants.

136 pages, softcover   Item # 069288

For current prices or to order visit us online at www.wilder.org/pubs

Funder's Guides

Community Visions, Community Solutions
Grantmaking for Comprehensive Impact
by Joseph A. Connor and Stephanie Kadel-Taras
Helps foundations, community funds, government agencies, and other grantmakers uncover a community's highest aspiration for itself, and support and sustain strategic efforts to get to workable solutions.

128 pages, softcover   Item # 06930X

Strengthening Nonprofit Performance
A Funder's Guide to Capacity Building
Paul Connolly and Carol Lukas
This practical guide synthesizes the most recent capacity building practice and research into a collection of strategies, steps, and examples that you can use to get started on or improve funding to strengthen nonprofit organizations.

176 pages, softcover   Item # 069377

Vital Communities

Community Building: What Makes It Work
by Wilder Research Center
Reveals twenty-eight keys to help you build community more effectively. Includes detailed descriptions of each factor, case examples of how they play out, and practical questions to assess your work.

112 pages, softcover   Item # 069121

Community Economic Development Handbook
by Mihailo Temali
A concrete, practical handbook to turning any neighborhood around. It explains how to start a community economic development organization, and then lays out the steps of four proven and powerful strategies for revitalizing inner-city neighborhoods.

288 pages, softcover   Item # 069369

The Wilder Nonprofit Field Guide to
Conducting Community Forums
by Carol Lukas and Linda Hoskins
Provides step-by-step instruction to plan and carry out exciting, successful community forums that will educate the public, build consensus, focus action, or influence policy.

128 pages, softcover   Item # 069318

Violence Prevention & Intervention

The Little Book of Peace
Designed and illustrated by Kelly O. Finnerty
A pocket-size guide to help people think about violence and talk about it with their families and friends. You may download a free copy of *The Little Book of Peace* from our web site at www.wilder.org.

24 pages (minimum order 10 copies)   Item # 069083
*Also available in **Spanish** and **Hmong** language editions.*

Journey Beyond Abuse: A Step-by-Step Guide to Facilitating Women's Domestic Abuse Groups
*by Kay-Laurel Fischer, MA, LP,
and Michael F. McGrane, LICSW*
Create a program where women increase their understanding of the dynamics of abuse, feel less alone and isolated, and have a greater awareness of channels to safety. This book includes twenty-one group activities that you can combine to create groups of differing length and focus.

208 pages, softcover   Item # 069148

Moving Beyond Abuse: Stories and Questions for Women Who Have Lived with Abuse
(Companion guided journal to *Journey Beyond Abuse*)
A series of stories and questions that can be used in coordination with the sessions provided in the facilitator's guide or with the guidance of a counselor in other forms of support.

88 pages, softcover   Item # 069156

Foundations for Violence-Free Living:
A Step-by-Step Guide to Facilitating Men's Domestic Abuse Groups
by David J. Mathews, MA, LICSW
A complete guide to facilitating a men's domestic abuse program. Includes twenty-nine activities, detailed guidelines for presenting each activity, and a discussion of psychological issues that may arise out of each activity.

240 pages, softcover   Item # 069059

On the Level
(Participant's workbook to *Foundations for Violence-Free Living*)
Contains forty-nine worksheets including midterm and final evaluations. Men can record their progress.

160 pages, softcover   Item # 069067

What Works in Preventing Rural Violence
by Wilder Research Center
An in-depth review of eighty-eight effective strategies you can use to prevent and intervene in violent behaviors, improve services for victims, and reduce repeat offenses. This report also includes a Community Report Card with step-by-step directions on how you can collect, record, and use information about violence in your community.

94 pages, softcover   Item # 069040

For current prices, a catalog, or to order call ☎ 800-274-6024

ORDERING INFORMATION

Order by phone, fax or online

Call toll-free: 800-274-6024
Internationally: 651-659-6024

Fax: 651-642-2061

E-mail: books@wilder.org
Online: www.wilder.org/pubs

Mail: Amherst H. Wilder Foundation
Publishing Center
919 Lafond Avenue
St. Paul, MN 55104

Our NO-RISK guarantee

If you aren't completely satisfied with any book for any reason, simply send it back within 30 days for a full refund.

Pricing and discounts

For current prices and discounts, please visit our web site at www.wilder.org/pubs or call toll free at 800-274-6024.

Do you have a book idea?

Wilder Publishing Center seeks manuscripts and proposals for books in the fields of nonprofit management and community development. To get a copy of our author guidelines, please call us at 800-274-6024. You can also download them from our web site at www.wilder.org/pubs/author_guide.html.

Visit us online

You'll find information about the Wilder Foundation and more details on our books, such as table of contents, pricing, discounts, endorsements, and more, at www.wilder.org/pubs.

Quality assurance

We strive to make sure that all the books we publish are helpful and easy to use. Our major workbooks are tested and critiqued by experts before being published. Their comments help shape the final book and—we trust—make it more useful to you.

CD-ROM INSTRUCTIONS

Hardware requirements

This CD can be used with Windows computers. It runs most successfully on Windows XP.

PLEASE NOTE: Because every computer is already loaded with different Windows files, you may receive an error message when installing the Integration Planning Software. If you receive an error notice, simply restart the installation process by double-clicking on the setup.exe file again. After this, the program should run smoothly.

Questions?

For more detailed installation instructions, open the file on the enclosed CD called INSTRUCTIONS.rtf.

If you have questions or problems with the enclosed disc, please contact Wilder Publishing at 800-274-6024. You can also download the same material from the publisher's web site if you have purchased this book. See the URL on page 6.

No Warranty

Wilder Publishing does not warranty this software or provide support for it.

Installation instructions

1. Begin installation by closing any programs you have running. The installation process may reboot your computer. This will cause you to lose anything you don't have saved.

2. Open your CD-ROM drive so you can see a list of items on the CD. (For more detailed installation instructions, open the file on the CD called INSTRUCTIONS.rtf.) Open the folder titled "Free Integration Planning Software" and double-click on "setup.exe."

3. Follow the instructions on your screen. If you receive installation errors, restart the installation process by double-clicking on the setup.exe file again. The setup will automatically put a shortcut for this program in your computer's Start menu.

4. Open the program by selecting "Integration Planning Tool" from your Start menu. Whatever changes you make in the plan will automatically be saved.

5. The worksheets, pre- and post-merger assessment tool, and audits have been created in Microsoft Word. To open and modify these documents you should copy them to your computer and open them with a word processing program.